The Agony and the Ecstasy

The Agony and the Ecstasy

Stephen Roche's World of Cycling

Stephen Roche with David Walsh

Stanley Paul
London Melbourne Auckland Johannesburg

Stanley Paul and Co. Ltd

An imprint of Century Hutchinson Ltd

Brookmount House, 62–65 Chandos Place
Covent Garden, London WC2N 4NW

Century Hutchinson Australia (Pty) Ltd
PO Box 496, 16–22 Church Street, Hawthorn, Melbourne, Victoria 3122

Century Hutchinson New Zealand Limited
191 Archers Road, PO Box 40–086, Glenfield, Auckland 10

Century Hutchinson South Africa (Pty) Ltd
PO Box 337, Bergvlei 2012, South Africa

First published 1988

Set in 11/13pt Sabon by Deltatype Ltd, Ellesmere Port

Printed and bound in Great Britain by
Mackays of Chatham Ltd

British Library Cataloguing In Publication Data

Roche, Stephen
    The agony & the ecstasy : Stephen Roche's
    world of cycling.
    1. cycling. Roche, Stephen. Biographies
    I. Title   II. Walsh, David
    796.6′092′4

ISBN 0 09 173684 6

Contents

PHOTOGRAPHIC AKNOWLEDGEMENTS

The authors and publishers would like to thank the
following for their permission to reproduce copyright
photographs (identified by caption):

Colour
Presse-Sports: With Marc Madiot; the 1985 Tour de
France
Billy Stickland: 1986 Tour de France; 1987 Tour de
France; the climb of Alpe d'Huez; a very happy
moment; back in Dublin for post-Tour celebrations
Graham Watson: the Aubisque, 1985; I have always
enjoyed time trialling; the crash which ruined a year;
Sappada stage of the Giro d'Italia; riding hard in the
'87 Giro; winning the Giro; leading up St Patrick's Hill

Black and white
Presse-Sports: on my way to the bronze medal;
attacking Kelly; 1984 Paris–Nice; Raphaël
Géminiani; 1985 Tour de France; Bernard Hinault;
1986 Tour de France; Paris–Nice, 1987; 1987
Criterium International
Billy Stickland: everybody needs a break sometime!;
the hectic moments before the start of a Tour de France
stage; the 1987 Tour is over and I am happy to speak
with all the journalists; back in Ireland with Sean;
friends and family turn up for the ceremony
Graham Watson: Paris–Roubaix; Roland Berland;
'two Irish lads in the bunch'; bronze medallist; Eddy
Schepers; Patrick Valcke; Roberto Visentini; Robert
Millar; Pedro Delgado; winning the Tour

'Freewheeling Champ' is reproduced by kind
permission of Davoren Hanna.

And Now?

It is the first day of the new year, 1988. In a sense 1987 is now very much in the past. The great prizes – Italy's pink jersey, France's yellow and the rainbow of world champion – are packed away in my wardrobe. They cannot help me in 1988. I am a little worried as I look into the new season. Six weeks ago I underwent the third operation on my knee and the recovery has been very slow. Most of all I am afraid that I will rush my comeback and try to do too much too soon. I think of all the preparation that I have missed and how all my rivals have enjoyed six weeks of good training. But the anxiety does not stay for too long and does not trouble me too deeply. I believe that I can have a good cycling career after 1987, that I can ride as well in the future as I did in 1987.

This is not to say that I will ever win the Tour de France again or that I can again become world champion. Years are different, races ride differently. The form I had in 1987 might not be good enough to win the 1988 Tour de France. That thought does not bother me. All I can do is my best. I know that I have ability and that if I am in good condition I will not be beaten easily. People tell me that because I am now considered a great champion I must be careful about putting my reputation on the line. They say that I should not ride this race and that race unless I am going well enough to win. I have never seen things like that and will not see them like that in the future. In cycling one race serves as preparation for the next and you get on with the job. For me the job is establishing a good foundation of training and building from there.

It is true that people should not expect that I can ever repeat what I did in 1987. Yet I have always been a dreamer and I believe that people need their dreams. Without dreams, the road is even harder. But I am not going to worry about what the road brings. I have been down before, so low that people were sure I could never get back up. Even in the depths of my bad years I did not lose belief in my own ability. It was this self-confidence that kept me going then. It keeps me going now.

PART I

Birth, Sweat and Gears

CHAPTER 1
The Roches

About the most likely story you will come across is that Stephen Roche's parents met because of their common interest in the bike. Bunny wanted to be part of a touring club, Larry wanted to help set one up, and that was it – romance. Five years later they married.

Larry's mother had come to Dublin from Cappawhite in County Tipperary and Bunny's father emigrated to Ireland's capital city from Scotland. Everything else about them connected to Dublin. They grew up in the Dublin of the forties and fifties, a time when jobs were scarce and wages low. As a teenager Larry liked the bike, enjoyed racing and followed the stars of the sport on the continent of Europe. Fausto Coppi, *le campionnissimo*, was the cyclist that Larry Roche admired most. From film clips of the Italian in action, Larry had noticed his rhythm, the way his ankles were always spinning round. Even when everything else went, Coppi's ankles revolved smoothly. That was something, thought Larry Roche.

Cycling was Larry's method of transport and the source of his fun. He and his friends would cycle behind buses in Dublin. Those buses had shiny chrome bumpers which reflected the young cyclists' ankles. Larry looked at his ankles spinning round and wondered about Coppi. Larry suffered from varicose veins, a complaint which cut short his racing career. But he stayed with the bike through the more relaxed pastime of touring. He heard about a group of girls who wanted to start their own touring club but did not know how. Larry was asked, or got himself asked, to help out. He told them what gear they needed and what food to bring, and he took them to wonderful places like Glencree, Enniskerry, and along the Dargle Valley. The distance was rarely more than 50 miles and Larry tried to ensure that there was no hardship. One of the girls in the group was called Bunny Samson. She liked Larry and Larry liked her, but they dared not let on at first. Eventually they became friends, dating partners, engaged and married.

After their marriage, Larry and Christine (the name which appears on Bunny's birth certificate) emigrated to London. Larry got work with London

Transport but there was a strike soon after he started. That was in 1958. For seven weeks the young couple lived on strike pay of £2 10s per week. Back in Dublin their families were concerned and wrote that the newlyweds should return home. They did. Without work in Dublin, Larry and Bunny stayed with Bunny's mother in her one-room flat in Lennox Street, off the South Circular Road. They slept on the couch. A friend of Larry's, Ignatius McCann, found Larry a job. Next they needed a place of their own. Bunny was pregnant and she and Larry wanted to have their own home before the baby arrived. As Larry was working they felt they could afford it. They looked and they looked. Larry Roche retains one vivid memory:

We went around with our heads pointing upwards, searching for empty windows. I remember a place in Hatch Street. We called because we knew the owner had a flat. Bunny was about five or six months pregnant at the time and was wearing a blue coat. I can see it all as if it were yesterday. The woman came out, took one look at Bunny and said no. We could not have the room. I have always associated that moment with the Holy Family. Calling to the different doors and being turned away. That moment has never left me and has influenced my attitude to our family. It was a bad time in Ireland and people did adopt that kind of attitude.

The Roches lived in a one-room basement flat in Ranelagh when Stephen was born on 28 November 1959. He was the second in the family, Maria having arrived before him. Carol arrived next. They lived for six years in Ranelagh, moving to a corporation house in Dundrum before the arrival of Jude. The fifth and sixth members of the family, Laurence and Pamela, were also born in Dundrum. When they moved to Dundrum they had furniture for just one room but both their families helped out and they got by. Nobody can remember scarcity at the table but the Roches were not well off.

They liked the outdoor life and most forms of physical recreation. Swimming was a particular favourite. Larry and Bunny liked to take their children down to Marian College for a swim but the family could not all go together. It was a shilling for each person and that meant one parent going with two children one week and the other parent going with two other children the following week. The younger Roches understood why there was a rota and nobody complained. When the family lived in Ranelagh, Bunny would push Carol in her pram to Sandymount beach each day during the summer. Maria and Stephen would be brought along. Mum and the three children would spend the day by the sea, to be collected by Larry when he finished work in the evening. It did not cost a penny and it contributed enormously to the Roches' happiness.

Larry Roche is an even-tempered man, sensible and organized. He works things out for himself. Life for him revolves around his family. His only concern when Stephen raced was that he would not seriously hurt himself. It is not in

Larry to want his son to be a champion. He sees his family as if on a ladder, thinks it would be nice if each member progressed to the next rung but has no yearning to see them arrive at the very top. Bunny considers herself more of 'a goer'. If she wants something, she will not give up until she gets it. Larry and Bunny, understandably, like to think that Stephen extracted what was best in both of them.

Academic education had not played important parts in the lives of Larry and Bunny. What they learned was picked up from life. Larry had grown up in the company of his father, treating him as a friend rather than a parent. He wanted his children to learn from him in the same way. It helped that Stephen shared his father's interest in stripping and reassembling the engines of vans, cars, motorbikes and scooters. Granddad, Dad and Stephen spent many hours providing new solutions for old engines. Three generations of Roche, bound together by a shared interest. Now, when Larry Roche casts his mind back to Stephen as a boy and an adolescent, most of the time he sees his son with a screwdriver in his hand.

Because he was the oldest boy in the family, it was Stephen who spent most time working with his father on the milk round. Provided that Stephen did not miss out on school, Larry liked to have him along as he went about his business of delivering milk. He welcomed the help, and Stephen was a good companion. Larry was especially taken by his son's willingness to listen: 'We would be out in the van driving along, I would be talking. Telling Stephen something. And no matter what I said, he would never reply, "I know." He was a good listener and I thought that was an unusual trait in a young fellow.'

Although brought together by their liking for the bike, Larry and Bunny were not enthusiastic about the idea of their son racing. Especially Larry. His friend Ignatius McCann raced and his career stood before Larry as a warning:

Nathy used to crash a lot. In his day it was dangerous, you could tell there was bike racing in the Phoenix Park by the number of casualties in Dr Steeven's Hospital across the road from the park. And just as Stephen was getting interested in the bike we had the experience of a man calling to our door in Dundrum telling us that Stephen had been in a crash on his way home from school. He had fallen, hit his head on the ground and was concussed. We were to go to the hospital.

But the Roches were not going to lay down laws for their son. When Stephen tried to convince them that he could handle a racing bike, their minds were open and soon they were persuaded that the youngster understood his bike and the dangers.

Stephen was a good pupil without ever liking or having an interest in school life. When he was fifteen his father used his contacts in Hughes Dairy, Rathfarnham, to get Stephen an apprenticeship as a maintenance fitter. That offer came shortly before Stephen was to take his Inter Cert examination at Dundrum vocational school. Stephen was in a quandary. The principal at his school, Mr Hogan, advised that he accept the job offer. Stephen did. After a few weeks at Hughes's, his bosses said he could return to school and do his examination. Stephen sat for his Inter Cert examination and passed it. His formal education was at an end.

His real education took place in the company of his father, with his friends on the bike, and at work. Friends recall hostelling weekends with Stephen. Five or six guys, aged between fifteen and eighteen, leaving their homes in Dublin on a Saturday morning in November for some far-flung hostel in Wicklow. They would arrive, cook up their evening meal, cycle off to a local pub, return to their beds and talk through the night. Next morning they would make breakfast and prepare for the long journey home. Once they got into trouble with the guards when one member of the group, Sean Fitzelle, was found in possession of a lamp which rightfully belonged to the Wicklow County Council.

On another occasion the gang proved to themselves that farts could be ignited. Well, up to a point. And Stephen discovered that a hearing aid, used on a dark and lonely country road, could be a forceful means of scaring one's companions. To his fellow travellers, Stephen was one of the group, no more and no less. Maybe he had more pedalling ability than the rest but that counted for little. Especially when the game was Kill! The idea was that each rider attempted to knock every other rider from his bike until there was only one survivor. Kill was great for laughs.

Once a group of seven were heading for a hostel at Clogher Head in County Louth. They chose a route which took them off the more congested tracks. It was hilly and hard. The two youngest members of the group were the Kimmages, Paul and Raphael. On a hill the *derailleur* on Raphael's bike became jammed in his back wheel. They were miles from anywhere. Raphael's bike needed a mechanic with tools. Stephen said he would see what he could do. Producing a small bag with some tools he set to work. Most of all he needed a link extractor to shorten the chain. Cyclists do not normally carry such instruments around with them but that day Stephen had one. The rest of the crew thought it 'typical' and everybody, including Raphael Kimmage, made it to Clogher Head in good time.

As their son made his way to the forefront of Ireland's amateur cycling fraternity, Larry Roche considered his apprenticeship at Hughes Dairy to be a matter of more importance. By the time Stephen made up his mind to pursue a career as a professional racer in France, he had established himself as one of the finest amateur riders produced in Ireland. Still Larry thought it most unwise to forsake secure employment in Ireland for the possibility of becoming a professional in France: 'I did not want him to leave his job. He had a good job, a nice car, good money. Why give these things up? He said he did not want to spend the rest of his life wondering if he could have made it. I still thought he was wrong but it was going to be his decision.'

That was the Roches, a solid, hard-working family. The parents graft conscientiously throughout their lives, always doing their best. Their eldest son serves his apprenticeship to be a fitter. He qualifies, finds employment and, soon afterwards, ups and leaves for France. To ride a bike. It was not Larry Roche's idea of sense. He could give his son advice and he did. But he could not deny his son the right to do things his way. And he did not try.

CHAPTER 2

Cycle? Why Not?

'Please,' says Bunny Roche, 'don't think of Stephen as a model child. He was not that. He would get into fights, rob orchards, swear. He was no angel.'

The thing that appealed to me about cycling was that you trained and you raced. As a boy I played soccer and hurling and I swam. All our family swam. My father would break ice to get into the water and my grandfather would not be far behind him. But I was not great at soccer or hurling and even though I trained I was not sure of getting in the team. When I swam in a race there were problems because I started in the middle and ended up crashing into the side wall. I was a strong swimmer but could not travel in a straight line. In cycling you did not have to qualify to get into a race. You trained and you showed up on the day.

I remember riding my first race. It was in Skerries, north of Dublin. My cycling gear consisted of trousers and a shirt. No shorts, jersey or cycling shoes.

At some point in that race I decided that enough was enough and stopped. They asked why I had stopped. I said I was tired. That may appear a trivial answer. For me it was the big thing about cycling. If I was tired, I could stop. If I wanted to train, I could train. I could race every day I wanted to race. This represented freedom and was the reason I gave up soccer, hurling and everything else. There were no second thoughts. I had found the sport that appealed to me. My parents had cycled in their day but never attempted to steer me into cycling. I found my own reasons.

I was thirteen when I took up cycling. Six years later the bike took me to France and I have lived in Paris for the last nine years. Ireland is still home but I am lucky if I get to spend two months at home in any year. Because I have lived away so long, much of what happened during the first twenty years of my life has slipped from my memory. Friends who were important during those years are not seen that often now and the things we did together are not recalled. Being away meant that I missed out on things in my own family. When I moved to France the three youngest in our family, Jude, Laurence and Pamela, were only kids. While I was away they grew up. Only now am I getting to know them fully.

My earliest memory goes back to when we lived in Ranelagh. At the time only Maria, Carol and I were around. It was Christmas. Our parents had gone to enormous trouble to get Maria a doll's pram, her present from Santa. But it was a second-hand pram. Our father had painted it blue and yellow. We could not understand why Santa had brought Maria a second-hand pram. Santa did not deal in second-hand toys. We questioned our parents until they got really embarrassed over it. Deep down, we knew why the pram was second-hand. We were at the stage where we believed in Santa and we did not believe in Santa. Even now it sticks in my mind, how selfish and cruel kids can be. Our parents always did their best but there were six of us and it was a hard job.

Maria was the oldest, a year older than I. Carol was next, two years younger. There was a gap of four years to Jude, Laurence next and Pamela the youngest. Because she was the oldest Maria expected to get her own way and often did. Carol was more easy-going and I got on especially well with her. As a child she was skinny and never wanted to eat her food. There was a famine in Biafra at the time and I spent mealtimes reminding her of the Biafrans in Africa, saying what a scandal it was that she would not eat her food. All the time she just wanted to pick up the plate and throw it at me. Right from those days we were close and it has stayed that way ever since.

I disliked school from the start. My mother used to take me to a nuns' school in Milltown when we lived in Ranelagh. I spent the morning trying to come up with a way of getting out of school. I would take a bottle of milk from my lunch box, hide it, wait for my mother to go a good bit down the road and then go racing after her, away from the school. I would explain that I did not have any milk and, really, I should go home with her. It never worked. I can see Nicolas, my son, behaving in exactly the same way now, doing clever things to avoid being left in school. After we moved from Ranelagh to Rosemount in

Dundrum I attended primary school in Dundrum. Things got a bit better but I never learned to like school. Some time later I told myself that it was a laugh and that was why I went. Like most of the boys who went to school with me, I could only see the value of school after I left it. In French class I would sit at the back and draw pictures. I learned two words, *oui* and *merci*. Four years later I went to France and suffered terribly in the first few months because I had not a word of French. Those French classes could have been worthwhile.

The only subjects which interested me at school were mechanical drawing, metalwork, woodwork and woodwork drawing, and I loved the gym. Anything else and I could not be bothered. I did other subjects because I had to. I looked upon examinations as something that I had to pass, it never went further than that. I calculated and did the minimum necessary to pass my exams. School was that part of your life which came before a job. I could not wait to get it over and get into a job. I was fifteen when the chance came to switch from school life to the working life. My father had a milk round and worked for Hughes Dairy. He knew the personnel officer, Sean Nolan, and found out that there was a vacancy for an apprentice fitter. I went for two interviews and got the job.

Long before that I had begun working with my father on his milk round. I was five when I started. When you are five you do not question your father; I was not going to ask him if I had to go on the milk round. I accepted the discipline from the start. I did not mind doing it and, looking back, I believe that the experience helped me in everything I did afterwards. I helped at the weekends and during school holidays. In the early days I put a bottle of milk into this house and that, nothing much. As I got older I was allowed to do more. We used to be out early in the mornings and during the winter it was always dark. Long, dark driveways scared me. Especially in Mount Merrion where there were many big houses with long driveways. I would hear a noise in a bush and presume the worst.

As I got older my father allowed me to share the driving of the electric van. Whoever was nearest to the van when it needed to be moved up the road would do it. Later, I would do all the driving. On the way home my father would sit in the driver's seat but I would steer, so that he could do his books. This meant that he did not have to do the books when he got home and that was important to us. He read out the names to me and I said what each had taken. When we arrived home all we had to do was unload the van and that was it. Everything was done. My father was serious about his work. He always worked on Christmas Day because if you allowed somebody to do relief for you, it would take three weeks to get the mess sorted out. Working for two hours on Christmas morning, he said, could save you lots of trouble.

I continued going out on the milk round after school and during my apprenticeship. Even when I was home from France, I occasionally went out. I look now at my two younger brothers, Jude and Laurence, and think that they missed out on something great. As they became old enough to go on the milk round my father gave it up. They were never going to come into contact with all the people a milkman meets and they were not going to spend hours just chatting away with our father in the van.

Much of my early life was spent over the engine of a car. My father and grandfather were both mechanically minded and I picked up a fair bit from them. Now I can do anything with a car. Welding comes fairly easily to me as well. When they first gave me a welding rod and explained how you weld two different materials together, how you must melt one to the same temperature as the other, how there must be so much current going through, I understood. My first weld was not as neat as it is today but I welded.

My grandfather is a remarkable man. He is seventy-five now. He retired from his job about ten years ago and as his sight was failing he bought himself a bike and sold his car. One of his last cars was an old Spitfire. He had always wanted a Spitfire and he passed on his love for old cars to me. His failing sight did not reduce his mobility. He is now on his third bike and getting around as well as ever. There is a mirror on the bike and a neat carrier. It is beautiful to see him on the bike, as happy as can be, not a care in the world. When he gets to a hill, he climbs off and walks. 'I am in no great hurry,' he says. That is his way. A big, heavy man, always joyful and giddy. The kind of grandfather that you read about in story books. Every moment I spent with him growing up was an education.

Although I was not interested in touring or racing, I had always had a bike. My father bought me my first when I was three or four, a second-hand bike that he painted himself. Soccer used to be my game, I was a full-back and felt that I was very good. But when Sunday came, the day of the match, I was on the sidelines looking on. Two of my friends, Derek Doyle and Davy Murray, had bikes and the three of us would cycle off to the Pine Forest, in the foothills of the Dublin mountains. For us that was the edge of the world. We had a little stove that we took with us. Up there we fried rashers and sausages, and went down to the nearby river for water to make tea. We had great times up there. The journey home was nearly all downhill and we flew it. Derek was a very close friend. He was a lot like me. We needed money and we both tried to come up with a way of making some. We got this brainwave that we would do a paper round together. We were told that there was one penny profit for us on each paper sold. On our bikes we canvassed all the houses in the Nutgrove and Rathfarnham areas. Five hundred families agreed to take a Dublin evening paper from us; that was 500 pennies. We were fourteen at the time and it was good money. As soon as school ended we would set off on our bikes to collect and deliver the 500 papers. It was heavy work and we also had to collect the money from our customers. My father thought it was too much for a fourteen-year-old and asked me to give it up. I did. Derek kept it going and expanded the business before selling it.

Soon afterwards I got interested in cycling and I did not see as much of Derek. Cycling did not interest him, he had a chopper and never went any further. Years later I came across him again when I worked in Hughes Dairy. He had bought a milk round and a juggernaut. He kept the milk round and the haulage business going at the same time. Towards the end of 1987 Derek emigrated to Boston, where he now works with a big contracting firm. He was a businessman from the start.

When I began my apprenticeship to be a fitter at Hughes Dairy I fully believed that I was entering a trade which would be my livelihood. I enjoyed the time I spent in the dairy and I remember clearly the guys I worked with. There was Paul Lennon, the genius of the dairy. He used to make the factory run by itself. He was very talented. At the time when I worked at the dairy some company in the motor industry introduced hazard-warning lights. Paul reckoned he could make his own and did. He used to make Christmas toys for his kids at work. When I am at home now I try to get around to the dairy to see the lads. When I do Paul will want to have a look at the car I am driving. He will scrutinize it and even if he does not know what something is, he will work it out pretty quickly.

But I served my time with John Woods. We called him Woody. He was more my kind of bloke. Paul would go to a machine and fix it. Instant solution. We would not have a notion of what he did, only that it was the right thing. Woody was the kind who would go to a machine, study it, analyse everything and think out loud before actually getting into it. He would get his screwdriver, his spanner, take his hammer, think about it again and then systematically try different things, slowly, trying to discover why the machine was not working. That was good for me because I was learning all the time. Woody and I used to work in the refrigeration room for a month each year. We were cold but dry.

Mick Nolan was another friend at Hughes's. He was the apprentice before me and was in his last year when I was in my first. He showed me the ropes. The apprentice had to make the tea, collect the tea money, clean the lathes, sweep the floors and look after the overalls on Thursday. Mick was a very genuine fellow, any time I needed something he was there to give me a dig out.

Johnny Hudson was our boss, the Hud to us. He retired last year and the lads told me that even up to the day he retired, the Hud was the same as he had always been. They were still afraid of him. We would see the Hud coming and if we were not doing something we would jump for a spanner. Each of us used to put a mirror over our workbench which reflected the door. If we were talking we would continually look up at the mirror to check that the Hud was not coming in. There was always tension in the air and, really, we could not hide from him. He would sniff us out. Towards the end of my apprenticeship I began to cycle seriously but the Hud was not very interested. I would race in England at the weekend, catch the boat back to Dublin late on Sunday night and be back in Dun Laoghaire at six the following morning. From there I would go straight in to work, my eyes deep in the back of my head from the lack of sleep. The Hud would notice my condition and put me out in the cold working on a tanker all that day.

In his own way Johnny Hudson did a lot for me. He gave me some time off when I needed it but it always came out of my holidays. He never actually hindered me the way some fellows might have but he did not help me the way others might have. After serving my three-year apprenticeship in Hughes Dairy I qualified and immediately got a job at Premier Dairies in Finglas. Things were completely different at Finglas. They were very interested in sport at Premier and they looked upon my cycling as an asset. They had their own football team, they played among themselves and there was a far better atmosphere there than at Hughes's. The work was still done. Premier had their mechanical genius as well, he was called Declan O'Brien and we became very good friends. Declan is now the gaffer in Premier because Jim Keenan, who was boss when I was there, went out on early retirement. Jim was very good about my requests for time off. He did not answer immediately, he thought about things and tried to find a way of letting me have what I asked for. Declan O'Brien played a lot of football and needed weekends off in the winter; I needed them off in the summer and we filled in for each other.

Because of the way my cycling career went, I ended up spending only nine months at Premier but they were good times. In the middle of that time I won the Rás Tailteann and the lads at work were delighted for me. A formal celebration was arranged by the lads at the Ashbourne Inn in Ashbourne. I was able to bring my girlfriend along and we all had a meal. It was a smashing evening. The atmosphere at Premier was extremely good. Nobody wanted to say no to anything. I was there as a qualified fitter and that was something new for me. It was a big ordeal to be left alone and expected to do the work of a fitter. But they all helped me. I never lost contact with those guys or the guys at Hughes's and when I was made a freeman of Dublin in September 1987, they were all there. I was very glad to see them.

I was thirteen when the bike first became more than a means of transport to me. It was an afternoon in 1973. A few of us were playing football on the green in front of our houses in Rosemount. I do not recall if I was injured or a reserve but I was sitting on the sideline when Pat Flynn came walking across the green. We knew her as a woman who lived down the road, wife of Steve Flynn who did some cycling. Pat, being a sociable type of person and one who knows most of what is going on, asked whether I would be interested in joining a cycling club. She told me that there were two guys, Paddy Doran and Noel O'Neill, who were organizing training spins from the H. Williams supermarket each Wednesday evening.

Join a cycling club? 'Why not?' I said. I was sitting idly as the others played football, so it seemed a good idea at the time.

CHAPTER 3

An Amateur

Noel O'Neill coached Roche from the time he joined the Orwell Wheelers. He remembers noticing special talent: 'A three-day in Wicklow, 1978. Stephen took too much out of himself on the first day, did even more on the second and could still ride away from the entire field on the third day.'

As an amateur racing in Ireland, I was not much good. But that never bothered me. There was a day's work to be done before going out racing and at the weekends I delivered milk before setting out for the race. There were Sundays when I was out from four or five in the morning with my father on the milk round. I got back to the house in time to go to 8 o'clock mass, have a quick breakfast and go off to the race. At the time I never thought a second time about my approach to bike racing. Cycling was only for enjoyment. Too many riders think too much about racing, instead of just going out and doing it. They feel that they will not be able to race unless they are in bed before nine the previous night. I was going out and getting hammered. I had no sense of tactics, just getting to the front and riding. And riding.

Coming home in the afternoon, I complained to my father that although I had ridden harder than anybody, I did not win.

He would calmly ask, 'Well, what happened?' I explained that I was the one who rode at the front all through the final part of the race but the other guy had sat in behind me and sprinted past at the finish. Even more calmly, my father would say, 'Well, if you brought him to the finish like that, that is your problem.' I spent Sunday evenings going through these races and fighting back the tears.

Fran Riordan was the same age as I. A good rider but a wheelsucker. Still, he could always beat me in the sprint.

My father's only worry was that I might become too involved in cycling and give up my apprenticeship. He advised me to do evening classes to help me in my apprenticeship and I did. A normal week for me at the time could have involved overtime at the dairy on Tuesday and Thursday nights, and evening classes in Bolton Street tech Monday, Wednesday and Friday. If I wanted to train it had to be for an hour before I went to work and that was only during the summer. As a result I never managed to find any kind of form until June or July when the lengthening of the days enabled me to do some training.

People now look back on my amateur career and pinpoint different performances or victories as being of particular importance. They think of the year 1979 and say, 'That was a good time to win the Rás Tailteann.' They are trying to find reasons for what happened afterwards. I cannot see things in that way because I know that at the time there was no way I was looking to go to the continent or to become a professional. I had a job, cycling was my sport and if I won a race, that made the sport more enjoyable. No more than that. There were no thoughts that I was better than the rest or that if I won such-and-such a race I might get an offer from the continent. All I wanted to do was go forward: if I had an ambition, that was it. This applied to my job, to cycling, to anything I did.

I wanted to go to the Olympics because I felt I was as good as the other Irish amateurs around but I never considered for a second the possibility of being a professional. At the time Sean Kelly was a professional, winning stages of the Tour de France, but the case of Kelly only proved that an ordinary Irish amateur could never become a pro. To us, Kelly was a superman. It was well known when we were racing as amateurs in Ireland that Kelly had gone over the Gap of Mamore in Donegal using an 18 sprocket. Everybody knew that you needed a 22 sprocket on Mamore but Kelly was a horse and could do things that nobody else would even consider. Only people like Kelly became professionals and there was only one Kelly in Ireland. We spoke about Kelly as you might speak about a legend. It did not bother me that he was so far ahead of everything we achieved because I had no intention of ever trying to follow in his footsteps.

If things did fall into place, it was by accident. I was nineteen when I won the Rás Tailteann. It was 1979, a year before the Olympics and a good time to win Ireland's most famous bike race. It meant that I was pretty sure of selection for Moscow at the end of 1979. Early in 1979 I completed my apprenticeship to be a fitter and this made me more flexible. I could put more time into my cycling and my new employers were more understanding of the needs of my cycling career. In some ways I saw the Olympics as being the pinnacle and I wanted to give myself every chance of doing well in Moscow. Because of this, I decided to take six months' leave of absence from Premier Dairies and cycle as an amateur in France. If I was to have any chance of performing well in the Olympics I needed the experience of racing against the best on the continent. Premier were very good when I asked for leave of absence. They said they would like to pay when I was away but they could not, instead they would give me a cheque to help me on my way. And to think I had only been with them for six months!

But the Olympics were a long way from the mind of the thirteen- year-old who turned up at the H. Williams supermarket in Dundrum for his first-training spin with the Orwell Wheelers in the summer of 1973. I had a Jack of Clubs bike which my grandfather had given me. Some time before this I had crashed and the dropped handlebars on the Jack of Clubs got all bent. I took them off and replaced them with straight handlebars. That evening I was the only one of the group who did not have dropped handlebars and I had to change that. I went home after the spin, fished out the dropped handlebars which were damaged, straightened them out a bit and put them back on the bike. I started my life as a cyclist on this old Jack of Clubs bike.

Orwell Wheelers had started up some years before but had gone into decline. Noel Hammond, who has since died, was the president of the club and he wanted to revive it. Noel O'Neill and Paddy Doran were not in the original Orwell but became involved in the club as it tried to get going again. Noel Hammond organized the club on the north side of Dublin while Noel O'Neill and Paddy Doran looked after the club on the south side. Occasionally we would meet the northside Orwell Wheelers and go for spins together. On those Wednesday evenings in 1973 we went over a five-mile circuit in south County Dublin. At first we did the circuit once and headed for home, after that we did two circuits, then three, and increased our miles as we got more experienced and stronger. Most of us were very young, Paul Tansey and I being the two oldest. Because of that we were the two who were allowed to race. Noel O'Neill owned a good racing bike and Paul Tansey had a bike that was quite good, but my Jack of Clubs was not really fit for racing. So Noel gave his bike to Paul and Paul gave his bike to me. Paul's bike had high-pressure tubes and tyres and a bent crank but that did not bother me.

I sensed that my father did not want me to race and tried to conceal it for a time. But it was difficult. Although I was not doing well in the races I kept getting mentioned in the newspapers because I was the best rider on high-pressure wheels. Given that every other rider in the race was using sprint wheels it was easy for me to be the best on high pressures. Still, I was happy to pick up my little prizes. Once I won a game of draughts and felt very pleased with myself. I went home with it, wanting to show everyone in the house what I had won. But when I got home I thought of how my father might react if he knew that I was racing and I hid the game of draughts behind a chair in the sitting room. My father read the cycling results in the newspapers and I knew that he knew. Maybe he wanted to pretend that he did not know because he never said anything about it to me and, eventually, it just happened that everyone at home accepted the fact that I raced.

My enthusiasm for the bike was helped by people like Noel O'Neill and Steve Flynn, who both lived quite near me. I went down regularly to Steve's house, asking him about my training and racing and anything to do with the bike. He is a postman and was free in the afternoons. When I arrived, he made a cup of tea and we talked. Sometimes we went for a training spin together and he gave me a hammering. I also spent an awful lot of time at Noel O'Neill's but that was probably because I had a fancy for Doreen, Noel's wife. With Noel I discussed the race we won, the race we lost and the race we should have won. We weighed one sort of training against another. I am sure now that I was getting in Noel's way most of the time, but when you are young you do not realize this. Noel and Steve had one thing in common. They both considered that I was a little above average on the bike and I had grown close to the two of them. But no matter how good they thought I was, they insisted that other things must come before the bike. They were old-fashioned in their outlook and I appreciated that.

When I was at school, my studies came first. When I began my apprenticeship, they told me that it was the most important thing in my life. I had to fit the bike into the rest of my life without disrupting things too much. I agreed with them and that was the way things were throughout my amateur career in Ireland. If studies or work meant that I could only manage 40 miles training in a week, I only did 40 miles. Their ideas on training were also old-fashioned but I found they suited me. Even during my professional career, many of those old ideas have served me well. Sometimes, people forget that cyclists rode at 40 miles per hour before the arrival of the heart meter. Noel and Steve believed in using a fixed-wheel bike as part of a rider's preparation, forcing him to ride entire training spins in a low gear. Over ten years later I still have a fixed wheel in the basement of my home in Paris.

Later on Peter Crinnion came to my assistance and provided me with encouragement and advice. Peter had raced as a professional on the continent but was not much involved in Irish cycling when I was starting out. One evening he went to the Eamonn Ceannt track and noticed 'a young lad with a bit of talent', as he later said. He reckoned that he could do something for me. He got back into Irish cycling, was made Olympic coach and ended up doing a great deal for me. We did not always see eye to eye. Peter's experience on the continent gave him one set of ideas but I felt that I could not be treated like other Irish amateurs, who did not have a job and were riding the bike full time. I was working and the idea of doing 20 or 30 miles after completing a race did not appeal to me. I rode a race, eyeballs out, and after that I could not do another thing. I could never get that across to Peter but we still got on well and his influence continued to grow.

Those who reckoned that I had some ability as a rider did so because of what I did in races and not because I won races. As an amateur I did not win very much. But when I got the chance to ride in international races I did well. Probably the most notable performance I achieved as a schoolboy was at the ESCA (English Schoolboys' Cycling Association) trials in England. They were held at a Butlins complex and I should have won but towards the end my chain went into my wheel and I panicked. Rather than stopping and having the problem sorted out by a mechanic I kept pulling and pulling, in the hope that it would just come right. It was this type of performance that got me a reputation for having some kind of ability. Because I did not win much at home I found it hard to get selected on Irish teams, but if I was picked, I always rode well. I was never happy to go and just be the best of the Irish team. I wanted to ride well and finish well up.

One of my first big wins came in 1976 in the Dublin-to-Drogheda handicap race. As a schoolboy I was off in one of the first groups. Behind there were the best amateurs in Ireland, including the Olympic squad for that year's Montreal Games. They chased and chased but could never catch me and it was a surprise to everybody that I stayed away to win.

At the start of the next season I had a serious problem with two ingrown toenails. They were so bad that I could not wear cycling shoes and I told myself that if I could not clear up the problem I was going to pack in the bike. One evening I cycled out to the Phoenix Park in my ordinary clothes to watch a race. When I got there I met a few lads and was pumping up wheels for one of them when I heard people speaking about me. I was at one side of a van, they were at the other, and they had no idea that I was around.

They were saying that this fellow Roche had been a flash in the pan. He had come along, done some good rides and now he was going to pack it in. I was furious when I heard this. I remember saying to myself, well, I'll fucking show you. I rode home from the park that evening determined to do something about my toes. The next day I went to hospital and that afternoon both of my toenails were removed. My feet were bandaged up and I was told I could leave. My father was with me. He left me at the exit while he went to get the car. I held on to the railing and remember seeing blue with the pain. Three or four days later I went back to the hospital to get the bandages changed. I was walking on my heels and the pain was still unbearable. As a means of making the pain less, I promised myself that I would win the Irish Junior Championships. My toes healed and I trained and I trained, as I had never trained before.

From the start, I had not been able to sprint. If there were four guys left at the end of the race, I was pretty sure to be third or fourth. It did not matter that the other fifty or sixty riders were eliminated because of the pace that I had set. In the Junior Championship of that year, I went from the line and got clear with a few lads. With two laps of the five-mile circuit to go, there was just Lenny Kirk and myself in the lead. I beat Lenny tactically. It was not because I was stronger or had more talent. If any rider in Ireland at that time had talent it was Lenny. As we shared the work I would fly past him and ease up. In his mind he was thinking that I must be flying. It was a little bluffing on my part. Then as he would go past me to do his share at the front, I increased the speed and made it really hard for him to come past. After doing that for six or seven miles I attacked on the last lap and Lenny blew. He lost over two minutes in less than five miles. Because I wanted to win that championship badly, the victory helped my confidence enormously. People began taking an interest in me. Being Irish junior champion did not mean a thing, the attention came from the manner of the victory. I think that was the last road championship I won before the 1987 World Professional Road Race in Villach.

At this time people were beginning to tell me that I was a good pedaller. I was never sure what exactly they meant by this as I did not feel that I had a talent for pedalling. It is only now, after all the years, that I am beginning to understand what they meant. It first dawned on me as I watched the 1987 Giro d'Italia on video. Italian television used a split screen in the time trials, showing Visentini in one half of the screen and me in the other. In that picture you see him fighting with his bike. His upper body is swaying from side to side as he tries to generate power. On the other side of the screen my upper body is hardly moving at all. There is a smoothness about my pedalling which does not exist in his. Similarly when French television showed Delgado and me time trialling together, you could see that he was having a bit of a battle with his bike and I was perfectly still on mine. I sat back watching this, telling myself, so this was what all the bullshit was about, Roche being a good pedaller.

Victory in the 1979 Rás Tailteann got me a lot of publicity as it was filmed by RTE television. At the time I did not consider the win to be very important. As was usual for me, my form did not come until June because I could not train much before the evenings got long in May. Normally, I was on good form for the Isle of Man, where I liked to ride well. In 1979 I did well in the Isle of Man and returned for the Rás as one of the favourites. I was not sure how I would do as I had never ridden a long-stage race before this. My sharpest memory of that Rás was the fact that Alan McCormack and I were team mates on the Ireland team and he was, by far, my biggest enemy in the race. It is funny to think that years later I had the same problem in the Giro when the stakes were higher and the ill feeling stronger.

Alan was a good rider and wanted to win. Whenever I meet any of the riders who were involved in that Rás, they always talk about the day Alan attacked. I was the raceleader and Alan had got away in a small break. When his lead on the bunch jumped to three minutes, my leader's jersey was under threat. I was not having that. I left the group I was in and went after Alan. After a hectic pursuit, I caught Alan and rode the legs off him all the way to the finish. Billy Kerr, who rode that Rás, remembers that day very vividly and talks about it every time we meet. According to Billy, I was in a group with him and a number of others. Alan was three minutes up. I decided what had to be done and left Billy's group as if I was going to the shops for a message.

An unusual thing about that Rás was my victory in the Westport stage. I won the sprint from a group of eight or nine riders. It was a slightly uphill finish and I led it out from a long way. I did not think I had a chance but as nobody was getting to me, I sensed I could win. In the end it was one long wait for the line to arrive. I reckon it was the only time in my career that I won a sprint which involved more than two or three riders.

Because I was wearing the yellow jersey, the RTE cameras focused on me quite a bit during that race. The film made it look as if I was really comfortable all through, which I was. I waved to people on the side of the road, people that I knew, different people in different places, and I felt obliged to say hello. That urge to acknowledge people on the roadside is in me, it is stronger than me. If you look at the video of the final stage of the 1987 Tour de France you can see the same thing. But in that 1979 Rás Tailteann I was riding well. I broke a spoke in the time trial and still won it by over a minute. My strategy was to get control of the race; that took the first four days. Getting into the right groups, staying there, eliminating one, then another, and when things started getting hot, I was strongest.

Later that summer I rode the Tour of Ireland and finished third. It was a very competitive race with people like Phil Anderson and Ron Hayman coming from their seasons in France to ride. I finished third overall and was happy with the way I rode. A year earlier I had ridden the Tour of Ireland and come up against Robert Millar, a Scottish rider who was competing successfully on the French amateur circuit at that time. That 1978 Tour of Ireland turned out to be a messy race with lots of fighting. Millar was out to prove how good he was. He was very sour. On the stage to Dublin I got away on one of the hills before Naas. Millar was on the same team as the raceleader John Shortt and was with me. Bernie McCormack was also there. Going up the dual carriageway from Naas to Dublin we had a tailwind and the gap was widening. This meant that I had a chance of taking the jersey from Shortt. Millar was not pleased.

At one time I moved across the road to speak with Peter Crinnion, my team manager, who had driven up alongside. As I did, Millar came through between me and the car, doing his best to knock me down as he went past. On another occasion I went to collect a bottle from a person on the side of the road and Millar again shot between us, knocking the bottle out of my hand. Getting close to Dublin he attacked and I said to myself, let him go. And I let him stay 100 yards clear rather than have to ride the remaining part of the stage with him. Millar won the stage and I got back over three minutes on Shortt but not enough to take the yellow off his back. How strange that years later Millar and I should become such close friends! I did not understand Bob in those days. Now I do and he is one of the soundest guys in the *peloton*. It is remarkable that the man who was trying to knock me in the 1978 Tour of Ireland was protecting me from being knocked off in the 1987 Giro d'Italia.

By the end of 1979 my career as an amateur in Ireland had come to an end. I did not know this at the time. For me the decision to go to France in 1980 stemmed from the need for good preparation for the Moscow Olympics. After the Olympics, I expected to be back in Ireland in 1980 or 1981. Although I did not realize it at the time, my career as an amateur in Ireland prepared me very well for what was to follow. By serving my apprenticeship to be a fitter, I gave myself the security of knowing that whatever else, I did have a trade. During my amateur career I did not train that much and so there was scope for significant improvement once I began racing full time on the amateur circuit in France. I was also fortunate that the people who helped me when I rode in Ireland, people like Noel O'Neill and Peter Crinnion, knew what the sport was about and understood the best way to bring on a young rider.

I had also come through a system which deepened my love for the bike. We were told from the start that the bike was not only about racing and we never treated it as such. During the winter months I greatly enjoyed taking off at the weekends on hostelling trips with my friends. Lads like Sean O'Grady, Paul Smith, Damian Long, Paul Kimmage and, now and again, Martin Earley. Occasionally Bernie McCormack and Fran Riordan would join us. We had fantastic times on those trips. At that time the Irish Cycling Federation was making a big effort to revitalize cycling in Dublin and the re-emergence of my club, Orwell, was a part of that. Interestingly, that effort had its reward in the fact that Paul Kimmage, Martin Earley and I all made it into the professional *peloton*.

CHAPTER 4
France

Before their son left for France early in 1980, Larry and Bunny Roche arranged a little get-together for Stephen and his friends. They had tea, sandwiches and cakes. At some point that evening Peter Crinnion, coach and friend to Roche, rounded his young protégé into a corner. 'Stephen,' he said, 'whatever happens in France, don't come back without giving it a real try. No matter how bad things are, stick it for one full season.'

I left for France on 11 February 1980. One of the reasons that I remember the date is that I worked at Premier the day before. Booked on the 8.05 flight from Dublin to Paris on the morning of the 11th, I was scheduled to arrive in Paris at around 10.20. The arrangement was that I would be picked up at Charles de Gaulle airport, shown my apartment and taken to the team's headquarters. In the late afternoon we were to leave Paris for the team's training camp in the south of France and we were not expected to arrive in the south before midnight.

I was a bit nervous about the whole experience. This was the first time I was leaving my parents. I did not speak a word of French and I did not know anybody in France.

ACBB was the name of the amateur team that I was joining. It had the reputation of being one of the top teams in France and great riders like Shay Elliott and Tommy Simpson rode with the ACBB before turning professional. Even so, being accepted by ACBB did not mean much. They were prepared to open their doors to most foreigners because they knew that if the foreigners did not measure up, they could easily be sent packing. From the beginning, I knew I would have to get them before they got me. It was simple.

Things could not have got off to a worse start. On the morning of 11 February there was a long delay on all flights out of Dublin because of fog. We thought every half-hour that it would lift but eventually did not get out of Dublin until mid-afternoon. It was after 5.30 in the evening when we landed at Charles de Gaulle. The person who was supposed to collect me at 10.30 that morning had long since left and I was on my own. I did not really know where I was and all I had was the address of the apartment at which I was to stay.

My luggage was heavy and I decided that a taxi was necessary. I showed the taxi driver the address and we set off. The apartment was in Boulogne on the west side of Paris and when we got to the street the taxi driver told me that it was one-way only and he could not take me to the door. I paid him and he dropped me at the top of the street. I had two very heavy suitcases and a shoulder bag. It was a long walk. I got to the correct number but the gate was closed. It was now about eight o'clock in the evening, I had not eaten since breakfast early that morning and was starving. When the bell was not answered I climbed over a big steel gate and got into the porch. There was another door and bell but still no answer. To hell with this, I thought.

Climbing back over the steel gate I picked up my suitcases, carried them down a dark alley and hid them. I went into the first restaurant I came across. I looked at the menu without understanding a thing. I chose what I thought was an omelette but when it arrived, it was a plate of green pasta. Served dry, without even a touch of butter or oil. I now regard green pasta as the making of a beautiful meal; with oil, cheese or butter it is wonderful. But that night I did not have a clue what it was. Coming from Ireland and a diet centred on potatoes, I had never seen anything like it in my life. I did not know enough to put a little salt on it. But it was what I had ordered and it had to be eaten. It was like eating leaves. This green stuff turned my stomach.

The waiter kept coming over to me asking if I was all right. 'Oh, I'm fine,' I replied. I struggled through half of what was on the plate. I got up and asked the waiter how much I had to pay. He enquired if I had enjoyed my meal. I told him it was great. 'Well then,' he said, 'it's OK. It does not matter.' I gave him a small tip and went on my way. Back to the apartment and more bell-ringing but still there was no sign of life.

It was now after ten o'clock on a cold winter's night in Paris, and things were not looking up. I fetched my suitcases, which were where I had left them, and got them in over the steel gate. Getting a tracksuit, leather jacket, hat and gloves out of a suitcase, I lay down on the porch and tried to sleep. But the coldness of the night kept me twisting and turning.

At four o'clock in the morning a car pulled up outside the steel gate. It was a Peugeot 104. Two lads, about the same age as I, got out of the car and opened the steel gate. They asked if I was Stephen Roche and said I was to go with them. We were going to the south of France.

There were two bikes on the roof rack and the boot was full. I put my two suitcases and my shoulder bag into the back seat and then squashed myself in alongside them. Sixteen hours later I was pulled out. We were in the town of St Maxime, where ACBB had their training camp.

It was a 600-mile journey and our stops on the way had been few. Some petrol, some peeing and some junk food that you can buy in any of the motorway restaurants in France. I did not know my two companions. One of them spoke a tiny bit of English, the other spoke none and I spoke no French. I learned that they were riders; one was from Belgium and the other was from the north of France. Later on I got to know them. Jean Louis Barrot was the Belgian and Pascal Cuvelier the other. They were typical of the kind of amateurs that one meets in France: guys who were interested in going out until all hours and trying to get up and race the next day. Cuvelier later helped me to meet Lydia and I remember him especially for that.

We arrived in St Maxime in time for the evening meal. During the meal I was introduced to Russell Williams and John Parker, two English guys riding with ACBB. There was also a Danish rider who spoke English, James Moler. Paul Wiégant was the ACBB boss and he used Parker as translator when giving me instructions. I was told where we would be training, what was expected of me and that my *voyage* had ended. Wiégant was an elderly *directeur sportif*, old-fashioned in his attitudes to the bike, and you had to earn his respect. At first, he came across as being distant. In one of my first attempts at conversation with him I referred to him as *tu*. He replied sternly, 'Mr Stephen Roche, Mr Wiégant is a colleague to you. When you speak to a colleague you say *vous*, you say *tu* when you speak with a friend. Mr Wiégant is not a friend. You must address him as *vous*, Mr Wiégant.'

Over the years I got to know Wiégant and have got on very well with him. I still say *tu* and he occasionally reminds me that it is incorrect. Sometimes he will even address me as *tu* but not very often. He ran the team like a military establishment but it was a wonderful school for any young rider. When you saw Wiégant coming, you jumped.

Everything he did was carried out with the appearance of importance. Never dressed in collar or tie but always full of authority. Out on the road, during a race, he impressed me greatly. It was the strength of his personality that made him so good at what he did. He knew how to get us motivated and nobody questioned his authority. Wiégant did not go to many races with the team because he lived in the south and Claude Escalon was the person who looked after us most of the time. But Wiégant came to some of the bigger races and when he was around, he was in charge.

St Maxime turned out to be hard. When I arrived there were just three days before the first race of the season. Before that race I was told what to do. There was a guy called Blagojevic in our team and he was the leader. We were all to ride for him. Blagojevic was a big name and was told by Cyrille Guimard that if he won a classic race, he would immediately get a contract with Guimard's pro-team, Renault-Elf. As the race got towards the finish, Blagojevic and a rider from another team were away. I was in the bunch but itching to attack. When the chance came, I went after the two leaders. I joined up with them and thought to myself that this was great. Here I was, in my first race, part of a three-rider breakaway and the finish was getting close. As well as that, one of the other two was a team mate of mine. I reckoned that either Blagojevic or I would win and I told myself it would be me.

I was strong and attacked a number of times. Each time I did the other two chased me. I wondered why Blagojevic would chase his own team mate. Yet when Blagojevic made his attack, the other rider would not ride after him. I knew that something was not right. I was so innocent. My first race for ACBB and I did not have a clue what was happening. As the attacking and pursuing went on I began to cop. The two lads were riding together, against me, even though Blagojevic was from my team and the other guy from a rival team. With about seven or eight kilometres to the finish the bunch was getting close to the three of us and there was a chance that we were going to be caught. Blagojevic attacked, the other guy rode after him for a bit and then eased up. I sensed that I was going to be stuck with this guy and that the bunch would swallow us up before the finish.

I waited for my chance and took off like a bullet, leaving the other guy well behind and closing the gap on Blagojevic. Blagojevic was about 100 metres ahead of me, I was the same distance clear of the other guy, and the bunch were about 200 yards behind him. The most likely outcome was that I would join Blagojevic at the front and that the bunch would catch the other guy. Blagojevic and I would be sprinting for first place. Wiégant saw things differently and he sped up past the bunch and slowed down alongside me. He told me to stop riding. I did not know what he meant or why he should tell me to stop. As I thought about it, he just ran me off the road and into the ditch. Such was the fright that the strength went completely from my legs. But I kept riding as best as I could and it was not until 100 metres from the line that the bunch eventually caught me. I think I finished last in the bunch.

After the race I was in a state of shock. Total shock. Paul Wiégant was not long in explaining things. He said that I had been told Blagojevic was the leader before the race and that I was not to ride after him. Everything had gone well until I counterattacked after Blagojevic and in doing this I had shown a bad example to the team.

I did not argue and for the next few races did not do very much. Then there was the Grand Prix des Issambres. This was an important race for ACBB as Wiégant has a house in Les Issambres and wanted his riders to perform well. The race goes six times over a circuit which starts and finishes in the village of Les Issambres. ACBB riders made up the majority in the race. Towards the end six riders were away, four ACBBs and two others. I was one of the ACBB riders in the break and because this was Wiégant's race, I wanted to win. But, again, when I attacked all five behind me chased. I could not believe that all three of my ACBB team mates were riding against me. It made me very determined to win. I decided to attack and give it everything. Even though the five were all riding behind me I stayed away and won on my own. The Grand Prix of Les Issambres. My first victory for ACBB.

Afterwards I found out that the other two riders in the break were part of an ACBB combine. An ACBB combine that did not include me. To them, I was a nobody. I did not exist. And I was so innocent. I did not know what a combine was. After winning in Les Issambres things became easier for me in the team as the others realized that I should be included in their schemes. I was recognized.

We spent three weeks in the south of France and Wiégant's strictness was the thing which made us sit up. In his younger days he had been a *directeur sportif* to Jacques Anquetil, and he is very professional in his ways. It was a good introduction for me. I had come from an Irish environment which was relaxed and carefree. At ACBB it was drilled into us that we were a part of an organized and professional set-up. Wiégant demanded that our shoes were clean when we raced, that everyone in the team wore the same clothes at mealtimes, that everyone ate the same things, that if 7.30 was the time agreed for evening meal, then it was 7.30. It was an excellent preparation for any rider who wished to turn pro. Years later I am doing things as they were done in that first year at ACBB. I do not like training in dirty shoes or in a pair of shorts that are torn. Sometimes I will go training on a dirty bike but I do not like doing it.

After surviving St Maxime and Wiégant I encountered my first serious problem in France and the only one that ever made me think about wanting to be back home. I had brought over a pair of Colnago cycling shoes which were comfortable and which I used for the first two weeks at St Maxime. At the beginning of the third week I was given a pair of Le Coq Sportif shoes and told to wear them in the next race. ACBB had a contract with Le Coq and their riders had to wear them. After wearing them in a race I found that one of my knees was sore.

I could not imagine that my sore knee had anything to do with the new shoes and decided that a little rest was all I needed. Two days later I returned to racing and the knee was still sore. Training camp had come to an end and we were ready to head back to Paris for the spring classics. Paris–Ezy is the first of the amateur classics and is important because of this. I rode well and found myself in a three-man break at the end. My team mate Pascal Poisson was there and the other guy was Alain Bondue. Again, I thought that Poisson and I should ride together but they were both in the French national squad and they combined against me. Bondue first, Poisson second and as we say in the *peloton* I was *flicked* again. The victim of another secret combine. But, worse than that, my knee was very sore again and I needed to have it seen to. I went to a doctor. Between missing a few days in the south and a few before Paris–Ezy I had been a week off the bike. The doctor told me to take another week off and I would be fine.

After resting it for a week, my knee was still no better. I was feeling down. Previously I had never read a book in my life but now it was my salvation. I could not train or race, I was on my own a lot of the time, staying in an apartment in Boulogne. I went through five books in less than three weeks. Towards the end of the three weeks I was getting really depressed. Thoughts of home were constantly in my mind and going home seemed like a good idea. But I remembered what Peter

Crinnion had said to me: 'Stick it out for a year.' I also knew that people in Ireland saw me as the soft city boy, totally different from Kelly, the hard boy from the country. If I had gone home they would have said, 'Ah, there's Roche. He went over to France, went once around the Eiffel Tower and came home. Ha, ha!' When homesickness was at its worst, I told myself that I could not go home and allow some people to say that I was too soft.

Three weeks off the bike and my knee continued to get sore when I returned to cycling. At my lowest, I decided that something had to be done. My work fixing machines was helpful as I put everything back to zero, that is back to the time when there was no problem with my knee. Coming from Ireland, I had brought my own saddle and bars but I removed them from the bike I used when ACBB provided us with saddles and bars. I retrieved the old saddle and bars from a locker at the team's headquarters and put them back on the bike. As a part of this process I went back to the old and worn Colnago shoes that had been brought from Ireland. Out for a training spin and my knee was perfect, no reaction. I soon worked out that the problem came from the Le Coq shoes, or the sole of the shoes. The Colnago shoes were leather-soled while the Le Coq shoes had a plastic sole. The important difference was that the leather sole would take the shape of your foot after a few days, but the plastic sole was inflexible. After a few days the sole of your foot began to take the shape of the shoe. As my foot adjusted to the shape of the shoe, it created some kind of imbalance which led to a tendon problem in my knee.

This experience made me very conscious of the importance of shoes and I kept wearing the old Colnago shoes for another eighteen months. When I won Paris–Nice in 1981, it was with the Colnago shoes. I was afraid to change them. The way around the shoe problem is to use new shoes during winter training as this gives you the chance to get to know them without being committed to wearing them in a race. Changing in mid-season is dangerous and something that an experienced rider should never attempt.

After sorting out my knee problem, everything else fell into place. I was riding well. Doing better than some of the lads in ACBB who were getting a monthly cheque. I asked Wiégant, what was the story? I was winning some races, riding very well and they were getting paid. He said, '*Mon petit*, when you win races, you win money.' And that was it. I did not get the slightest satisfaction from him. In his own way he was telling me that lads like Blagojevic and Poisson were getting a monthly cheque, maybe £200, because they had won races in previous years. After that I never asked Wiégant for a penny and I never got a penny. Once, actually, he gave me a present of about £40. But we were very close all the same and kept in touch after I left ACBB. For the Grand Prix des Nations I will normally go to Wiégant's house in Les Issambres and prepare there for a week before the Nations. It is a good house for the cyclist: you eat at the same time each day, the routine is never broken. One night in the week Wiégant gives you a little extra at mealtime, maybe a little bit of ice cream. He knows when to talk cycling and knows not to talk cycling all the time. The moment has to be right.

Our apartment in Boulogne was comfortable but a little crowded. There were two bedrooms, a sitting room and a kitchen. I was one of the guys who slept in the sitting room – the French riders had got to the apartment first and taken the two bedrooms. To get to their bedrooms, the French had to come through the sitting room. They often stayed out late and came through the sitting room at around two in the morning. But I was a heavy sleeper and they did not wake me *every* night.

For three months it was chaotic as seven of us shared. Then the process of elimination began: two of the seven realized that they were not getting anywhere and left. Another guy just disappeared. That left four of us: Parker, Moler, a French guy and myself. At the weekends confusion returned as ACBB drafted in riders from the country for the classics. These guys would come to the apartment, ransack the fridge late on the night of their arrival, do the same early next morning, and we never saw them again. They took things we had bought for the race. I was there struggling on my own, a long way from home. These guys spent six days of the week with their mothers and on the seventh they came along badly prepared for a race and robbed stuff from people who had worked hard for the money to buy it. But the guys who came and robbed our fridge never lasted too long. If they were the kind who expected food to be provided for them, they were not going to make it at ACBB. They were too soft, too easily put off.

I got on with French people as I would have got on with people from any country I was in. You make your friends and get on with it. In Boulogne I made some good friends, particularly the butcher François Hervo. Claude Escalon introduced me to François. I went to him for my meat every day. He did not speak English and I did not speak

French but we got on really well. He always had a special piece of steak set aside for me and no matter what he gave me, he would only charge me ten francs. Half a beast and he still charged me just ten francs. I brought the English pros John Herety and Sean Yates down to meet him and they began getting their meat there. François got a television and put it in a room at the back of his shop so that when the lads came they could make themselves a cup of tea and watch some television.

After I left Boulogne another English rider with ACBB, Dave Akam, started going down to François's, but when he made himself a cup of tea he left the cup unwashed and almost ruined things for everybody else. Later I saw François and he said that if it were not for me he would never have continued to look after the cyclists, but he kept hoping that he would meet another one like me. François came to my wedding in 1982 and now my younger brother Laurence is living in Boulogne, riding for ACBB and going to François for his meat every day. The experience I had of meeting people during the years working with my father on the milk round helped during the early years in France. On the milk round I learned not to bat an eyelid if somebody was contrary. It was important to do the same in France.

Back in my Colnago shoes and without the slightest problem in my knee, it was time to prove that I could do something on the bike. May and June were just around the corner and I knew that was my time of the year. I went to the Route de France, an important stage race for amateurs, and finished second overall. It was a good performance because I was a member of a composite team, Peugeot Troyes/Peugeot ACBB, and one of our team, Jerome Simon, led the race from start to finish. There was very little we could do except defend the jersey for him. I lost two minutes on the stage that finished on the Puy de Dôme but kept getting a little time back each day until the last, when I won the concluding time trial and jumped up to second overall, behind Simon. Wiégant was our *directeur sportif* on that race and immediately after it ended we left the town of Vichy for Paris. On the next morning Paris–Roubaix was starting and would be a big test. Wiégant folded down the back seat of the car and told me to sleep. We arrived in Paris around midnight and were up again five hours later, on our way to the start of Paris–Roubaix.

Paul Wiégant always impressed me. I remember him that morning wrapping bandages around the wrists of the ACBB riders so that they would be better able to cope with the jarring sensation of riding kilometre after kilometre over cobblestones.

For an amateur in France, winning Paris–Roubaix is a big thing. Normally the race is dominated by Belgians and the roadsides will be full of supporters from Belgium who have made the journey to cheer their riders on. Belgians have the reputation for being hard riders and, with all the cobbled lanes to be crossed, Paris–Roubaix is a race for hard men. I had never even seen cobbles or *pavé* and when I now consider what happened on that day, it seems to me unbelievable. I rode in the gutter at the side of the *pavé*, on the actual *pavé* itself; I went from left to right to the middle as if I had been on *pavé* all through my career. I was more surprised than anybody by the ease with which I went over the *pavé*. As the race started to get near Roubaix there were four of us going well: the Belgians Ronny van Holen and Dirk DeMol, a French amateur called Michel Larpe and myself. Van Holen tried to get away but I went after him and the others followed. On one severe section of *pavé* I went berserk and only DeMol could stay with me. We got clear and the final battle was to be fought out between the two of us.

He decided that I was strong and that he would sit in my slipstream and never come past. Wiégant was driving the team car directly behind us. His front windscreen was broken and he was screaming at me through it. I can still see through the broken glass, a big overcoat wrapped around him and a Peugeot hat on his head. 'Hey, you, what are you doing?' he screamed. He was concerned that I was doing too much work and playing into the hands of DeMol. I replied that there was nothing else I could do as DeMol just refused to come round me. Wiégant told me that if I did not win I was going home. I moved over and waited for DeMol to pass, but he did not budge. The other two were not that far behind and I had to keep up the pace to make sure they did not rejoin us. I did not see what else I could do. With about three kilometres to go we were riding down a big boulevard in Roubaix. There was a traffic island in the middle of the road. I had towed this guy for miles and was hearing Wiégant's voice every two minutes: 'You are going home.' I had to do something. Otherwise DeMol was sure to win.

Approaching the traffic island I shifted into a higher gear and got out of the saddle but instead of going right around the island, which was the correct way and a good bit shorter, I veered off as if I intended to go left. DeMol followed me for a bit until he became convinced that

I actually meant to go left. He shot off suddenly to the right, as he did I braked and jumped my bike onto the island and crossed to the other side, latching on to his back wheel as I did. He was now in front of me and it was my turn to sit tight in his slipstream. He led for the last three kilometres, leading me into the velodrome where the race finished. We had to do a half lap and then one complete circuit. With one lap to go I used the area of concrete at the finish line to pass DeMol on the inside. He tried to push me further out and into the grass but I held the inside and was just in front of him. Both of us were tired and for the entire lap I stayed just a fraction in front of him, winning by less than half a wheel. The biggest win of my career so far. I was delighted.

Victory came at a good time. Premier Dairies contacted me a short time before, wondering if I knew whether I was coming back to my job, since it was getting towards the end of my six months' leave of absence. At the time, I had not been sure. I went to Wiégant and asked him if I had any chance of getting a pro contract. He asked, what had I done? I listed all my placings, third in Paris–Ezy, ninth in Paris–Troyes, seventh in another, fourth in another. 'Ah, *mon petit*,' he said, 'what are they? They are no reference.' But after Paris–Roubaix his attitude changed. He told me there was a good chance of a pro contract. A week later, still on the same form which enabled me to win Paris–Roubaix, I won Paris–Reims. The Paris–Reims performance attracted attention. I was sent the wrong way at one point during the race and there was a breakaway group up the road. Everything was lost. On a long, steep hill I left the pack, caught the breakaways halfway up, counterattacked and was clear at the top. I rode the last 40 kilometres on my own and won by a minute. Doors suddenly started opening for me. I could now ring Premier and tell them that I would not be returning to Dublin, that they would have to replace me.

Even though I went to France in search of preparation for the Olympics, the Moscow Games decreased in importance as I settled into the ACBB set-up. My mind was set on a pro contract and I knew that would come from what I did in France. About this time I rode the Tour of Liège with the Ireland team. It was our final preparation race before the Olympics and most of the European countries were using the Liège race as a last test for their Olympic teams. I lost out in the prologue and on one other day. I was eighth overall, four minutes down, as we set out on the last day. As I was leading the mountains classification and wanted to strengthen my position, I attacked at the foot of a hill soon after the start. Getting clear, I crossed that first mountain on my own and when I looked behind all I could see was another green jersey. Afraid that he would tow the others up to me, I was waving frantically at him, telling him to go back. He was screaming at me to hold on for him. It was Billy Kerr.

Billy and I had ridden together on a number of teams and he was a very good rider. He was well into his thirties but was as good at thirty-six as he had been at any time in his career. When he showed up at the start they had asked him whether he was the Irish manager. They thought he was joking when he explained he was a rider. Because of his age, they refused to let him take part. There was a bit of a war and the organizers were told that Billy was a good rider and was representing Ireland at Moscow. Eventually they agreed to make an exception to the rule that over–35s could not race as Category One amateurs and Billy was allowed to take part.

As I told Billy to go back and he kept asking me to wait, we compromised. I half waited and he half sprinted. Once he joined me we were a happy tandem. Rain lashed down all through the stage, roads turned into rivers and in one field caravans floated off in the opposite direction to us.

Herman Nys, a Belgian with a deep interest in Irish cycling, lent Peter Crinnion a Mini and Peter drove it on the race that day. All he needed was oars to keep the Mini going. Herman has never forgotten that Peter ruined his Mini that day, for it was never the same again.

Billy and I were strong and we did not mind the rain. Our lead increased steadily until it was over five minutes with about 10 kilometres remaining. At that point Billy and I were sent the wrong way and on the finishing circuit we met the bunch coming in the opposite direction. We turned round, joined them and finished in the same time. I started the day eighth but because of bonuses picked up by others, I dropped to twelfth overall. And I was nowhere on the stage. Without the mishap I would have won the overall, the points, the mountains and finished second to Billy on the last stage. Billy would have been second on general and second in the points.

Everybody sympathized and said how unfortunate it was. But there was also an attitude that, really, it did not matter much. To Billy and me it mattered. We spoke with Peter, telling him that he had to do something. He protested to the race *commissaires* and there was a formal meeting to consider what had happened. They said how sorry they were but that they could not declare me the winner. They agreed to give me the prize money for first and award me each of the jerseys that I would have won if it had not been for the mistake in setting us on the wrong route. It was some recognition of the bad luck which had robbed Billy and me.

After Liège, we went to Moscow for the Olympics. I did not feel well in Moscow and was totally off form for the road race, performing well below my capabilities. It was not as big a disappointment as might be imagined because my biggest aim at that time was to become a professional. There was talk that Peugeot were interested and when they came with an offer I had no hesitation in signing. My feeling was that as long as I was getting as much for cycling a bike as I was for maintaining machines in the factory, I was better off on the bike. In Ireland I had earned £100 a week in the dairy. I did not smoke or drink. Everything I had went on the bike and, at the end of the year, I did not have a penny in the bank. Riding for Ireland I still bought my own tyres, shorts, paid my own travelling expenses, paid for my own meals and practically had to hire the green jersey I wore. Peugeot offered me a starting salary of £450 a month and all of my bike equipment would be supplied. If I had been in the factory my salary would have risen to £125 per week in 1981 and so I asked Peugeot for £500 a month. They agreed to that and I signed. After all the usual deductions I was left with £430 and my tax had to come out of that. It was not a fortune but I was a professional.

Right: My sister Carol's first communion – myself, Carol and Maria with Laurence and Jude

My youngest brother Laurence and I bury our dad alive but he does not look too unhappy about it

Above: Looking cool after my first big win – the 1979 Rás Tailteann

Right: They call Paris–Roubaix *l'enfer du Nord* and they are right

Roland Berland, my *directeur sportif* at Peugeot was not all bad but we had our problems

Sean and I were always seen as the 'two Irish lads in the bunch' and we were happy to be seen as such

Above: Bronze medallist at the world championship in Switzerland, 1983. Van der Poel (silver) and LeMond (gold) had even more to smile about

On my way to the bronze medal at the 1983 Worlds

Left: Attacking Kelly in the 1984 Paris–Nice. But he is one difficult man to shake off

Below: Holding on as Hinault applies the pressure in the 1984 Paris–Nice

CHAPTER 5
Meeting Lydia

'The first things I noticed about him,' says Lydia Roche, 'were his blue eyes and his chubby cheeks. I liked him.'

Growing up in Dublin, I did not have many girlfriends and they did not last very long. I left school when I was fifteen and between work, overtime, evening classes and the bike, there was not much time left over. The lads that I hung around with were the same. If one of them started going out seriously with a girl it generally meant that his interest in the bike dropped off. When we went on our hostelling weekends to Wicklow we had great fun but there were never any girls. It was not that we were not interested. We were. But the weekend was hard, long hours riding through the mountains and cooking our own food in the hostels that evening. Part of the fun for us was that it was so hard. Girls did not fit into this life. Maybe if there was a club dinner we would have to go and find a partner but that usually turned out to be nothing more than a good night out. Next day was for training and racing and training.

For me, things changed in France. It was June 1980. I was getting comfortable at ACBB and proving that I could hold my own against the best riders in France. One evening we were riding a criterium in Longjumeau on the south side of Paris. Before the start all the ACBB guys were talking about a girl who was there. Before the end of the race, all eyes were on this girl. All through the race I was watching her. I wanted to win and attacked every time there was an opportunity. Each time I was recaptured until I went away and stayed clear. After winning I made sure that I saw this stunning-looking girl before going home.

Back at the apartment in Boulogne I asked Cuvelier about this blonde-haired girl. He told me that she was Thierry Arnaud's sister. Thierry was a racer that we both knew. Cuvelier reckoned that I wanted to see her again and said that as Thierry was riding a criterium at Mantes-la-Jolie that night, Lydia was likely to be with him. Neither Cuvelier nor I was riding at Mantes, which was a good bit out on the west side of Paris. I asked Cuvelier if he would give me a lift out to Mantes. He owned the Peugeot 104 which took us to the south of France on my first night in France. He agreed and, dressed in jeans, we went to Mantes in search of the girl with the blonde hair, Thierry Arnaud's sister. Walking around the course, Cuvelier and I found the lady we were looking for. She was with another girl. I did not know her name but as she was wearing an ACBB jersey there were no problems. 'Hello, ACBB,' I said.

We began chatting and I tried to impress with the little bit of French that I had learned. Lydia was trying to make conversation as well and asked how many laps were left in the race. I knew and knew the French for it. So I immediately said *quinze tours*. My Irish accent made it sound like *casse-toi* (go away). Lydia could not believe what she was hearing and listened more carefully. I said it again. Eventually she understood. We said our goodbyes and Cuvelier and I headed for home. At a traffic light we noticed that Thierry was driving the car alongside and had Lydia and her friend in the car as well. I asked them to join us for a drink, and we stopped at a café up the road. We had our drinks and conversation and I realized that I did not have any money to pay the bill. Thierry paid and we, again, said goodbye. Soon afterwards I joined up with the Irish team for the race in Liège and from there I was off to the Olympics. I did not see Lydia again until the Olympics were over.

Lots of guys were interested in Lydia. One of them, Philippe Badouard, was chasing her for a long time. Lydia mentioned to him that she had had a drink with me, and he said, 'Stephen Roche? Sure I beat him.' Lydia did not know enough to contradict him. After the Olympics Lydia was on holiday with her parents at the Ile d'Oleron and I went on holiday with ACBB to a town called Espelette, near Biarritz. I rode criteriums down there and as I was in the company of French riders only and nobody spoke English, my grasp of French improved greatly. Back in Paris, the quest for Lydia continued. I would see her occasionally and we would have short conversations. She said that she would like to be able to speak English and I suggested that the best way to learn would be for her to come to Dublin and I would teach her.

Things began to happen in August at the Grand Prix de Garches, a three-stage race close to Paris. There were two criteriums and a road race. In the first criterium I was away with a team mate of mine, Yves Renaud. Another team mate, Jean Louis Barrot, who stayed with us in the apartment at Boulogne, abandoned the criterium after a few laps and got changed quickly. After changing he went out to watch the race and ended up sitting on the side of the road, on one of the hills, talking to Lydia. They were getting on well and each time Renaud and I passed, I noticed the two of them together. After four laps of watching this, something had to be done. Casually slowing down on the hill, I moved over to where they were and, nodding towards Lydia, I said, 'Hey, Jean Louis, she's mine. Hands off.' Half joking, half serious. Quickly I rejoined Renaud. He told me that he was from Garches and that it would mean a lot to him to win. I did not mind who won in Garches and let Yves have it.

I did not ride the second stage, which was the road race, but decided that I would put on a big show in the second criteruim. I knew that Lydia would be present and so my new tyres were put on and the bike was cleaned until it sparkled. But one of my new tyres rolled off the wheel on the very first corner and I crashed. So much for the big show. Knowing the ACBB boss, Claude Escalon, I picked myself up and set off on a two-hour training rather than go to where Lydia was watching the race. If I had gone directly to Lydia he would have suggested that I crashed deliberately in order to be with her.

When I did meet up with Lydia after the race, she had a shock for me: 'Stephen, I have spoken to my father and he says that I can go with you to Ireland to learn some English.' What I originally had said was in the course of conversation, something that a fellow says to a girl he is chatting up, not thinking for a second that the girl might take him seriously. As Lydia was going to be coming to Ireland with me, I thought that I had better ask her out. We went for a drink with a group of friends that evening and I asked for a date. She said she would ask her father. She came back to say that her father gave his permission on the understanding that I would collect Lydia and take her home by a certain time. My first date with Lydia was for the following Tuesday and I was to collect her at 4.30 in the afternoon.

One of the guys in the apartment lent me his car and at 3.30 on that Tuesday afternoon I set out with a map and an address in Conflans, where the Arnauds lived. Our plan was to go to the pictures at around 5.30 and return to Lydia's house for the evening meal at around eight.

I took a few wrong turnings, got caught up in the Paris traffic and arrived at Lydia's house three hours late for my first date. In fact I was only just in time for the evening meal. After eating it was time for me to be getting home.

Although that first date had not been a success, Lydia and I began to see much more of each other. Her two brothers, Thierry and Michel, were both racing and Lydia travelled with her father to watch. Afterwards we met. Once Monsieur Arnaud was dropping me back in Boulogne and he asked me if I would like to come along with them and eat in Conflans. I said I would but how would I get back to Boulogne? He told me to bring my bike and I could stay the night. That was the first of many such nights.

Lydia came to Ireland that winter, as promised. It was one of our best ever times together. As boyfriend and girlfriend still developing our relationship, we had great fun. In another way it was a very difficult month for Lydia in Ireland. She got on fairly well with my people. But she was very good-looking and still lacking maturity. Although she looked far older, Lydia was only fifteen. Coming to Ireland with me, she felt that I would be able to give her nonstop attention. She got excited very easily and my parents, as parents will, were noticing everything. So far away from home and unable to speak English, Lydia was vulnerable. My parents wanted to like her but because they could not communicate, it was very difficult for all three of them.

Things were made worse by the comparison so many were making with my situation and that of the late Shay Elliott. Shay had been to ACBB, had been a star on the French amateur circuit and later a star in the *peloton*, once winning the yellow jersey in the Tour de France and winning a silver medal at the World Championship road race. He married a good-looking French woman and the marriage did not work out well. Cycling people in Dublin believed that the marriage had been bad for Elliott. People were looking at my situation, relating it to Shay's and advising my parents to stop it before it went too far. They wondered how I could go to France and fall for a girl when in Ireland I had not had a girlfriend. Some people even treated Lydia coolly because they reckoned that she was going to ruin my life, take all my money and run. Throughout my life I always listen to what people have to say and, at that time, I contributed to the problems by listening to these people. I should have told them to stay quiet. The important thing was that Lydia was able to live through all of this and stay with me.

Lydia was not being too well received by cycling people in France, either. Daniel Dousset, who was then manager to all ACBB riders, invited Lydia and me around to his house to eat. During the evening Dousset managed to separate Lydia and me; he ended up with Lydia in the dining room and I with Madame Dousset in the sitting room. He lectured Lydia for an hour on the facts of the cycling life and how she could ruin my career. When you are sixteen years old and going out with a boy that you like, there are things you do not want to hear. Similarly Maurice De Muer, *directeur sportif* of the Peugeot team, believed that Lydia would ruin his young professional. If Lydia showed up at a race, De Muer would attribute anything that went wrong to her presence. He and Dousset were very much of the old school. Women and cycling did not mix.

I am also a bit of a traditionalist. It is not good for the rider to have his wife or girlfriend present at races. Lydia understands this and agrees. Being on a race is a 24-hour-a-day job: the time you spend sleeping and resting is as important as the time you spend on the bike. But back in the early eighties when Lydia and I were going out together, getting engaged and planning to get married, De Muer and Dousset were not helping anybody. They were chastising a girl of sixteen, telling her that if she did anything wrong, I would not do well. Lydia was getting upset, repeating all these things to me, and I was then getting upset. They were fucking everybody up. It took me until 1983, a year after we were married, to get a grip on things. I began answering back. I was not prepared to take any more of the criticism.

PART II

The Learning Years

CHAPTER 6
A Day in the Life of a Pro

Thursday 24 May 1983. It is nine o'clock in the morning. Miribel-les-Eschelles, a village in the southeast of France, shows but the faintest signs of life. Pleasant sunshine and the gentlest of breezes brighten and freshen the village. From the village hotel, Les Trois Biches, four young men emerge. All athletic in appearance, dressed in the style of professional bike riders. Their clothing and bikes reveal that they represent Peugeot. Their flippant cheerfulness reveals good humour. They are joking about some mountain pass or other, Alpe d'Huez. They agree that whichever one finishes last at the summit of this mountain will have to buy a bottle of champagne at the evening meal.

Some young mothers begin to appear in Miribel, taking their little ones to school. They notice the four bike men but do not think their presence in any way strange. Food is packed into the back pockets of the riders' jerseys. Apple tarts, fruit cake, biscuits, wrapped with care and stored away for later in the day. At around twenty-five minutes after nine an older man, dressed in shorts and T-shirt, tells the riders to mount their steeds, and the jibing momentarily stops. All four slip onto their machines and ease away from Les Trois Biches. The older one gets into a newish-looking cream Peugeot car and accelerates away after the riders, for already they have disappeared from view.

The four Peugeot riders are Pascal Simon, Stephen Roche, Robert Millar and Philippe Martinez. They have come to Miribel-les-Eschelles as part of their preparation for the Tour de France, which begins in five weeks' time. The driver of the car is Roger Legeay, assistant *directeur sportif* to the Peugeot cycling team. Three of the riders, Simon, Roche and Millar, are considered to be above average. Martinez, the fourth, is not well known.

The three good ones, Simon, Roche and Millar, are potential winners of the 1983 Tour de France. Injury will keep Bernard Hinault out of the Tour and make it a very open race. Simon, Roche and Millar know how open the 1983 Tour is and imagine themselves on the Champs Elysées podium. But, first, there is the question of leadership of the Peugeot team. Simon, Roche or Millar? They have been training in the Alps for almost a week, staying at Les Trois Biches and climbing all the mountains they will face in the Tour. Today is their final training spin and it is not a coincidence that their ride will end with the tortuous ride to the summit of Alpe d'Huez. Perched 1860 metres above sea level, Alpe d'Huez offers the riders one of the most punishing experiences in the sport of cycling. At the first hairpin there is a sign which says Virage 21. From that point to the top the riders must climb 1054 metres in thirteen kilometres and work their way around a further twenty hairpin turns.

Simon, at twenty-six, is the oldest of the three. Tall and strongly built, he has proven that he can ride the Alps. Now close to the zenith of his powers, Simon believes that he can make a big mark in this year's Tour. Today's spin is important to him. Roche is the youngest of the three, just twenty-three. He is now in his third year as a professional but has disappointed. When he was a first-year pro in 1981 they said he could be the next Hinault but since then they have lost interest in Roche. He did not seem quite what he was cracked up to be. Millar is a year older than Roche and in his fourth professional season. He is a proven mountain climber but his engine is not considered big enough for a race like the Tour de France.

The fourth member of the training party, Philippe Martinez, is tall and lean and sits elegantly on his bike. Looking at him setting off with the others, you would not guess that Martinez is nearing the end of his brief and unsuccessful career. But the others know about Martinez. He is always taking one form of medication or another. Always coughing, or suffering from a runny nose. Never able to find his form. Martinez will be let go by Peugeot at the end of the season and the others know that no other team will touch him. They are glad that his old man is fairly well off.

As the four settle down to the business of the day, you notice Roche's style. His legs do the cycling, smoothly revolving as if automated. His shoulders and arms sit still. Not a flicker of movement where there should not be movement. Legeay, once a professional rider himself, remarks that what Roche has is not learned: 'Stephen was born with that ability to turn the pedals. You cannot teach yourself to do it the way he does.' Legeay says that Roche is not ready for the Tour. Maybe Simon, not Roche. His physique has not yet developed sufficiently. Millar, says Legeay, is like Roche. He, too, has not attained the physical maturity necessary to win the Tour.

The hours slip by peacefully. First the riders climb the Col du Coq, 1434 metres above sea level and situated in the heart of the Chartreuse. At the very top there is an unpaved section, a gravel and dust reward for the riders who get thus far. At the beginning of the Coq, the four are in a line, like four beads joined by an invisible string. Martinez loses his hold on the string halfway up. The others show neither interest nor mercy. He is left on his own. Legeay frowns to himself, makes a mental note of Martinez's troubles and drives up behind the other three. He, too, is uninterested in Martinez. Near the top, the three riders notice patches of old, sheltered snow and something clicks uncomfortably in their ears.

After crossing the summit of the Coq, the three wait for Martinez to catch up and all four flow down the descent in a line. Onward they go, seeking out the next mountain. The Côte de Laffrey is not as long as most other Alpine passes but it makes up for its lack of length in steepness. Again Martinez is shed as the other three carry on towards the summit. Their pace is strong but controlled. Each knows that the only place to ask questions is on the climb to Alpe d'Huez. And, again, Martinez is allowed to rejoin as the others make the descent. They have been on the road for over four hours and only Martinez shows any sign of frailty.

Once clear of the Laffrey the Peugeot quartet makes its way up the Romanche valley. Called the Valley of the Dead because it is for ever in the shadow of the surrounding mountains, the Romanche valley is eerily quiet on this May afternoon. Through the villages of Schilienne, Gavet, Les Glavaux and Riouperoux, the racers travel and there is not a stir. Open doors but no people. A sleeping dog here, a shuttered window there. Like life the day after.

Still onwards the four go, rising gently with the road until they find themselves in the town of Bourg d'Oisans. Beyond Bourg d'Oisans, a mountain stands upright and towering. The Alpe to the racers. The one and only Alpe. Looking closely they can see a lightly coloured line which begins at the bottom and wriggles and loops its way to a village near the top. That is the climb to Alpe d'Huez. Suddenly time passes quickly as the riders fly through Bourg d'Oisans and arrive at the foot of the Alpe. Simon, Roche and Millar are about to find out things about themselves and the others. A week's training had come to this final, searching examination. Legeay sits back in his car seat, smiles and pretends that it is all just another training spin. Soon, he is leaning forward again.

Martinez is the first to feel the competitive instincts of the others as he loses his place in the line at the second hairpin. Millar and, especially, Simon want to get rid of Roche. They know that he is most vulnerable on the steep early slopes. Up goes the pace, Simon and Millar at the front, Roche trying to hang on. Simon and Millar persist; a gap of four, maybe five, bike lengths opens between the two and Roche. Perspiration drips down Roche's face, a measure of his pain. Legeay encourages Roche to fight, Simon and Millar try harder. Roche can hang on no more and visibly eases. Soon the other two are gone clear. Twenty metres, thirty, forty, fifty and then one full hairpin ahead of Roche. Legeay is quiet, pensive, disappointed. He encourages Roche as he drives past. As he has left Martinez earlier, he leaves Roche because there are others cycling faster up the road.

Simon and Millar ride side by side. Both punch aggressively on the pedals, taunting each other with strength. They have forgotten Roche. Three kilometres from the summit Millar attacks, leaving Simon on his own. Once his surge subsides, to be replaced by a steady rhythm, Millar is thirty metres ahead of Simon. Legeay exhorts Simon to pursue. He does and soon catches Millar.

Suddenly aware of his limitations, Millar loses some of his self-esteem and is now an easy adversary for Simon. Simon's attack comes soon; Millar does not, cannot, respond. Away flies Simon, Millar settles for second, afterwards Roche and, last, Martinez.

Simon arrives alone at the rendezvous at the summit of Alpe d'Huez. Exhausted but satisfied. Point proven. A minute later Millar makes it. Three minutes after Millar, Roche pedals to a stop. Disappointed but not demoralized. Eleven minutes after Roche, fifteen later than Simon, Philippe Martinez battles with the last gradient.

Legeay takes the riders to a restaurant. They all drink simple mixtures, mineral water and ice. They remount and begin the long cycle home. Soon the four have showered and dressed. Spirits rise at Les Trois Biches. A hard day's training over, nobody wishes to gloat or agonize over the events of Alpe d'Huez. Martinez is not asked to buy champagne for, now, champagne does not seem such a good idea at all. As darkness envelops Miribel, Roche slips away from the dinner and calls Lydia in Paris: 'Oh yeah, things went fine today.' Later that evening he analyses his performance on Alpe d'Huez. In a one-to-one with Simon and Millar, he would always have problems. But when it is the Tour de France, he would expect to be ahead of both. His spirits, knocked a little, are nowhere near the ground.

The owner of the hotel and Roche have become good friends. When the others are distracted the patron invites Roche to return with Lydia for a vacation. Roche promises.

Strange the way things work, but an outsider who watched Roche, Millar and Simon go about their business that evening would have presumed that Roche was the champion. It was something in his bearing, something in the way the patron deferred to him and something in the way Roche accepted the patronage. At about 10.30 the riders funnelled upstairs and disappeared into their bedrooms. Quietness filled the hotel and four men closed their doors on another day's self-exploration.

Standing starkly against the feeling that Roche might be a champion was the punishing evidence of the Alpe. Four minutes to Simon in less than twelve kilometres. So exciting as a first-year pro in 1981, so disappointing in 1982 when he did not win a race, Roche now hung somewhere between the promise of 1981 and the depths of 1982. Most likely, he had found his true worth in 1983. Talent, yes. Greatness, no. But to admit that was to ignore that something in Roche which was indefinable. Maybe star quality. Maybe not. Whatever it was, the patron of Les Trois Biches recognized it.

CHAPTER 7
Instant Stardom

Serge Beucherie won the French professional championship in 1981. That same year Beucherie looked around and saw a newcomer, Stephen Roche. Beucherie was impressed: 'I was not the only one to think that we had one super rider in our midst. A specimen that one encounters only once in a decade.'

Looking back on his career, a cyclist will always see things more clearly than he did at the time. Now I can easily explain why I had so much success in my first two years in France and so many problems afterwards. At the time, I did not have a clue.

The success I achieved as an amateur with ACBB and as a first-year professional with Peugeot was based on the completely different way of life I had in France. As an amateur in Ireland, I had done far less training and I would never have considered taking time off work to prepare for a race. My body was allowed to develop without the strain imposed by excessive training and the victories which came my way in Ireland resulted from the natural ability I possessed.

Once I arrived in France, everything changed. Given the chance to compete as a full-time cyclist, I wanted to get as much as I could from the life. I trained seriously and settled into the life of a committed bike rider. The improvement in my performance was bound to be enormous and it was. With ACBB in 1980 I won nineteen races, which, for a non-sprinter, was something. The benefits of racing full time and training properly continued into 1981, my first season as a professional. Only three weeks of the season had passed when I won the Tour of Corsica. From there we went to Paris–Nice and I also won that. No one had ever won Paris–Nice as a first-year pro and nobody has done it since. But, in some ways, the huge success of 1981 made my life difficult afterwards.

There was a lot of pressure on me after Paris–Nice as expectations went sky high. I was being held up as the successor to Hinault and I was immature enough to go along with the idea. My head was on my shoulders but I was still a bit of a dreamer. I did not have the intelligence to realize that what I did as a first-year pro, while it was fantastic, was only the first part in my development as a professional rider. I had not served an apprenticeship but I was foolish enough to believe that I could become a fully fledged, successful cycling star without one.

For example, I had no idea how to handle journalists. In my mind I was the star and there were obligations which the star had, like talking to journalists. A journalist would call and ask to see me that day, I would suggest that he come to my house, he would say that he could not and I would agree to meet him somewhere in Paris. An hour-long interview ended up taking the whole day.

My own attitude did not help. I recall somebody asking me in one interview what I thought of Hinault. I replied that the guy was only human 'with one head, two arms and just two legs, like the rest of us'. That was my attitude because I had got things so easily myself. I did not mind saying something like this, it was not meant to hurt anybody and there was no disrespect intended towards Hinault. It was simply that I had come from nothing to be a star: there was no apprenticeship. Now I can say the same things that I said in 1981 but in different words and nobody notices a thing.

I was also being unfair to Lydia. Because of my racing commitments during the summer I had not been able to see her very much and then during the winter I was always going to receptions or to see some journalist, and Lydia was becoming very dissatisfied. We came close to breaking up. Lydia was the only one who could see how things were going and she told me. But I knew too much and was not listening.

Even if things happened too fast for me in 1981, it was still a memorable year. It all began at the Peugeot training camp in Seillans. Because I wanted to be in reasonable condition for the training camp I spent the previous week preparing at another south-of-France location, Narbonne Plage. I was with Robert Millar and as he had ridden for Peugeot in 1980, he was showing me the ropes. On arrival at Seillans the first thing was to meet Maurice De Muer, *directeur sportif* of the Peugeot team. I knew De Muer only by reputation and he had a name for being strict and old-fashioned. Walking into the team hotel in Seillans we met De Muer. He asked Millar who his friend was.

Robert said, 'Stephen Roche.'

'Roche, the rider?' asked De Muer, trying to sound shocked.

'Yes,' said Millar.

'But this individual is three stone overweight. How is he ever going to ride a bike?'

So, there it was, I had met Maurice De Muer. The man who would be my boss for the next two years.

From the start it was made clear that De Muer was not much bothered about me. He wanted me to know that I had brought too much weight to training camp and that there would be a price to pay. And he was going to show me that there was a big difference between amateur and professional racing. After a week at Seillans we began racing in the south and in one of my very first races I came face to face with Hinault.

It was the Tour of the Mediterranean and on one stage Hinault was about 100 yards clear of the bunch. Different riders tried to get across to him but failed. I saw a chance to go, took it and got across to him. As soon as I reached his back wheel he growled, 'Ride.' I said I would as soon as I got my breath back. I rode with him and he rode hard. When it was over, I wanted to collapse. *Le blaireau* had given me a lesson.

From the Tour of the Mediterranean we went to the Tour of Corsica. Hinault took the jersey in Corsica and with the backing of the strong Renault team he looked likely to hold on to it. On the penultimate day my team mate Jacques Bossis attacked and was 100 yards clear of the *peloton*. I counterattacked and joined him. The entire Renault team was chasing at the front of the bunch but Bossis and I were flying and we stretched the lead to one minute. It was up and down terrain and that suited Bossis and me. Our lead moved from one minute to 55 seconds, down to 45 seconds, back up to 50, and it went on like that for 120 kilometres. Bossis was going to take the leader's jersey from Hinault so he did not mind allowing me to win the stage. My first win as a pro. Bossis got the leader's jersey, I was second overall and Hinault third. The race finished with a time trial the next day and the presumption was that Bossis would beat me in that test and only have Hinault to worry about. But next day I beat Bossis, Hinault only beat me by a handful of seconds, and I was the overall winner.

We flew directly from Corsica back to Paris for Paris–Nice began just two days later. Lydia came with her dad to see the start of the race and I spoke with her before my ride in the prologue. I should have produced a good time in the prologue but my chain slipped and I was well down. De Muer told me this was the kind of thing that happened 'when women were brought along to races'.

As always in Paris–Nice the team time trial is the first important test. At the foot of the hill in the team test we were 20 seconds down on the Italian team Bianchi, having waited for Graham Jones, who punctured. On the hill I went to the front and set the tempo, constantly looking behind to make sure that nobody was being left on their own. At the top of the hill we were told that we had taken over the lead and were ten seconds up on the Bianchis. After the hill I still did far more than my fair share of the work and at the finish in Bourg-en-Bresse we were the fastest team of all.

Our team time-trial performance enabled Michel Laurent to take over the lead in the race and the rest of the Peugeot team all moved up. For Laurent it was a very happy occasion as he is from Bourg-en-Bresse. After Laurent got the jersey he went to Duclos-Lassalle and embraced him. I felt a bit let down because it was I who had done most work in the team-trial, far more than Duclos, and I was not being recognized. I was a nobody and others were happy to take the credit for what I had done. This was not because they had anything against me. It had to do with the fact that I did not have a reputation, I was a new pro and nobody expected very much from me. The Tour of Corsica was a small race and when you were in the middle of Paris–Nice it did not seem very significant. It was only when Paris–Nice was over and I had won that people, my team mates included, looked back and said, 'But remember the ride he did in the team time-trial, that proved something.' From that first Paris–Nice I gained the reputation for being a strong man in a team time-trial, a rider who could hold things together.

With Laurent in the jersey, Peugeot were happy to defend for him. He was a strong rider and we knew that he was very determined to win. In his early career he had been very good but had suffered two bad years and was now in a sort of comeback year. When we hit the mountains, the race changed completely. On one of the hills he punctured and I waited for him. I was the only Peugeot rider who waited. I brought him back to the bunch, riding up the hill on the right-hand side of the road, and we took up positions near the front of the pack, in about tenth and eleventh places. Almost immediately there was an attack from the front; Fons de Wolf was the one who started it. I shifted into a higher gear, got out of the saddle and went *phyff*! I joined the breakaways and we ended up taking 12 minutes out of the pack. A pack which included Michel Laurent. I took over leadership of the race.

When the break was away the Peugeot team did not know what to do. They were considering riding after the break and called up De Muer to ask what they should do. De Muer said 'the young fellow' should have his chance. From De Muer's position, I had ridden a good time trial in Corsica and Paris–Nice was likely to be decided in the concluding Col d'Eze time trial. De Muer understood too that the other teams in the race would be happy if Peugeot chased down the break. The break did not contain any big name riders and none of the other teams felt that it was their responsibility to organize the pursuit. De Muer decided to play his Roche card.

That evening I had the race leader's white jersey and felt very satisfied. Not everyone in the Peugeot team was happy. The Peugeot doctor came to my room to tell me that Michel was very upset and actually crying in his room. I told the doctor that I had not done anything wrong and that if there was anything I should do, I would be happy to do it. The doctor suggested that I go to Michel's room and speak with him. When I got there, Michel was still crying. I could only say that I was *désolé*. 'Don't be,' he said, 'you did your job. You were the guy who waited for me when I punctured. It was up to the other teams to ride after the breakaway group. They didn't. You were the beneficiary. I only hope that you can now win the race.' He left it at that.

Later that evening there was a team meeting. De Muer got to the point quickly. 'OK, there are two possible courses of action. Tomorrow, on the Ventoux, we can have fireworks with attacks going in every direction. Or we can defend Roche. What do you think?'

There was a silence for a few seconds. A voice said, 'We defend Roche.' I looked around. It was Michel Laurent. I almost fell through my seat. Leader of Paris–Nice and I was going to have the full backing of the Peugeot team. This was heavy stuff for me. Having come from a relaxed amateur career in Ireland, I knew very little about team tactics or pressure or having a team riding for you. As well as all these things there were journalists and television cameras. Everybody present to see how Roche reacted.

That night I did not sleep. It was the only time in my career that nerves have affected my sleep. At the start of the stage I felt unwell: shivery and cold one minute, warm the next. By the time we reached the foot of Mont Ventoux I felt very warm and decided to discard some clothes, taking off my arm warmers and hat and putting them in the car. As we climbed the Ventoux, rain started to fall but I was surviving. Farther up the rain turned to snow and it became very cold.

Near the top Adri Van der Poel, who had been in the break with me, attacked with some other riders and claimed the forty-five seconds' bonus at the summit. That was enough to give him the leader's jersey. At the top there was three inches of snow on the road and I was about a minute behind the Van der Poel group. I was also freezing and asked De Muer for my arm warmers. He just screamed, 'Get down that mountain fast and get yourself onto the tail of the leading group.' Van der Poel descended well but, somehow, I managed to get back the minute and join up with his group. I did not know where I was as I took chance after chance, on that descent.

After the descent we rode in the shadow of the Ventoux and I became even colder. I felt sick and exhausted. Other riders knew how I was and there were many attacks. I could not close the gaps immediately and survived by gradually increasing my speed and eventually recapturing those who had broken away. There was another hill after the Ventoux and as we began climbing again I felt as if I had been hit with a hammer. I could not go any farther but I knew I could not stop. Most of my team mates were around me: Chalmel, who had been told to stay with me all day, Duclos-Lassalle, Linard and Perret. They were doing everything possible to keep me in touch with Van der Poel.

I eventually got to the finish line in the same group as Van der Poel. I had lost the jersey to him but not by very much. It was freezing cold and the rain was still lashing down.

I went to our team car, held on to the roof and ate an entire box of sugar lumps. I could not move. I was crying and utterly exhausted. There was a sense of loss as well. Everybody had put everything on me and I had been defeated. We did not have the jersey any more.

That night De Muer came to my room. He reminded me that I had lost the jersey but I must get it back. Something had to be done. His plan was that Duclos-Lassalle and Bossis would lead me to the top of the final climb on the next day's stage and from there I was on my own. I was to go mad on the descent into Mandelieu. He said I could kill myself if I wished but I was to get the jersey back. He did not care how I got it back as long as I did it.

Next day I went mad on the descent, almost went over the edge a few times but kept upright and finished 25 seconds up on Van der Poel. That was enough to get the jersey back.

Once I had got the jersey back, everything went fine. Next morning was the last day and there were two stages: a morning road race to Nice, and the Col d'Eze time trial in the afternoon. On the climb of the Col de Tanneron in the morning Laurent, Clere, Vandenbroucke and I got away and rode very hard all the way to the finish, taking a minute out of Van der Poel. The race ended well for me when I won the Col d'Eze time trial. I got the feeling that De Muer was, at last, acknowledging that I had something. That I was not just another ordinary, overweight new pro.

De Muer was not unlike Wiégant except that he was even stricter. Wiégant tended to keep things to himself; De Muer never minded walking straight into your room and telling you things. Even though I began the 1981 season on very good form there was tension between De Muer and me. Maybe I resented his attitude towards me, he wanted to ensure I appreciated how hard the life was. He may well have found me presumptuous and resented the fact that so much success had come so quickly. A pretty major row was inevitable.

It happened on the night before the Flèche Wallonne classic. In the first two months of the season I rode as many races as I had done in my entire career before then. At the end of March I went with Lydia down to her family's holiday home on the Ile d'Oleron and we spent a week there. While there I rode the bike each day but took things relatively easy. I was sure that a break from serious competition was necessary. I returned to Paris just in time to ride Paris–Roubaix and on the night before the race De Muer came into my room and asked what I had been doing. I told him I had taken a week's break. 'Ah, a tourist,' he said. He proceeded to castigate me for going to the south.

The next day I was to ride for Duclos-Lassalle. Getting towards the end we were both in the lead group when he punctured. I gave him a wheel and waited for the team car to service me. It was a mess because I was going far better than Duclos and quickly caught up with him. He did not recapture the lead group and was soon blown out of our group. I was fine until about twenty kilometres from the finish when I ran out of energy and lost about twenty minutes by the time I reached Roubaix.

I rode hard all through that Paris–Roubaix and was shattered at the finish. De Muer came over and said maybe I would now 'think again before taking my holidays in the middle of the season'. I was furious because I had given so much and this was all he could say.

From Roubaix we headed towards Belgium and two days of preparation before Flèche Wallonne. On the night before the race we were having our meal in the cellar of a restaurant and after the main course was served, there was a general silence. De Muer suggested that as we were all together and sitting at one long table it was as good a time as any to discuss tactics for the race. Most of Peugeot's big riders were there: Duclos, Bernaudeau, Laurent and I. De Muer began, as he always did, wondering who was in the mood to make the race. As usual nobody spoke up, so he looked at Jean René Bernaudeau and said, 'Bernaudeau?'

'Oh, I'm OK,' said Bernaudeau.

After Bernaudeau he turned to Laurent. 'I'm OK,' said Michel.

Duclos? 'Yes, I feel OK too.'

I watched and thought about what to say when it came to my turn. 'And Roche, what about you?'

'Me,' I said, 'I'm taking a camera with me. I'm going touring.' It came out half joking, half seriously. I was trying to get at him. Everybody at the table knew it and there was a silence.

De Muer stood up and started shouting at me. I stood up. We were face to face.

'Listen, Monsieur De Muer,' I said, 'I have a lot of respect for you but I am Stephen Roche and my legs belong to me. I know when they must stop. You can never tell me.'

The argument went on for half an hour. The waitress came to serve dessert but saw what was happening and went away without serving. Everyone else stayed sitting, not saying a word. Between De Muer and me, the words went back and forth. The mood was as cold as ice. Eventually I sat down. He continued on and on. At the end of it all I told him that if he ever wished to speak to me like that again, he was to come to my room. I did not like it that he was saying personal things to me in front of the team.

I got up from the table and left. All the other riders walked out behind me. On the stairs to our bedrooms I discovered that all the lads admired me for having stood up to De Muer. They could not believe that anybody would. Jacques Bossis, in particular, was amazed. If I see Bossis now, it is all that he ever remembers.

That night helped me enormously with De Muer. He appreciated somebody standing up to him. He had grown tired of people saying, 'Yes, Monsieur De Muer, no Monsieur De Muer.' After the row I found it easy to be straight with him.

Almost a year later we were at training camp in the south of France and many of the lads had their wives and girlfriends staying in the hotel next door. At training camp it was expected that husbands and wives would sleep separately but after the evening meal the lads would go to their rooms only to slip out through the windows and meet their partners. Towards the end of the week Lydia was due to come down and I went to De Muer and asked if it was OK if Lydia and I went to Cannes for three days. He wondered why I sought permission. I told him it was because I was not afraid to ask. Years later he told me that he admired me for having asked to go to Cannes and that he did not have any time for the clever guys who thought they were fooling him by slipping out the window.

The row that preceded the Flèche Wallonne in 1981 was but one of many between De Muer and me. But they ended well and after De Muer lost his job as *directeur sportif* I was the only one who went to visit him in his retirement. Duclos used to be his great mate and I am not sure but I don't think Duclos has been in touch with him since. Afterwards De Muer said that the difference between me at twenty-one and Duclos-Lassalle at twenty-seven was the difference between a man and a child. Duclos forgets that, tomorrow, when he stops cycling, he could need the help of Maurice De Muer. Anyway, it costs me nothing to give De Muer a ring occasionally and see how he is. If I am away for a long spell, he will ring Patrick Valcke, my mechanic, and enquire how I am getting on.

After Flèche Wallonne I continued to ride well and recorded my third stage race victory in the Circuit d'Indre et Loire in May. Victory came in very unusual circumstances. On the final stage I was in a breakaway group of five who were all very close on general classification. We knew that the time bonuses at the stage end would decide things. Eddy Planckaert, Herman Friou and I were the three principals. It was raining and everybody wore their raincoats. I kept trying to get clear of the other four but could not do it. Six or seven kilometres from the finish I pulled off all the extra clothing, stripped right down to my short sleeves. The stage ended in the town of St Augustin, down a great big boulevard, a U-turn and a sprint up the far side to the line. Going down the boulevard I attacked again but they caught me on the corner.

They cut across on the corner and I jumped onto the last wheel. They sprinted, Planckaert appeared to have it from Friou on his left. I went really late and to the right of Planckaert. He was only watching for Friou on his left and right on the line and I got past him. The fun was only starting.

I received the bouquet for winning the stage and Planckaert received the race leader's jersey. The bonus he picked up for finishing second gave him the overall victory. But there was an irregularity in the sprint and Planckaert was disqualified for switching Friou. Promoted to second on the stage, Friou picked up additional bonus seconds and that put him on a better overall time than Planckaert. As Friou was from St Augustin, there was great joy when it was announced that he, and not Planckaert, was the overall winner. De Muer and I were leaving in the car and knew nothing of what was going on. Just as we were pulling away we heard over the public address of Planckaert's disqualification and Friou's promotion. De Muer screeched on the brakes and said, 'Oh no, no, no, no, no. Friou is *not* the overall winner. Roche is.' He raced back to the podium and explained to the organizers that Friou and I were level on time, I had more points and so I was the winner. There was no argument from the organizers. A mistake, that was all. It was the most embarrassing experience of my career as I took the bouquet out of Friou's hands and the race leader's jersey off his back. And in his home town too.

The exceptionally good start tempted Peugeot into believing I was ready to ride the Tour de France in my first season. De Muer was sure that I should ride the Tour. His attitude was that you raced when you were going well. Not surprisingly he has a reputation for having burned out a few riders. Fundamentally I agree with the philosophy that a rider must race when he is going well but that cannot be applied to a first-year professional. In my mind I was just twenty-one years old, I was still growing and developing and I should be allowed to do this without being exhausted all the time. I was determined to get out of riding the Tour. I knew it was not right for me. The Dauphine Libere proved that I was correct.

Because it races over many of the most difficult Alpine passes, the Dauphine is a very good preparation race for the Tour. I expected to have real problems in the Dauphine. I did not want to ride the Tour and I was not even ready for the challenge the Dauphine represented. The first couple of stages were flat and I did a fairly respectable time trial, finishing fifth. But in the mountains I was murdered. My loss each day varied from a half an hour to 45 minutes. I was really wiped out, finishing with Ludo Peeters each day. My first experience of the Alpine passes in midsummer and I was going to remember it.

On the day we climbed the Ventoux we approached it from the unsheltered side and the sun was beating down on us. On a long climb like the Ventoux I can get into a rhythm and maintain that rhythm indefinitely. I was actually hoping to finish well up on the Ventoux stage. It was proposed that because of the intense heat and the severity of the Ventoux we take it easy. Hinault said that was OK by him and everybody expected a controlled ride to the summit. After two kilometres of a controlled pace, Mariano Martinez took off and that was it. Everyone went like the hammers. I ended up finishing alongside Martinez, both of us 45 minutes down. He went all out and won the sprint for 141st place. A madman. But that finished all notions of my riding the Tour in 1981. After the Dauphine even De Muer accepted that I was not ready.

During the 1981 Tour I rested and returned to racing in the Tour de l'Avenir. My team mate Pascal Simon dominated and there was nothing I could do. But my form was good and it enabled me to finish second in the Grand Prix des Nations time trial, beaten by the Swiss time-trial specialist Daniel Gisiger. It was not common for a first-year pro to finish so high in the Nations. Further proof that I had maintained my form came in the Etoile des Espoirs which was my fourth stage race victory in my first season. Right at the end of the year I rode the Tour of Lombardy and was very strong, finishing about eleventh but being in the sprint for first place. It was a good end to what had been a spectacular season. Any rider who wins Paris–Nice in his first season will be considered a star by a public that always wants new stars. I was young, innocent and a long way from being mature. They said I was the next Hinault. The problem was that I believed them.

CHAPTER 8
Problems at Peugeot

At a time when his morale was low and his results depressing, Stephen Roche spoke with the experienced Dutch pro Gerrie Knetemann. 'If a rider has true talent,' said Gerrie, 'and has proved that he is really good, then he can be good again.' Roche willingly embraced Knetemann's theory.

Now, when I look back on the years 1982, 1983, and 1984, I see them as the years of my apprenticeship. Without them, I do not believe that I could have achieved the success of 1987. They were not years when I was down all the time – 1983 was a good year with many notable victories. They were, however, three years in which I learned much. With a different mentality, I might easily have gone under from lack of success in 1982, the bitterness of my contractual dispute with Peugeot at the end of 1983 and the disappointment of failing in the 1984 Tour de France when it appeared sure that I would ride well. Some of the time I created my own problems, on other occasions it was the fault of others, and sometimes I simply had bad luck. But the cause of the problems did not matter very much. The reaction of people to the fallen star was the same. I had to learn from the troubles and, most of all, I had to be able to pick myself up and fight back.

It is easy now to look back and decide that the extraordinary success of 1981 led, in its own way, to the letdown of 1982. Success had come too quickly and too easily. When I should have been preparing on my bike for 1982, I was living the life of the star. Seeing this journalist, going to that reception. I went to training camp with about 500 kilometres in my legs when the minimum I needed was 1500. As soon as the racing began I was picking up a cold, then bronchitis and another cold. But there were expectations and I continued racing. I kept forcing and forcing even though I was getting nowhere.

Towards the end of March, two months into the season, I sensed that something was wrong. On the mountainous stage of the Criterium International I was just behind the leaders as they went over the brow of a hill. I could see there was going to be a split and knew that I had to tag onto the end of the lead group. But I could not get onto it, everything was ready but I could not make that extra effort and go. I continued in search of that something which would lift my performances. I was not being wiped out but neither was I going as well as I hoped or as others expected. In the back of my mind there were questions but the pressure to keep going was stronger than my desire to find out precisely what was wrong.

De Muer came to me every second day, asking what was wrong. He begged me to tell Lydia to take it easy. He used to tell me that Lydia was going to kill my career. If something was wrong with my racing, De Muer was sure it had to be Lydia. Others blamed Lydia as well. They could not accept that I was not going well and that was it. I did some good rides, especially in the Amstel Gold Classic when I finished second behind Raas. But a one-off performance like that only confused things. I knew that something was lacking.

The Dauphine was, again, a turning point. Each day I was being dropped and left minutes behind by the leaders. Three days from the end I was again left behind and was in a group about 20 minutes back when the leaders stopped riding. Slowly but surely, the group I was in got back on. It was an amazing turnaround. As soon as we got back on there was an attack and I went with it, finishing fourth on the stage. De Muer read it all wrong: 'Great, you're coming round. There's nothing wrong with you, you can ride the Tour.'

I knew he was wrong but what could I say? My legs did the talking for me. On the next day to St Etienne I took another hammering. Enough was enough. I called the team doctor to my room that evening and told him that something was wrong with me. I could not go on and what could the team do? The doctor said I should be sent to a special institute in Cologne, Germany, which Peugeot used to test their riders. De Muer came into the room. I told the doctor that the only way De Muer would agree to my going to Germany was if it came directly from him. On hearing it from the doctor, De Muer said that if it was necessary then I should go. I was on my way to Cologne the next day. They did tests in the institute and found that I was suffering from 'chronic fatigue'. Two years of constant racing and an inadequate period of rest during the winter of 1981/82 accounted for my condition. I was in no state to continue racing and was ordered to rest.

After resting during the Tour de France I came back and rode the World Championships in Goodwood without any preparation. I surprised myself and many others by riding prominently and helping Kelly to get his bronze medal.

As I tried to organize my comeback there were very few journalists who wanted interviews and I was left on my own. What really shocked me was what happened when I finished the Grand Prix des Nations. A year earlier I was the neophyte who finished second to the specialist Gisigier and had to fight my way through the journalists and photographers to get to the team car. Now I was second from last and when I went past the line there was not one person to give me a towel to wipe the sweat away. Nobody wanted to know me. I wanted to tell the journalists how I suffered, how bad preparation meant that the 89-kilometre test was one long struggle. To me, this was important but there was not one pressman who had the slightest interest. Maurice Champion, who used to work with Guimard and Gitane, saw me on my own and handed me a bottle of Perrier. 'Stephen,' he said, 'make sure you learn from this. Last year a hero, today a nobody.'

I had not the strength to agree with him. I just took the Perrier. Drained and exhausted, I went to the car and sat down. Devastated. I told myself that it was my own fault.

I tried to learn from the experience of 1982 and prepared well during the winter. But the atmosphere in the Peugeot team during 1983 was bad. The team was beset by problems. Roland Berland was the new *directeur sportif*, having replaced De Muer. Everybody on the team, it appeared, wanted to be leader. Anderson, Laurent, Duclos-Lassalle, myself. There was a lot of shit. Many of the guys were on the last year of their contracts and this led to feelings of instability. If you did not ride well during the final year of a contract you had problems for the following year. Laurent, Anderson, Duclos, Millar and myself were all on our last year. But my feeling was that things started to go wrong with Berland's direction of the team. He was not correct in certain ways and stirred things in the wrong direction within the team. For De Muer, we had respect. If there were problems, they were sorted out around a table. There was no secret back-stabbing.

Berland came to Peugeot with Jean René Bernaudeau. Both rode for Gitane but Berland had come to the end of his career. It is said that he went to Peugeot and suggested that if they signed him as assistant *directeur sportif,* he could persuade Bernaudeau to join as well. Peugeot went for it but it was obvious that Berland was not satisfied to be number two to De Muer. He wanted to be the number one. Towards the end of 1982 the signs were very clear. De Muer visited the riders' rooms telling them which races he wanted them to ride. After he left, Berland came to the rooms. He asked riders which races they were doing, and on being told he would say, 'De Muer said you must ride this, that is too much for you. You should be riding less than that.' He disagreed with everything De Muer proposed. This created insecurity in the team. Whom should the riders talk with? Berland was closer to the riders in age and a few years before rode against many of them: Duclos, Laurent, Bossis and Bernaudeau. They found it easier to speak with Berland than with De Muer, who might close the door in their face. They went to Berland and he received them. Encouraged by the attention, he made his case to the Peugeot bosses and, one day, De Muer was not needed anymore. I believe that the decision to dispense with De Muer and appoint Berland brought about the downfall of the Peugeot team.

Roland Berland was not all bad but I found it difficult to like him. When he spoke to you he looked towards the ground, at your toes. When I talk, I like to talk to the other person's eyes. Berland never looked you in the eyes when he spoke with you. He liked to show off when driving, going too fast on narrow roads. You received a letter telling you that you were riding this race, but two days later you had a phone call saying that the plan had been changed.

Even with an unhealthy ambience in the team some of the results were good. Anderson won the Amstel Gold Classic and I won the Grand Prix of Wallonne and the Tour of Romandie. They were important because they were my first victories since winning the Etoile des Espoirs at the end of 1981.

In 1983 I rode my first Tour de France and was encouraged by how I performed. Although I was left far behind on the two Pyrenean stages and on the first Alpine stages, I rode exceptionally well on the mountain stage to Morzine and I time-trialled well throughout.

After the Tour ended, negotiations with Berland for 1984 reached a vital stage. Originally I wanted to leave Peugeot but Berland persisted in trying to get me to stay. It went on for months and by the end of the Tour I decided to remain at Peugeot. When I consider all that was to pass before things were eventually sorted out, my conclusion is that

Berland tried to screw me. I asked that my contract with Peugeot for 1984 be settled after the World Championships in Altenrhein, Switzerland. It was clear that I was prepared to stay at Peugeot and it was only a question of striking on the right money and the right conditions. I wanted a car, an advance on my wages to cover the purchase of a piece of land on which I intended building, and I needed this advance by a certain date. He got me most of what was asked and the only outstanding problem was the money. We agreed on a figure which would be my salary, unless I did anything at the Worlds. If I did, we were to renegotiate. I gave him my word that I would re-sign under the conditions we agreed. He said he needed more than that. So I agreed to sign my name on the last page of the contract. In my own mind I had committed myself, in principle, to riding for Peugeot in 1984. All this took place shortly before the Worlds and I felt sure there would be no problems. I was working on the basis that if I did a ride at the Worlds, I got extra. I did not sign the contract in all the places I was supposed to and did not believe that I was contractually bound to Peugeot.

At the Worlds I finished third, taking the bronze medal behind LeMond and Van der Poel. Berland was one of the first to congratulate me. Back in Paris a few days later I rang him and asked about the contract. He said there was no problem. He intended talking to me at the Grand Prix d'Isbergues, which was the next race. He did not come to Isbergues. A few days later I rang again, and he said things would be sorted out at Paris–Brussels. But he had the flu or something and did not show at Paris–Brussels. I was getting anxious because I needed to be able to show the owner of the land my contract. I got in touch with Berland again. He said he was in the process of having the contract typed up and he would leave it at a hotel and all I had to do was look at it and sign it.

I went to the hotel next morning and collected the contract. Having brought it home I realized that it was for even less money than we agreed. I rang Berland straight away, pointing out that the salary was less than we agreed, even without the World Championship perform-ance being taken into consideration. He said, 'That is the way it is, you sign it or leave it.' I told him there was no way I was signing it. He said he would talk with me at the Grand Prix des Nations. We met and I outlined what I wanted. He said there was no way my demands would be accepted. I said I was not signing the contract as it was. He intended to make the document which was already signed the official contract.

We argued at length. I did not believe that he could use that one signature on the last page of the original document to make me stay at Peugeot. But he thought he could and intended doing so. From his point of view I had signed a contract and that was it. There was no point in talking any further.

A week later we did talk again and I tried telling him that if he did not do something I intended negotiating with other teams. But the door was closed. I explained that I would run the risk of a court case. There was no way I could accept what he was doing to me. It was cheating. He was not worried, believing all the time that he could make the original document stand. Peugeot was Peugeot, Stephen Roche was Stephen Roche, he reminded me. He tried to pressurize me into accepting by mentioning the fact that I was buying land, that I had debts over my head and that, in the event of my going elsewhere, my Peugeot car would be taken back immediately. I thought a solution would be found but Berland let things drag on. He knew what he was doing because the longer it went on the more difficult it was going to be for me to find another team. He used to ring my home when I was not there and speak with Lydia. We had been married less than a year at this time and he tried to use Lydia to put more pressure on me. He told her that if I went ahead with my decision not to re-sign for Peugeot I was putting both her and myself under an enormous strain. That Peugeot would take me to court and demand £400,000 compensation. This got through to Lydia and distressed her very much. When I came home she told me about the phone calls and would break down as she was recalling them. It upset me that she was being intimidated. I decided that whatever happened I would never work with a man who could behave like this.

The La Redoute team wanted me to be their leader. I explained the problem I was having with Peugeot and that I could only sign for them if they agreed to pay the costs of any legal battle that might ensue. They agreed and we signed up everything. They were trying to improve their team and had taken on some good riders but I knew that they were still a small team. But I was happy to find an alternative to Peugeot.

The saga went on for over two years with Peugeot. They tried to sue for compensation and La Redoute were defending the case for me. We lost the first part of the case but both La Redoute and I were convinced that we were not being represented very well and changed our legal people. At the end of two years I was sick of the case and La Redoute were getting out of cycling sponsorship. I was on my own and the

Peugeot issue was not resolved. When negotiating at the end of the 1985 season I explained to teams that were interested in signing me that they would have to sort out the Peugeot problem.

I spoke with Peugeot and asked my criterium manager, Daniel Dousset, to act on my behalf with Peugeot. At the end of our discussions we agreed that whatever team signed me would have to have 'Peugeot' inscribed on their shorts for two years. I did not consider this a big price to pay but then I wanted to finish with this problem once and for all. From Peugeot's point of view they were moving from a demand for £400,000 to a name on the shorts for two years. I do not think they were too confident of eventually winning the court case. Carrera, whom I agreed to join at the end of 1985, accepted the solution to the Peugeot case. They claimed that it cost them £150,000 to have 'Peugeot' on their shorts but I felt that was an exaggeration. Once or twice it was mentioned but I never batted an eyelid. They knew what they were getting themselves into.

After leaving Peugeot at the end of 1983 I met Berland at different times. In my view Peugeot went from being a top team to a nothing team under Berland. Eventually Peugeot replaced him as *directeur sportif*. During a race Berland liked to calculate for his riders, which I believe is very dangerous. If I calculate for myself and I lose then it is I who have lost. Berland wanted to be recognized as a strategist. It cost Robert Millar the Tour of Spain in 1985. The problem for Millar in that race was that he did not have the personality to overpower Berland. Throughout my life I have tried to forgive and forget. Sure there will be arguments and conflict, but it is not my way to carry these things around with me after they have happened. Of all the people I have come across in cycling, Berland is the one person I cannot easily forgive and forget.

On the bike 1983 was a good year for me. As well as winning the Tour of Romandie and Grand Prix of Wallonne I had ridden a satisfactory first Tour de France and won a bronze medal at the World Championships. Even after the Worlds I rode a good end of season, winning the Etoile des Espoirs and Paris–Bourges and playing an important part in Sean Kelly's first classic victory in the Tour of Lombardy.

From my first year in the pro *peloton* Kelly and I hit it off well. At first there was mutual respect and also respect for the fact that we were the only Irishmen in the bunch and, as such, we should try to help each other. It helped that there was no competition between the two of us. He was not interested in being the best Irish cyclist on the continent, and neither was I. Towards the end of that Tour of Lombardy Kelly was in a bit of trouble after his team mate Grezet was dropped from the lead group. There were about eighteen riders in contention and, after Grezet was left behind, Kelly did not have anybody to keep things together and so allow him to use his sprint at the end. My chances of winning were very slight as I did not have the power to get away from the others and my sprint was not going to get me anywhere. I decided to help Kelly. Going to the front I kept the pace up, discouraging the others from attacking and keeping things together for Kelly. Munoz, the Spaniard, did get away but I rode hard in pursuit and led the group up to him. I led all the way into the finish at Como and it was only at the final corner that the sprinters started to come round me – Kuiper, Seiz, Moser, Van der Poel – and I was wondering what had happened to Kelly. I reckon eight or nine passed before Kelly flew by. I was not at all sure he could make it, but he did. By inches.

Afterwards Berland was furious, complaining that I had ridden for Kelly and had not tried to win myself. I passed it off by saying that I was riding for my Peugeot team mate Anderson and not Kelly. Berland did not understand the way things worked in the *peloton*. He did not realize that among the riders one good turn leads to another. Today I help Kelly, tomorrow he will help me. I knew how much the Tour of Lombardy meant to Kelly. He had been a professional for six years and was one of the best around. It was unbelievable that he had not won a classic before this and it was a pleasure for me to be able to help. A good way to end the season and my three years with Peugeot racing team.

Although happy to be out of Peugeot, I was not joining a completely happy family when I began riding for La Redoute in 1984. There were problems from the start but, thankfully, I was not directly involved. Basically it came down to who managed the team. Maurice De Muer was appointed general manager and Bernard Thevenet was the *directeur sportif*. Normally that should have meant De Muer over-seeing things in the background and Thevenet making the decisions affecting the riders. But De Muer was a much stronger personality than Thevenet and wanted to make the decisions. People could see that Thevenet was weak. A very nice fellow, a very good fellow but as a *directeur sportif* Bernard did not have a clue. He found it difficult to take decisions and he had to make a mistake more than once before he learned from it. It was not easy for him as he was coming almost directly from being a champion rider to the position of *directeur sportif*. I know that if I had to make the transition I would not be able to cope. Nobody makes the transition overnight and for Thevenet there was an added problem. As a bike rider he was so strong that his legs did the thinking for him, he did not need to use his head. As a *directeur sportif*, he needed his head all the time. Things that he could see instinctively when riding himself, he could never see from behind the wheel of a car.

In some ways Thevenet was never really given a chance. If De Muer had been supportive, if he had allowed him to do things on his own and gently pointed out where he was making mistakes, it is sure that Thevenet would have done better. But that was not De Muer's style. He was not going to be a quiet fatherly figure in the background. The problem was not helped by De Muer's wife Jacqueline. Concerned that the team was not being run properly, Jacqueline used to ask the riders how they thought things were going. Before you got the chance to answer she would say, 'Bad, aren't they?' You tried to play down the problems and she would then say, 'But he hasn't a clue, has he?' Again, trying to play things down, you said that Thevenet was young. Jacqueline could not accept that. 'But he will never learn. Look at Maurice, he should be driving the car and making the decisions.' Even though the riders knew that Thevenet was weak, Jacqueline's efforts to change things did not go down well. Because this battle for control of the team was going on, there was a sense of unease all round.

My form in 1984 was good but the year was spoiled by a bad experience in the Tour de France. At the start of the year things were fine as I won the Nice–Alassio race early in the season, rode very well to be second to Kelly in Paris–Nice, and was third in Criterium International. My preparation for the Tour was satisfactory and I went into it hoping I could do well. La Redoute wanted their team to do especially well in the Tour and there was a great deal at stake. The Tour began satisfactorily and I performed well in the long time trial to Le Mans, finishing fourth behind Fignon, Kelly and Hinault. A year earlier I had finished thirteenth in my first Tour and expected to be a top-ten finisher now, possibly even top five. But a crash on the stage to Bordeaux, two days before the first day in the mountains, killed my Tour. In crashing I damaged my calf and rode the rest of the race on one leg. It was a misery. I suffered terribly from the leg all the way to

Raphaël Géminiani, my *directeur sportif* at La Redoute, improved my time-trialling preparation. Here I am on my way to a time-trial victory in the *Dauphine Libere* race

Everybody needs a break sometime!

Attacking on the 17th stage of the 1985 Tour de France

Left: Sharing the pace with Bernard Hinault. *Le blaireau* was a great champion

Below left: Leading on a climb in the 1986 Tour de France. Millar on my left, Criquielion on my right. Not a race I remember fondly

Below: The futile chase, Paris–Nice '87. A puncture cost me my place in the leading group. With Leali I tried to fight back but never made it

Right: Kelly and I got away on our own in the 1987 Criterium International. He stayed on my back wheel even though he had to hurt himself to do so. But in the end he won.

Four of those who played a crucial part in the 1987 Giro d'Italia:

Eddy Schepers

Patrick Valcke

Roberto Visentini

Robert Millar

Paris, eventually finishing an also-ran in twenty-fifth place.

I was in a bad way and cancelled all my post-Tour criteriums. I pulled out of the Worlds, which were on in Barcelona, and people said Roche was gone again. Up in 1981, down in 1982, back up in 1983 but back down again in 1984. The most common view was that I was not going to make it. I have never listened to that kind of talk. I see the positive side in everything that happens to me. Once recovered from the injury picked up in the Tour I was soon competitive again, finishing third behind Hinault and Kelly in the Grand Prix des Nations. Right at the end I went to the Tour of Lombardy and finished fifth. There was not too much wrong. My philosophy then and now was that if things go wrong, you start again. Everything that happened between 1982 and 1984 was a part of my apprenticeship – a part of growing up.

CHAPTER 9
Gém

'In 1985 this Stephen Roche filled me with wonder. There was something in the way he carried himself: a class, a magnificence. The one who came closest to Jacques Anquetil. Stephen believed it was his destiny to be a champion.'

Raphaël Géminiani

Before meeting him, I felt Raphaël Géminiani was not my kind of man. A successful racer in the fifties, Géminiani remained in cycling and was *directeur sportif* to different teams. From what I heard and read, I did not like him. He was a talker, he did not seem proper. My image of him was of a man who stayed up late every night, talking and talking. People used to say that wherever Géminiani had gone, the enterprise folded up soon after his arrival. If he was boss of a team, I would not have joined that team for anything. His strong, outgoing personality would clash with mine. During my cycling career I wanted to avoid people like Raphaël Géminiani. Anyway, after Berland and Thevenet I was entitled to a *directeur sportif* with whom I could work well.

It was clear to the riders in La Redoute that the sponsors were not happy with the performance of the team in the 1984 Tour de France. Normally when a team arrives in Paris at the end of the Tour there is a happy reunion with the sponsors and a celebration evening in Paris. On the day the 1984 Tour ended the La Redoute bosses came, said little and left without saying goodbye. Everybody suspected that something was going to happen but, even so, we were not prepared for what was to appear in *L'Equipe* on the following morning. The paper said that Raphaël Géminiani was taking over the La Redoute team and that Bernard Thevenet and Maurice De Muer were being let go.

A bombshell. It bothered me that although I was leader of the team nobody consulted me at any time about Géminiani. Nobody even discussed what was going wrong at the team. We were landed with Géminiani whether we liked it or not. I did not like it but as there was still another year of my contract with La Redoute to run, there was not much that I could do.

We did not see much of Géminiani towards the end of 1984 and at our team presentation in 1985 very little was said between the two of us. A week at training camp and still there was only the minimum communication. Something had to give and at the Tour of the Mediterranean it did.

It was at a hotel in Antibes on the morning of a race. Two of my team mates, Vandenbroucke and Bondue, complained that I had not shared the money I won from the Pernod and Credit Lyonnais competitions in 1984. My policy in relation to prize money was to allow my team mates to have my own share of the normal money won in races but I held on to money that I won in season-long competitions like the Pernod and Credit Lyonnais. Bondue and Vandenbroucke were making a serious allegation. Nice lads in their own way, but very quick to point the accusing finger.

The rest of the team were sitting quietly, waiting for the row which was sure to follow. Trying to be logical about it, I explained that having won a number of races in 1984 I decided to leave my share of prize money in the kitty to be divided up among everybody else. But when it came to money from the Pernod and Credit Lyonnais, I reckoned I was entitled to keep that money myself. They disputed this. I argued that if they wanted a share of the Pernod and Credit Lyonnais money they must return the money I had left for them in the kitty during the year. The argument went on.

Jean Louis Gauthier, a very experienced and capable team rider, spoke up. He had been with many leaders in his career, most recently with Zoetemelk. According to Gauthier, Zoetemelk only forfeited his share of the Tour de France prize money and never, ever, gave up Pernod or Credit Lyonnais money. And Zoetemelk's riders thought they were doing well. Jean Louis offered the opinion that I was a very fair leader and that the two lads should not push it. Vandenbroucke continued, talking about the big salary I was earning and how things were OK for me. Jerome Simon got up and left, saying that he had heard enough and that he was entirely happy with the arrangements as they were.

Eventually I made it clear to Vandenbroucke and Bondue that they were not getting a centime for 1984 but if they wished to change the arrangements for 1985, they could. They were to think about it and come back with an answer. The subject was never brought up again. Vandenbroucke and Bondue were like that, the type who cried over pennies. Jean Louis Gauthier earned less than they and he was able to stand up and admit I was entitled to what I received.

When the riders had all left the table, I was there with my meal still in front of me. Géminiani was sitting directly across from me. Just the two of us. There were things on his mind. He complained that I was ignoring him. He did not know what I thought of him but he said the two of us were going to have to work together for one year and we should get on with it. So I told him everything I thought of him. It was not very complimentary. We argued for an hour and a half. He put me in my place, I put him in his. And that was it. After that we got on fine. Raphaël Géminiani, or Gém as I came to know him, was to play a very important part in the development of my career.

Once we decided to get on, Géminiani watched everything I did, analysed what he saw and came to the conclusion that there were not many riders with the talent I had. He admired the way I went about my work, regarding me as very professional. Over the years there were many times when I argued with Wiégant, De Muer and Géminiani but, deep down, I believed in the things they preached. They were old-fashioned and I agreed with many of the old ideas. For example, it was always said that in Merckx's team every rider went to the table in their hotel wearing identical shirts. That makes sense to me. A sponsor pays big money to put a team on the road; it is not always possible for the team to win races but it is possible for the team to look totally professional at mealtimes in their hotel. If a visitor walks into the hotel and sees every rider at the table wearing the same shirt, he will say, 'Ah, look. There is the Carrera team.' It creates a good impression.

Géminiani knew Merckx and the big stars from other eras and he understood what I was trying to achieve. He also came to realize that I could be trusted. If I went home to rest and train, Gém knew that I would be competitive when I returned. As far as I'm concerned, his great strength as a *directeur sportif* was his belief in me and his ability to motivate me. Before a time trial Géminiani got behind me and nobody else existed. He would allocate Patrick Valcke, himself and my *soigneur* to cover all my needs on the day of a time trial. Looking at the schedule for the day he might decide that there was not enough time to ride the circuit so he would have a lunch packed for me and we would take off in the car, stopping on the way for me to eat my food in some bar. For about five hours before the time trial he motivated me. He kept others away and I would not see a soul until my *soigneur* came and greased my shorts and back. Gém never used to say 'good luck' before I headed off. He knew I was on my own and luck was not going to have much to do with how I went.

I enjoyed a super 1985 with Géminiani, it was my best year since 1981. After clearing the air with him on the first day of the Tour of the Mediterranean, my performances improved. Although still some way short of full fitness, I was third in the Tour of the Mediterranean. From there we went to Paris–Nice and I was second to Kelly, for the second consecutive time. Géminiani had total belief in me and when it came to the Criterium International, he convinced me that there was no way I could lose. His logic was simple: third in the Mediterranean tour, second in Paris–Nice and first in Criterium International. Géminiani was very superstitious. When we got to the race we found that my number was twenty-three and he saw this as further proof that I was going to win. Two from three equalled one and there was the significance of my race number. He was so delighted when I did win the Criterium International that he insisted on taking me to a nightclub in Cannes on the evening the race ended.

There was nobody in the club when we arrived as it was Sunday night and it did not open on Sundays. But Géminiani knew that and had only brought me so that he could introduce me to the proprietress, a Chinese lady. Géminiani told her that he had brought the winner of the Criterium International, as promised. I could not understand what was happening but found out later. She had a pet mouse. On the night before the race began Géminiani was in the club and the Chinese lady, whom he had known for a long time, told him to pull the tail of her mouse. If the mouse squeaked when the tail was pulled, whatever Géminiani was thinking would come true. Géminiani pulled the mouse's tail and it did squeak. He then told the lady that if what he was thinking came true he would bring her the winner of the Criterium International two nights later. And that was why I was hauled off to an empty nightclub in Cannes on a Sunday night in March 1985.

Géminiani was again at his best when we went to the Tour of the Midi Pyrenees. One of the stages in that race finished at the Pyrenean ski resort of Guzet Neige. A year before, Guzet Neige had been the first mountain-top finish in the Tour de France and, as it came just two days after my crash on the Bordeaux stage, I had a very bad time climbing that mountain. Eventually I finished over 18 minutes down on the winner and, in one day, killed my chances of doing well in the 1984 Tour. Géminiani said that performance did not reflect me and that I owed it to myself to prove that I could climb Guzet Neige well. He looked at the profile of the climb and deemed that it was one which suited me. And as all the best climbers were riding the Midi Pyrenees, Géminiani believed it was an ideal opportunity for me to show that I could climb the big mountains. By the time the stage to Guzet Neige began I, too, was convinced I could win. When I attacked I believed that I would get away and so it happened. I finished alone at Guzet Neige, got the leader's jersey and held it all the way to the finish. For me it was all down to Géminiani's faith.

He used the same approach in the Tour de France, pinpointing the stage to the summit of the Col d'Aubisque as the one I was going to win. That victory should get a special place in the history books because, for three months, Géminiani had been telling anyone who was prepared to listen that I was sure to win on the Col d'Aubisque. Every other rider in the race waited for me to make my move on the Aubisque and still I was able to get away with it. Géminiani understood how I climbed. If I could get a gap my natural climbing rhythm was usually strong enough to maintain my advantage. The problem for me was getting the gap for, as Géminiani said, I attacked like a diesel in the mountains. But for the Aubisque stage of the 1985 Tour, it was hammered into me that I had to make my attack count.

Géminiani made up a special one-piece racing suit for me, with the normal bottom and a cotton and silk top. Because the stage was so short, 52 kilometres, he wanted me to treat it like a time trial and wear the special suit rather than the normal shorts and jersey. His idea was that once I had the gap, it would be a time trial for me from there to the top. He even went to the trouble of having my number stitched onto the jersey. Great care was taken with the wheels, the bottle, the food, everything. That was how Géminiani operated. Before starting I felt that if I did not win I would be letting many people down, people who had worked hard to help me.

I set out on the stage to the Aubisque believing that I simply had to win. At the bottom of the climb Lucho Herrera attacked; somebody else then left the bunch but nobody was seriously going after Herrera. I shifted my chain to the big ring and zoomed out of the pack. I did not want any companions. Soon I got to Herrera and just carried on by him. From there it was the time trial that we had planned for.

Géminiani, being the man he is, wanted me to do the same in the afternoon stage which went over the Aubisque again before dropping down into Pau. But it was much hotter in the afternoon and I was not too interested in suicide missions.

That 1985 Tour was a very important breakthrough for me as it proved that I could survive a long, hard stage race without having one big off day. In 1983 and 1984 there were some days when my deficit was close to 20 minutes. But I rode consistently well throughout the 1985 race and my third place overall suggested that I had the potential to win a Tour de France. And third place in that Tour ensured that 1985 would be remembered as a successful year. As La Redoute were leaving cycling at the end of the season and everybody on the team was searching for a new employer, the Tour de France third place was a very relevant item in my credentials. La Redoute had never made it into the league with the other big teams. We remained small. There were not many in the team who were able to support me. Jerome Simon was good, Jean Louis Gauthier did a lot for me and Paul Sherwen did as much as he could. Not surprisingly, Bondue and Vandenbroucke were not my most hardworking team mates. But the ambience in 1985, under Géminiani, was far better than it had been in 1984 and we all had good fun.

I wanted to bring Géminiani with me to whatever team I joined in 1986. I owed him something and I was sure he could continue to help me, no matter which team I joined. He understood me better than any other *directeur sportif* had and a very good relationship existed between us. Patrick and he got on very well too and that increased Géminiani's value, because Patrick was my mechanic at Peugeot in 1981 and had stayed with me ever since. The three of us knew how the others thought, how the others worked, and each allowed the other two room to do their own things. As a threesome we were fantastic. When it was decided that I would join Carrera I spoke with them about the possibility of Géminiani being taken on. He spoke good Italian. But they considered their *directeur sportif*, Davide Boifava, to be very good at his job and they did not have a place for Géminiani. I sensed that it would not have worked anyway. My feeling was that Géminiani would never work well with an Italian star, particularly Visentini.

Géminiani and I went our separate ways. We parted on the understanding that if the chance came to reunite, we would. But I do not suppose that it will happen now. Before joining Fagor I tried to get them to take Géminiani but they were not interested. Gém will do OK. He is a survivor, always doing a bit here and a bit there, and he owns half of Seillans in the south of France. He will never be stuck for a franc. He was, of course, a bit of a nutter. Driving along the road, listening to disco music. I used to have a Walkman, he used to borrow it. He was only a child really. If you did anything wrong to him, he would cry. A very nice gentle man, good to be with. Very good for me.

CHAPTER 10

In the Dark

'People have asked me,' says Sean Kelly, 'whether I felt a little jealousy as Stephen won so much and became the hero in 1987. I couldn't. I had seen Stephen in 1986, when he was in a dark tunnel, no light, and he was not sure he was going to get out. After that, he deserved any success that came his way.'

It should have been a good year, 1986. Moving to Carrera meant that, at last, team support was not going to be a problem. My performance in the 1985 Tour de France established that I could ride the big tours and hope to win. Never did I draw a line under the Tour de France or any other tour and say, 'That is a race I *have* to win.' But I did think that the Tour was a race I *could* win. Others were not so sure, but third place in 1985 changed their view.

A month after the Tour ended I rode the World Championships in Italy and finished seventh. At one point on the last lap it looked as if I might win but the hill was not long enough and the descent was too long. Before the season ended I agreed to ride the Paris Six-Day with the English rider Tony Doyle. Some argue that the road season is so long and so hard that riders should stay clear of the Six-Day track races. Maybe it is the view of a dreamer but I have always believed that a complete bike racer should be able to ride on the flat, in the mountains, in the time trials *and* on the track.

The crash I suffered towards the end of the Paris-Six in November 1985, which led to such disappointment in 1986, has not altered my belief about the complete bike rider. At the back of my mind there is still something that makes me want to go out and win a Six-Day. It was a nasty crash but, as far as I could make out, no serious damage had been incurred. I went back to Ireland and started to get concerned when the soreness in my left knee was not going away. Physiotherapy was recommended and I felt fairly sure that things would be fine for the start of the season two months away. I was not too worried because everywhere I went they guaranteed me that they would cure me. My sights were set on Paris–Nice, it was to be my comeback race.

Paris–Nice came and went and my knee was not right. I tried to tell myself that missing out on the early season races would leave me fresh for the Tour. Géminiani, with whom I remained in touch, quoted examples of riders who had done nothing in the early season but then came along and won the Tour. Everyone tried to keep my morale up. Deep down, I was worried. From my earliest career, I enjoyed racing and needed plenty of racing to get me on form. I was not going just to come out and win the Tour de France. It took far more than that. I was also worried because, in my absence, Roberto Visentini and, especially, Urs Zimmermann were doing well in the Carrera team. When I returned I would have to fight to regain my status as a team leader. In one sense it helped that they were riding well because their success took pressure off me.

During the early season races I was at a physiotherapy school in Cannes, being guaranteed that I would be cured. We started on a basic programme of combining physiotherapy with a little work on the bike. I went from one hour on the bike to two, three, four, five. Everything appeared fine. A few kilometres up the road Kelly was winning Paris–Nice for the fifth consecutive time and, a day later, he came to Cannes for some training. A few of his team mates were with him and I began training with them every second day. One day we decided to do a long spin, seven hours. For six hours I was fine, on the seventh I started to suffer pain in my knee. It had been a long and extremely hard spin. All the improvement was undone. I was back to scratch. Three days later I began the programme all over again. As it had worked once, I figured it would work again. This time I would not be so foolish as to attempt a full-scale seven-hour training spin before I was ready. So it was back to the physio, the gym exercises and the slow build-up on the bike. I was confident the programme would work.

But, at this time, Carrera were panicking. They insisted I go to Italy to ride three races. I rode well in the second and third, particularly the third, which had an eight-kilometre climb where I was very strong. The next day my knee was again sore. Carrera took their panic a bit further. I had been given my chance to cure the knee, now they wanted theirs. They sent me to a number of specialists in Italy. One of them, in

Genoa, said that an operation was necessary. Fearful of an operation, for it was now two months into the season, I got in touch with my Paris doctor, Jean Baptiste Courroy. He advised against an operation, saying that it was foolish to undergo surgery in the middle of the season. When I went back to Italy they were saying I had to have the operation and that it would take place within the next two days. I rang Courroy for a final opinion but he was away on holiday and I underwent the operation on 4 April. I was not sure what they were actually doing to my knee but was assured that everything would be perfect after three weeks' convalescence. At the end of the three weeks I was thrown straight into the Tour of Romandie.

There were times when I wanted to disagree with what Carrera were proposing but I was in a difficult position. They were paying me a big salary and for what? I was not even riding. But their anxiety to get me back racing was not a help. Before the Tour of Romandie I was twenty days off the bike and there was no evidence that my knee was any better. As happened earlier, my return to competition was premature. I rode well for the first two days in Romandie but two days from the end my knee was as bad as ever. Carrera thought more racing would cure me and I was in the team to ride the Giro d'Italia, which began a few days later. I nursed the knee all the way through the Giro, getting physiotherapy and injections every day. Two days from the end I could go no further and pulled out. My performance in the race was way below what it should have been and I was not able to climb at all. After the Giro there was ten days' rest and then the Tour de France. Again I needed daily treatment on my knee to get through the Tour. I was not remotely competitive and ended up in forty-eighth place.

Such was my physical state after the Tour that I cancelled all my criteriums and took three weeks off the bike. Of what value is a quick dollar today when, by being patient, you can earn far more tomorrow? There were fifteen criteriums in all and they involved quite a bit of money. I wanted to ride, but only when I was fit to ride.

I went to see Courroy again. He wanted new X-rays of my knee but the X-ray clinic at his hospital was closed. It was August, the great holiday month in France. The X-rays were done at a hospital near where I lived in Sagy. When the X-rays were brought to the doctor there he analysed them and called me into his office. He asked what I intended doing when my career ended. As my career still had another five or six years to run, I was not sure what I would do when it ended and told the doctor so. 'You must think of bringing forward your retirement,' he said. 'You have another year, maybe two, and then it will be finished. Even at that, you will not be able to ride at your best. If I were you, I would consider my future immediately.'

I was shocked. The doctor told me it was arthritis in the knee joints that caused the problem. He showed me the problem areas on the X-ray and called in a colleague of his, who agreed entirely with the analysis.

I left the hospital, went home, wondered how much it would cost to finish my new house in Sagy, and counted up every penny I had, everywhere. I estimated how much I would get for selling the house, how much for the car. I wondered what I could turn myself into. Could I do some work as a journalist or a broadcaster? Maybe I could be a mechanic and own a garage? I was too scared to tell anyone, even Lydia. Dr Courroy was away on holiday. It was a Thursday and he was not due back until the following Tuesday. Five days when I counted the hours pass. I was never as low in my life. The doctors had given me a report with the X-rays and I dared not show it to anyone. I knew what it said.

First thing on Tuesday morning I went to Courroy. He went through the X-rays. I watched his eyes and listened. 'That's OK, that's OK, and that is also OK.' Was there not something there to worry him? 'No, nothing.' What about the report? 'Well, you know, I'm a doctor too.' And the arthritis? 'That's not important. All cyclists have that. Old people who suffer from arthritis are encouraged to cycle if they can.' I then admitted that the other doctors advised me to give up cycling. 'Ah, no, that won't be necessary. The other doctors are wrong.' I sank back into the chair and allowed myself a big smile.

Different people spoke to me about Courroy, telling of how highly regarded he was in France. I had total confidence in him. He had played rugby in his day and saw things from the sportsman's point of view. He is young and very dynamic and has a wonderful manner. If he feels there is somebody better qualified than he to do a particular job, he will admit it. He suggested that I continue training through September and see how things worked out. If another operation was necessary it could be performed at the end of the season.

I considered trying to return for the World Championships in Colorado in early September but although my training was going quite well, I was not strong enough to ride the Worlds. If I went to Colorado I was going to want to do a good ride and that might have pushed me too far. In September I moved to Patrick's house in Lille and trained really well there for a month, one day riding a kermesse in Belgium and riding behind Patrick's car on the way home, the next day going for a long training spin on my own. I was building for the Baracchi Trophy, which I was to ride with Visentini.

Two days before the Baracchi I rode my final preparation race in Belgium and was very pleased with my form. The next morning I could hardly walk. My knee was again very sore. Having prepared for the Baracchi so thoroughly, I could not bring myself to pull out on the day before. With Visentini the Baracchi was hard but I dug in and survived. Boifava watched the performance and concluded that I was at last clear of the problems. He came over to me after I crossed the line and said how glad he was that things had eventually come right for me. He began to speak about a programme for the end of the season. I interrupted, 'Davide, you can put the word *finis* on my season.'

Boifava was amazed. He had just watched me ride well in the Baracchi and I was now saying that my season was over. What he did not know was that I could not walk and the pain in my knee was bad. I told him that I would be giving up a good contract to ride the Tour of Ireland and he had to accept that my knee was in a bad way.

I stayed on in Italy, at Carrera's request, and saw some more specialists. One opinion was that it was a cartilage problem and that surgery was necessary. They said that the French were experts in the kind of operation they were proposing. There was no need to say another word. I told them that I was going to see Dr Courroy in Paris and that it would be better for me to be under a French surgeon as I was based in Paris. They said that if Dr Courroy came to the same conclusion as they had, there was no reason why he should not perform the operation. A couple of days later I saw Dr Courroy and the operation took place in early October. At last, I was on the road to full health.

During 1986 there were many dark moments. I did not win a single race and there were times when I worried if there was any way back. Resting, training, racing and having to rest again, back into training and another series of races before being forced to rest again. The worst time of all was during the 1986 Tour de France. What I wanted to do was to stop racing completely and get to the bottom of my problem. But I wanted to do it without hurting anybody. Carrera had invested a considerable amount of money in me and there was no way they were going to allow me to stop just like that. I tried not to feel guilty about my lack of results. Carrera received good publicity from the time they first expressed an interest in signing me. There were lots of stories about my injury and that was publicity as well. Within the team itself there were the problems that you would expect when the highly paid star rider is not producing results. My contract with Carrera was good and there were some additional benefits. The team were paying my air tickets everywhere and I was able to pick and choose my races far more than most other riders. This all led to a build-up of tension.

Urs Zimmermann, who rode exceptionally well in 1986, resented that I was being so well paid when, although he was producing very good performances, he was still earning far less. After riding well in Paris–Nice, Zimmermann won Criterium International and he was being encouraged by his *soigneur*, Claudio Albasini, to complain about things. Albasini was a trouble-maker. Forever complaining, saying what he would do if he were boss. During a race in the south of Italy between the Giro and the Tour we were at the table and Zimmer-mann was going on about how he was doing the winning and I was getting paid for it. This was the usual kind of bullshit and there were always a few Italians to agree with him. That evening I was tired of it and, in front of everybody, I asked Zimmermann his name. He could not understand the reason for the question and said I knew his name. Raising my voice I pointed out that I was Stephen Roche and over my professional career had won between thirty and thirty-five races, and that, apart from the Tour of Switzerland, he had not won a damn thing. I was getting paid for what I had won in the past, not for what I should win. I deserved what I received. And I reminded him that he was getting paid for what he had won in the past and that he should count himself lucky to be getting what he was.

At least that got things out in the open. Casani and Bontempi were others who made comments about what I was getting and how little I was winning. Things were dirty but it was better to get them out in the open. During the Giro there was an extra *soigneur* employed and he was not on the list of people who would get the house *prime* from Carrera at the end. So it was decided to let some of the prize money from the race go to him. Visentini, who won the race, said he would leave his share of the winnings so that the extra *soigneur* would have something. I said I would leave mine too. Casani straight away remarked, 'You don't need it, Steve, you're getting 250,000 lire a month.' Angry but not prepared to let it show, I replied, 'And, Davide, that does not include what Carrera give me under the counter.' At least it silenced him but I found remarks like that very unpleasant.

Eddy Schepers was the one guy on the team who was totally supportive. Years ago Eddy rode with Merckx and he knows the sport. From my results over the years, he could tell that 1986 was explained by the knee injury. He tried to help me off the floor: 'With what you have done in the past, you can never be written off. The last few years proved you were good and there is no way you are burned out. You will be back.' When I was going badly in the Giro and later in the Tour, it was Eddy who waited for me. He paced me up the hills. There were times when Eddy should have been helping Visentini, especially when Visentini was going well in the Giro, but he wanted to stay with me. Occasionally I told him to go to Visentini and then, of course, he would. Eddy is the best kind of team rider. At the end of 1986 Visentini did not want to keep him in the team, even though Eddy had helped in the final week of the Giro. I insisted that Carrera keep Eddy. It developed into an argument but eventually they agreed to keep him. Out of the disappointment of 1986 and my work to keep Eddy at Carrera our great friendship developed. He was loyal to me in 1986 and extra loyal afterwards. A first-class professional.

Of the other guys in the Carrera team, Erich Maechler was the only one I wanted to take with me when I left. Maechler is a good lad. He was the most human person on the team. He did his job well and tried to mind his own business. If I was down because of my knee trouble in 1986, Maechler understood. He never complained. Others looked over their shoulders to see how the other guy was doing, not Maechler. As a leader I like to mix with all the riders and I did get on fairly well with people. But, behind your back, Italians were Italians. Even Bruno Leali, whom I got on well with and liked. I knew what Bruno might say behind my back.

As Carrera's *directeur sportif*, Davide Boifava helped me through 1986. He was very sympathetic. I had known Boifava for a long time. We met at races and he used to ask when I was going to come to Italy. He always insisted that Italy would suit me and that I would do very well on an Italian team. He was likeable, although it was easy to see that he did not have the authority of a Maurice De Muer or Raphaël Géminiani.

Against that, Boifava was an excellent organizer, much better than De Muer or Géminiani. There was never anything second class about Carrera: the hotels were good, the transport arrangements were first class. We travelled by air when that was possible and we never ended up spending seven or eight hours in a car when there was an alternative. The rider came first with Boifava and he worked on the principle that we should arrive at the race with the least fatigue possible. During the crisis with my knee, he emphasized that I do things correctly. He trusted me completely. I am sure he was being harassed by the Carrera bosses but he remained supportive of me. He was not the type to push me. If I had refused to ride the Giro or even the Tour in 1986, Boifava would have agreed. We had a good relationship. I liked him. The year 1987 was destined to bring much success and many problems with Boifava but I did not change my view of him. He was a good man. At the time of our last parting, when it was certain that I would leave Carrera, he cried, saying that he loved me. He never wanted confrontation but in 1987 it did not matter whether he wanted it or not, it came.

PART III
Le Nouveau Roche

CHAPTER 11

From the Ashes

It was the kind of evening you do not forget. A Friday evening, halfway through the Tour de France, after the Pyrenees and before the Alps. It was going to be a sad evening, we knew that from the start. What athlete wants to crawl back over the ground which caused so much pain and inflicted such defeat? The name of the hotel was the Campanile. Roche lay on the inside bed, his team mate Bruno Leali lay on the other. Roche's eyes looked sickly, his expression full of grey resignation. The fallen champion. The time had come to relive the fall and dissect the corpse.

He began piecing the story together with the method which runs through his life. You had to see the last week of the 1986 Tour de France in the context of his season. A troubled season from the beginning. He arrived at the Tour's start, limping. If not physically, certainly psychologically. His knee was hurting all the time. But he was a dreamer and pain killers help you dream. He got to the first major battleground of the Tour, the long time trial at Nantes, in one piece and pretty close to the yellow jersey. They said that Nantes would tell.

Third in Nantes and he caught everybody by surprise. Up to second overall and Roche was not going too badly, after all. He could produce something. A year before he was third with no team, now he had the Carreras. Hinault and LeMond better watch out. Nobody wanted to notice that at the end of his time-trial ride into Nantes Roche lay across the bars of his racing machine, racked by exhaustion. Not the ordinary panting which precedes recovery but a body taken way beyond its customary limits. If you had been able to stand and look at Roche without the distraction of seeing a potential Tour winner, you would have said he was in a distressed state.

But the heaving mass of excitement and confusion is no place for objectivity and we all flew with the Roche dream. He was in second place, the raceleader was his team mate Pedersen, who would be surrendering his tunic in the Pyrenees. Of the men who mattered, Roche was best placed. On the night of his time-trial performance Roche spoke with his friend and mechanic Patrick Valcke. They considered the possibility of Roche winning the Tour. This year was salvageable. They looked at it this way: second overall going into the mountains, and a year before the same mountains had not been a problem. Why not? Why not indeed?

On the morning of the next stage Roche found his legs heavy and lifeless. He was glad that he had two days to shake the tiredness out of his legs before the Pyrenees. He did not want to be climbing on dead legs. Worryingly, his legs never lost that heavy feeling. On the morning of the first Pyrenean leg to Pau, Roche still seemed the most likely heir to Pedersen's yellow jersey. Inside, Roche knew that his miles were numbered. The Nantes time trial had been the last, violent contortion of Roche's 1986 Tour. The remains were scattered all over the Pyrenees.

He was with the leading group on the Burdincurutcheta climb, suffering but surviving. Then Bernard Hinault glanced around, quickly assessing the number and quality of his companions. Hinault considered the company unsuitable and accelerated. Four went backwards; Roche was one of the four. Suddenly aware that the battle could not be won, the rider submitted. People began to pedal past Roche. People who could not climb for nuts. By the time he got to the final climb of that day, the Marie Blanque, Roche was eleven minutes behind Hinault and friends. At the summit of the mountain, Roche's deficit had increased to 21 minutes. On that mountain he says he 'blew his brains'. He just could not focus his mind on what needed to be done. It was a suffering blur that went on and on.

That evening it was agreed that the racer who trundled a laborious passage through the Pyrenees was not Stephen Roche. Not the real Stephen Roche. The champion, they said, should leave the race and come back when he was better. Another time.

But Roche stayed. For him there was no shame in his pursuit. You do not always win and there were good reasons why, on this occasion, victory was not a possibility.

Things were even worse on the second day in the Pyrenees. As champions will, Roche positioned himself in the front line as the climb of the Tourmalet loomed. About halfway up, he died. As on the day before, he watched as the race went by. Exhausted and helpless. Paul Kimmage, the young Irish professional and a friend of Roche's, came upon the fallen star near the top of the Tourmalet. 'Stephen was in a bad way. I could not help feeling sad. Through my career I have idolized him. He should not have been where he was. As I rode alongside him, I put my arm around him. Trying to encourage. It was all I could do.'

Onwards Roche went. Faltering. Halfway up the final Pyrenean climb of Superbagneres, he stopped. Got off his bike, had a pee and sat by a bridge over a rushing mountain stream. He thought it was all over for him. But just as easily as he had climbed off, he remounted. What was the use of carrying on? What was the use of stopping? Ride on and make up your mind later. Over the final four kilometres of Superbagnères he was touching the depths. Staring blankly at the thousands on each side of the road, praying that they could read his thoughts: *Poussez-moi*. Many did and they pushed Roche forward. Cycling up that mountain on his own had hurt so badly. And it hurt even more when they pushed. A different kind of hurt. Never in his career had Roche solicited a push on a mountain and when well-meaning spectators took it upon themselves to push, Roche spurned their help. They were a nuisance. But not now, not on Superbagneres.

One of those who pushed Roche on Superbagnères was a fat man. He kept pushing for about 100 metres which, given the gradient and the heat, required considerable effort. As the fat man pushed he spoke into Roche's ear: 'Stefan, I would push you all the way to the top if I could. I help you today because I know you will never need this kind of help again.'

Roche drew inspiration from the fat man's belief. He needed to. That day at Superbagneres he was 33 minutes behind the winner, Greg LeMond. Thirty-three minutes is a long time, only seven minutes less than the stipulated time limit for that day's stage of the Tour de France. In just two days he lost over 50 minutes and went from being a Tour favourite to a shadow of the racer. The ashes of a former fire. We felt sad for Roche and on that Friday evening we came to the Hotel Campanile to keen at his bedside.

But Roche was far from dead. At least in his own mind. All his problems in the Pyrenees related not to weakness of mind or limb, but to the circumstances of the time. He did not climb with Hinault and LeMond because his lingering knee injury killed his Tour preparation. Whoever won a Tour de France without preparation? He catalogued the disappointments of the season. Roche did not feel defeated. But why compete when not in a position to compete on the same terms as one's rivals? Why not, like Fignon had done four days earlier, pack up and leave? Because something could be achieved by sticking it out. Roche believed that three weeks of suffering on the Tour de France would help take him in the right direction. You get strength from riding the Tour, even when you suffer on the way. Especially when you suffer on the way.

And Stephen Roche stayed with it all the way to Paris. He never found climbing legs but survived well enough on the flat. He even sniffed around at the front of the *peloton*, searching for the opening that might provide a stage victory. On the few occasions that he bolted, LeMond and Hinault personally went after him. Roche was not a rider that you allowed to go free. Not even a Roche on one leg and almost one and a half hours down on general classification. If Hinault and LeMond considered that Roche was still Roche, it cannot be thought surprising that Roche's self-esteem remained intact. He cycled into Paris in the pack. Officially, forty-eighth. Officially, an also-ran. In his own mind, the Tour had been a painful and useful exercise.

That Sunday afternoon Roche's team mate Bontempi won on the Champs Elysées, Greg LeMond became the first American to win the Tour de France, and we stood for 'The Star Spangled Banner'. Ceremonies completed, the Tour heroes were summoned to the various television broadcasting points. The

Americans, CBS, had a makeshift studio on the Champs Elysées, and so had the French station Antenne 2. LeMond was on his way to Antenne 2, who also wished to speak with Roche. As Roche moved across a platform to the Antenne 2 people there were lots of balloons scattered in front of him. He playfully kicked the balloons as he walked, sending them whizzing into the air. Just at the end there was one balloon he had missed so he pivoted round and set that last balloon dancing. We looked and thought: the fallen champion. But it was only in our eyes that he had fallen. Not in his.

CHAPTER 12
Getting Ready

Eddy Schepers regards himself as an above average team rider. He rode for Merckx in 1978 and waited for another *patron* to come along. In Roche, he found a successor. 'I knew he was a champion when he made a 100-kilometre break in the 1987 Paris–Nice and still had the strength to go with the counterattack when he was recaptured.'

Once I accepted that I could not race again until my knee injury was properly healed, things were sure to improve. During 1986 I spent much of the time fooling myself and allowing myself to be encouraged by false hopes. Crossing the line in the Baracchi at the end of September, feeling the pain in my knee, knowing that I would not be able to climb off my bike and walk back to the hotel – that was the moment when the deception had to end. Surrendering myself to Dr Courroy was the easy part. In early October he operated on my knee at the Policlinique d'Epinay. He expressed himself as fully satisfied with the state of my knee and said that with proper preparation there would not be any problems in 1987.

Soon after the operation Carrera's general manager, Franco Belleri, asked me to come to Verona, the company's headquarters, for a meeting to discuss clothing for 1987. On arrival I discovered that he had set up a meeting between the Carrera boss Tito Tacchella, Boifava, himself and me. As soon as I entered the room, Belleri said, 'Stephen, we want to cut your money for 1987.' There was a coldness in his voice which suggested that he meant business. He said that Carrera were paying me in full for 1986 but, because my results were so bad, they wanted to cut my salary for 1987.

My feeling was that Carrera and I were quits at the end of 1986. I did not owe them anything except gratitude. They had been support-ive during a difficult year. Tito Tacchella did not complain about my failure to deliver and I appreciated that. If, in 1987, my knee had prevented me from performing, I would have gone to Carrera and asked that they terminate the contract. But I deserved the chance to prove myself in 1987 and was not prepared to agree to a cut in salary before the year even began. Their plan was that I should begin 1987 at one third of the salary agreed in my contract, that it would be increased to a half when I won a race and my full salary would be paid when I was back at my best. I could not accept that. Who decided when I was back at my best, they or I? I could be going really well but might not win a race. What then? Would my salary jump from one third to a half? If they insisted on imposing this cut, I was not going to stay with the team. 'If you cut my salary, you must tear up the contract and allow me to negotiate with other teams.'

They were not prepared to let me go. It was a worry for me. There were other teams ready to take me on and the operation on my knee had been a success. Carrera argued and argued, claiming that if I rode well there would be no problem, I would be paid in full. But they insisted they needed to be protected against a situation where my knee would affect me again. In arguing this point they refused to trust my honesty. Another year like 1986 and there would have had to be a renegotiation. I did not want to be paid on the basis of a contract I was not in a position to honour.

A key person in the discussion was Boifava. If he had felt that I was not going to return to my best form, Carrera would have let me go. Boifava believed I would come back and, in the end, Tacchella trusted his judgement. Despite Belleri's best attempts to arrange things differently, it was decided that I would be paid in full at the beginning of 1987 but that if things were not going well by May, we would all sit down and review the situation. That satisfied me completely. Before leaving the meeting, I asked to be left alone to get on with the preparation for 1987. There were over three months before I would be racing and it was important that I be allowed to get on with things in my own way.

The preparation for 1987 went very well. My targets were not ambitious. After giving the knee prolonged rest and gentle exercise over the five weeks following the operation, I returned to the bike on 15 November. At first I did a 30-minute spin which, basically, meant riding down to the traffic lights a mile or so down the road and back. Visitors to the house noted all the preparations that went into a spin, saw that I was back within 30 minutes and wondered whether I was mad. Their analysis never bothered me. I progressed to 40-minute spins, to one hour, up to one and a half hours. It pleased me that the preparation could be organized in such a proper way. During the season I had constantly been forced to take short cuts. Now I had the time and intended using it. Once I progressed to three hours on the bike, I was able to do anything. I wanted 1987 to be good; partly for Carrera, mostly for Stephen Roche. The sponsor, no matter how understanding, can choose to close the door tomorrow and walk away from cycling. The only way for the rider to open another door is through results. A professional rides first for himself, secondly for his sponsor.

Joining up with the Carrera team for the early season races in 1987, I reckoned that there was some ground to be made up before my position as one of the team's leaders was re-established. I was prepared to ride for Visentini, Zimmermann and Bontempi, the guys who rode so well in 1986. In a sense, I was going to use them to get back to the front line, just as I used Michel Laurent and Duclos Lassalle in my first year at Peugeot. Perhaps *use* is the wrong word. I would ride for them, defend a leader's jersey, and if by some good team riding I got the opportunity to do something myself, I would take it. But it never came to that.

Visentini was not going for a message, Bontempi and Zimmermann did not have any form. I suspected that Zimmermann would have problems after the Tour he rode in 1986. It was one hell of a hard tour for him and I imagined he would need to be a tough man to recover. He was not helped by his diet. You cannot eat muesli with peppers and hope to survive on that alone. But Zimmermann did. The Man above did not give us cabbage, potatoes, carrots, mushrooms and all the other vegetables simply to have them replaced by muesli and dried fruit. An unusual man, Zimmermann. He does not take much care of his appearance. He wears old jeans and dirty shirt, and an old pair of flip-flops that he won in some schoolboy race back in Switzerland. He got an offer of a car from Fiat and chose an Uno when he could have had any car in the Fiat range. That is the way Urs is. As a rival in my team, I did not worry too much about him. If I got my legs back in the time trials, I was better than he. Races like Paris–Nice, Criterium International and others are often decided in the time trial. I believed I

could stay with him in the mountains and that I read races better than
he. As things turned out, Zimmermann never found any form in 1987
and suffered as much as I had in 1986.

I felt sure Visentini was going to try to do something in the early
season, if only to remind people that he was the rider who won the
Giro in 1986, and Carrera's most successful leader. The Giro would be
his number-one objective but I expected him to challenge for races as I
attempted to make my comeback. But when he did ride the early
season races, he generally climbed off, and as well as doing nothing
himself, he was of no assistance to any other rider on the team. Even
with a very thorough winter's preparation behind me, I did not want
to put myself under too much pressure in the early part of the season.
Liège–Bastogne–Liège, my favourite classic, was pinpointed as my
first important rendezvous. It came in the middle of April and I wanted
to be on my best form for that. But things happened much more
quickly than that.

From the very first races of the season, my form was much better
than anyone, including myself, expected. Towards the end of February
we rode the Tour of Valencia in Spain and I won. That success helped
my confidence because in addition to riding well on a mountain stage, I
had to win the race in a time trial. Kelly and Vandenbroucke, two very
good riders against the clock, were my rivals and beating them was
encouraging. Time trials are always a good indication of how well you
are riding and I came away from Valencia pleased and relieved.

From Valencia we went to Paris–Nice and my form was getting
better. I should have won Paris–Nice, having had the leader's jersey,
lost it, and regained it only to lose it because of a puncture on the last
day. There will always be argument about what happened when I
punctured. At the time we were climbing the Col de Vence and Kelly's
team was making a strong tempo because the Spanish sprinter
Gutierrez was dropped and Kelly wanted to make sure he did not get
back on. We were close to the top when I punctured and as soon as it
was known that I had to have a wheel change, the pace increased even
more. There is a custom in cycling that you do not profit from the bad
luck of the raceleader and some said that Kelly should not have ridden
at the front when I was in trouble. His team mates, yes. But not
himself. I never blamed Sean. He was riding at the front when I
punctured and was entitled to continue doing so. Without mistakes on
my own part, there would not have been a problem. After getting a
wheel change I set out after the leaders, convinced that I would catch

up before they crossed the summit of the hill. Consequently I took things too easily on the climb. At the top we had not got to them, so I panicked and went down the descent like a madman. Which might have been OK if I had caught them but I didn't. Instead I only succeeded in losing two of my team mates. After the descent only Leali was still with me and even though we got to within 100 yards of the leaders, we could not get across to them.

My only bad memory of that day was the behaviour of Christian Rumeau, *directeur sportif* of Kelly's team. He was behind Leali and me, zigzagging across the road to prevent other cars from getting past him. If those cars had got past we would have been able to use them to get back to the front. But the disappointment was minor. I did not set out in 1987 to win Paris–Nice and the race at least proved that my form was very good.

The race also provided me with the motivation to attempt an exploit. On the Mont Faron stage I calculated badly and lost the jersey to Jean François Bernard. That annoyed me so much that I decided to attack from the line on the next day's stage to St Tropez. It was not a very clever thing to do; tactically it made no sense and I ended up having to ride for about 100 kilometres on my own at the front. But at the end I was still with the leaders, Bernard was blown out and I was back in the jersey. For me that was an exploit. A little adventure that I will treasure. Cycling is a sport where it often pays to be cautious. Once every so often it is exciting to forget caution and shock everybody by attacking when they least expect you to. Through my career I have done this a number of times and on every occasion it has given me a great thrill. Even when the exploit has not come off. Later in the year I would try another such exploit in the Giro d'Italia and it would lead to the most controversial episode of my career.

Even though Kelly did not do anything wrong in Paris–Nice I was a bit upset for about two days. He told me he was sorry the way things worked out and, over a long training spin at Cannes-sur-Mer three days after the race ended, we sorted things out. His friendship is much too important to allow the events of one race to come between us. Out on our bikes we talked it through; you can always make more sense when the conversation takes place on the bikes. Sean is a big boy and I am not a kid.

From Paris–Nice the show moved on to the Criterium International. Again, it came down to a battle between the two Irishmen. Sean stayed on my wheel on the mountain stage and beat me fairly in the afternoon time trial. First for him, second for me, but there were no complaints. He was the best around at the time and finishing second to him was not a disgrace. I was riding well and was on course to mount a big challenge in Liège–Bastogne–Liège.

On the night the Criterium International ended I travelled home to Paris. It was my first visit home since setting off on the early season races seven weeks previously. Although I had not won as much as I should, things had gone very well and I felt entitled to an evening on the town. Ringing Lydia on the way, I asked her to meet me in a restaurant that we both knew. That night I treated myself to a pizza and ice cream – things that must never be touched in the normal run of things. I wanted a fling and this was it. We had a most enjoyable evening, getting home around eleven. I took things easy the next day but returned to a serious routine a day later.

In preparation for Liège–Bastogne–Liège, I rode the Tour of the Basque Country in Spain and again rode well without winning. On the evening before Liège–Bastogne–Liège Boifava came to my room to speak with me about the race. He believed that my style of riding was making it hard for me to win. In a leading group I tended to ride at the front too much and this made it easy for others to beat me in the finish. There were a number of examples from recent races. On the Ventoux and Mont Faron in Paris–Nice I climbed with Kelly on my wheel; he had also stuck to me in the mountains stage of Criterium International and the Basque Country and each time he ended up winning the race. Boifava advised me to be cuter, not to do so much work and, ultimately, I had to be prepared to lose in order to win. In other words, if my breakaway companions were not contributing I was to stop working as well. If that meant that some pursuit group behind caught us, that was OK. There was a fair amount of sense in what Boifava was saying.

The crucial move in the 1987 Liège–Bastogne–Liège came on the Sprimont climb when Criquielion attacked. Argentin went in pursuit, then I. Argentin got to within three lengths of Criquielion's back wheel but could not go any farther. I accelerated past him and joined Criquielion. We rode together from there, and once over the Côte des Forges we were clear. We shared the work until we arrived in Liège. Our advantage was sometimes a minute and then down to 40 seconds and back up to 50. We could not afford to be complacent. Once we hit the streets of Liège it did appear that we were going to stay clear and both of us began to consider the sprint. Neither Criquielion nor I is a particularly good sprinter but in a one-to-one we would be fairly fast. Two years previously we sprinted with Argentin at the end of this race; Argentin won easily, Criquielion was second and I third. But I felt stronger now than then and thought I had a good chance of beating Criquielion. Boifava's advice was going through my mind: be prepared to lose to win. Into the last kilometre and I was refusing to ride at the front, Criquielion was also trying to save his energy. It was silly as the two of us rode through the last kilometre, not doing much more than 15 miles an hour. As I moved wide of Criquielion to make my sprint I felt pretty strong and went past him easily. Victory was going to be mine but just then Argentin came flying past me and won. I could not believe it. I knew he was not that far behind but never considered that he might actually rejoin us.

I am not a bad loser. It is probably a fault. Rarely do I feel down after losing. But I take the victories very much in my stride as well, not being able to enjoy the moment of success as much as others. My aim has always been to be a good professional. When I sit down and try to work out my attitude to winning and losing it comes out thus: I am not a bad loser, it is just that I prefer to win. But after Liège–Bastogne–Liège I experienced something totally new to me. Defeat knocked me out. It disturbed me. I lost my head and could not accept second place. I suppose the big thing was that victory was lost through the stupid behaviour of Criquielion and me in the last two kilometres and it was mostly my fault. What Boifava advised was not wrong but I made the mistake of acting totally on his advice and forgetting all that I had learned in the previous ten years.

I cried at the end of Liège–Bastogne–Liège, the only time in my career that I cried after losing. After changing quickly in Liège I drove home to Paris, a horrible car journey as I replayed the finish of the race a million times in my head. I found myself jerking my foot on the accelerator, travelling at less than 60 miles per hour and incapable of getting to Paris in the shortest time. On the way I stopped at a motorway restaurant and rang Lydia, saying I was on my way and asking that whatever else there was to be no mention of the race when I got home. The race was not mentioned that night.

On the morning after a hard race I will train lightly, no more than two hours. The day after Liège–Bastogne–Liège I went out for two hours and returned after five. That race had to be ridden out of my system.

By now it was clear that I was riding very well, better than at any time in my career. There were not too many victories but that did not bother me. Once you start noticing the races you might have won but did not, you begin to put pressure on yourself. And that makes winning more difficult. My final race before the Giro d'Italia was the Tour of Romandie and, as my form was so good, I went there to win. Twice previously (1983 and 1984) I had won Romandie but the victories were lessened by the circumstances of both races. In 1983 it was said that I won only because of the help my Peugeot team mate Phil Anderson had given, and in 1984 I was lucky. Having finished in the same time as Grezet, I won because of a better points total. Now I wanted to win and leave no question marks and there was also the incentive of becoming the first rider to win the race three times.

I was the favourite from the start and was prepared to ride hard from the first stage. My team also rode their best. I pushed them to the limits and, most days, there was only Eddy and I left at the end. On the final day there was a morning mountain stage and an afternoon time trial. I wore the leader's jersey and there were many who were planning to attack me that day. I made the team ride at the front on the morning stage, keeping things together until we got towards the end of the race. This suited the other contenders who were able to sit and wait for the final climb. On a descent before we got to the climb there were a couple of dangerous corners and I changed our plan by attacking. Suddenly all the big boys behind me had to start riding after me and they were not getting an armchair ride to the climb.

They caught me before the climb to the finish and, almost immediately, Ruttimann attacked and went away with Cornillet. I imagined that the other top men would be chasing but they decided that Carrera could do it. Eddy was at the front, I disappeared back into the pack, losing myself in the bunch. When the others did not know where I was, I returned to the front and attacked. I caught the two leaders on the descent before the final hill and rode with them on the climb. I was at the front all the time and was afraid they were going to attack me. Trying to discourage them, I rode harder and harder and suddenly there was a gap. I was not going to let them get back to me and so went even harder, winning the stage on my own.

That afternoon I also won the time trial. Two stage wins in one day and the overall victory. I had never ridden as well in my life.

Winning the Tour of Romandie in this way meant that I went to the Giro d'Italia a few days later as the clear favourite. That did not bother me. I was riding well and looking forward to the challenge.

CHAPTER 13
Visentini

Angelo Zomegnan covers cycling for the Italian daily newspaper *La Gazzetta dello Sport*. 'Roberto Visentini,' he says, 'is a modern guy, into good motor bikes and fast cars. Cycling is not the only thing in his life. He likes to ski. He can live without the bike. It is, for him, a sort of hobby. For Roche, it is different. He is a champion.'

When I joined Carrera I appreciated that they already had a leader in Roberto Visentini but I was not worried by that. Whoever was going best at any particular time would get the support of the team and I was happy to take my chances. I did not know Visentini very well. I had seen him on the Tour de France a couple of times. He did not speak French and I did not speak Italian, so there was very little communication between the two of us. My memory is of his pulling out of the Tour, a crash or something, but I do not remember him getting to Paris. The only things I heard about him was that he was rich and did not have to ride a bike for a living. His father was supposed to have a big undertaking business in Brescia and Roberto, it was said, was Daddy's boy. He also had the reputation for being a bit of a playboy. Otherwise, I knew very little about him.

During my first year at Carrera I did not come across Roberto very much. My knee trouble meant that I was not competitive and there were no situations where we were both looking for the support of the team in one race. There was talk before the 1986 Giro that I would be a threat to him but that was never likely to materialize. He was going well and I was not. I got a glimpse of what he could be like in the team time trial during the 1986 Giro. He simply blew the team apart. After three kilometres his pace had got rid of two of our men. He continued to blow one rider after another until there were just four of us left:

himself, Casani, Eddy and I. The team's time was based on the time of the fourth rider to finish and we needed to cross the line together. I was feeling really bad, on my last legs, and the test finished on a hill. On that climb Visentini rode about 20 yards ahead of the three of us. I was suffering, just managing to stay on Eddy's wheel. Visentini was looking back, screaming at us to get up to him. To everybody on the roadside and to the journalists it looked as if we were slowing Roberto down but, in reality, he was at fault. If he had stayed with us we could have gone up the hill at a nice tempo and much faster than we did. As it was we finished second to Del Tongo in the test.

But we were all blamed. I was criticized for not being able to stick with Visentini on the hill, Leali was criticized for being blown out on the way, and most of the team were criticized. To me the time trial proved that Visentini did not have a sharp brain for working out race tactics. His original pace was nonsensical. There was not much that I could have done in that time trial. I was not going well and not in a position to start giving orders about how fast or how slow Roberto should have been going.

Because we were never rivals, there was no bad feeling between him and me in 1986. He was a very reserved person, saying very little and not allowing any great friendship to develop. I attempted to have some kind of relationship and often spoke with him. He was interested in fast cars – Ferraris, Porsches – and once I got to drive his Mercedes. Even though I was not going well in races I did what I could for him and there were a few stages in the Giro when I did some good work for him.

At the end of the season I was contracted to ride the Baracchi Trophy with Roberto and maybe that race proved that there was a certain amount of tension between us. I went to the Baracchi knowing that my knee was not right. It was so sore that I did not go for a spin on the morning of the race and I knew that if I even tried to loosen up it would be very painful. Normally when you ride a time trial with another rider you will both go for a short warm-up just before setting off but I was so concerned about my knee that I did not even warm up with Visentini.

At the start of the race my knee was stiff and sore and I was going very badly. On the hills the Italians would shout, 'Forza, Roberto!' and he would make it really hard for me to hang on. It was obvious that I was in a bad way and he certainly knew it. But rather than nurse me through and making sure we did the best possible time, he was humiliating me before his public. On the hills he sprinted through to do his turn at the front; I surged to take his wheel, but as soon as I did he eased, forcing me to go through and not allowing me any time to recover. Once I got to the front he accelerated past me, repeating the process again and again. We could have ridden a good time trial together but he was not interested in that.

As the race went on I began to come round and he started to weaken. Now it was his turn to suffer and I treated him the way he had treated me. Right at the very end there were a number of very sharp turns before the finish and even a section of cobbles. I could hurt Visentini on the cobbles and so I went as fast as I could. I sensed he was losing contact and went harder again. Afraid to look behind, because he might still be there, I pedalled as if there was no tomorrow. I wanted to show him that he could not do what he had done to me in the first part of the race and get away with it. If he had been decent in the first part of the race we would have finished together, as is normal for the two-man teams in the Baracchi. But this day I wanted to finish alone, wanted people to wonder what happened to Roberto, the man who was so strong in the first part of the race. At the line I was alone, he was about 200 yards behind.

It is very unusual to leave your partner in the Baracchi but I did it to Visentini. It was the last race I rode in 1986 for such was the pain in my knee afterwards that it was perfectly clear I would not be able to ride again unless the problem was taken care of.

There was a party after Visentini won the Giro in 1986. I had pulled out of the race a day before it finished and was feeling miserable, watching the last day on television. Seeing the entire Carrera team on the podium, knowing that I should have been with them and feeling bad because I wasn't. Visentini won the race and the team were getting this award and that award and the only person in the hotel's TV room watching with me was Visentini's father. The only reason I was still on the race was that the Carrera bosses specifically asked me to stay, they were having a big banquet and they wanted everybody there.

That evening we went to the restaurant for the banquet but before the main course arrived Visentini got up and left. His neighbours had painted the roads in Brescia and wanted to have a homecoming party. So he left the men who had ridden with him for three weeks and went off. The lads who had waited for this banquet had to drive back to Milan and pick up flights to their homes. I got myself a flight to Paris, arriving home two days later than was necessary. Everybody was dissatisfied: the Carrera bosses, Boifava, and the riders.

At the start of 1987 I was able to meet Visentini on equal terms. My knee had healed and my form was right. I saw every race as an opportunity to re-establish myself in the Carrera team. Roberto's attitude was that the Giro was *his* race and that the rest did not matter. He went to the Tour of the Basque Country, crashed, went home and said it was unimportant. What was the Tour des Pays Basque? He said he did not like Liège–Bastogne–Liège. He went to the Tour of Romandie and on the last day he rode up alongside me and said he was available to help me defend the leader's jersey. I think it was the first time I saw him on the race.

After Romandie came the Giro and there was no plus side to how I felt about Visentini. Any chance that he had to help me, he did not take. He was foolish because he was going to want me to help him in the Giro and he was doing nothing to earn that help. If the roles were reversed I would have done anything to mark up points with a person whose help I wanted in a future race. But Visentini was not like that. I went to the Giro feeling that he deserved nothing from me.

CHAPTER 14

I Want to Win the Giro

On the night the Tour de France ended the Carrera team was partying at the Lido in Paris. Lydia Roche found herself seated alongside the Carrera boss Tito Tacchella. In the course of conversation Lydia recollected the Giro d'Italia. What went so wrong? 'An Italian had to win,' replied Tacchella abruptly.

Tours that go on for three weeks or more are hard. No matter how you ride them. That is the principal reason why I have never been able to go along with the idea of riding one long tour as preparation for another. I know that others use the tours of Spain or Italy as preparation for the Tour de France. For me, it does not make sense. If I go to a tour that is three weeks long and has difficult mountain stages it is not because I want some good training. Before the 1987 Giro d'Italia my *directeur sportif* Davide Boifava and Roberto Visentini were saying things about what my attitude to the Giro should be. Things with which I totally disagreed. Boifava suggested that I help Visentini in the Giro and Visentini help me in the Tour de France. In other words that I accept a compromise in which the Giro would be his and the Tour mine. On the other hand Visentini was saying that as he was riding only the Giro d'Italia and as he was the defending champion of the race, he should have the backing of the Carrera team.

Boifava was trying to tell me Visentini would help me in the Tour; Visentini was admitting he had no intention of going to the Tour and using this as a reason why I should ride for him in the Giro. My response at the time was that I was hoping to win the Giro d'Italia and that the leadership of the Carrera team would be decided by the strongest legs. I was very satisfied with my form, for the previous four months I had been Carrera's leader and during that time Visentini had done nothing to earn my friendship or respect. Now that the big race had come round I was not prepared suddenly to move into the background. Carrera were never going to say publicly that they had a preference for Visentini over me in the Giro. But I was conscious of the fact that it was an Italian race, they were an Italian sponsor and Visentini was an Italian rider. Boifava probably anticipated the difficulties which were to follow and that is why he tried to get me to ride for Roberto. A major consideration for me was the other Carrera riders. In the event of a conflict between Visentini and me, whose side were they likely to take?

During the year I had been good to the riders, never taking my share of the prize money. Believing that I would get it back with their loyalty later in the year. In the early part of the Giro they helped me pretty well. But there were indications that they would have preferred to be riding for Visentini. I cannot explain why this was so. When I spoke with them they did not have many good things to say about Visentini. He did not treat them very well. In the restaurant he did not behave properly and he was not the kind of fellow that could be relied on for help. Earlier in the year he did not produce anything and they were openly critical of him. I do not know. Maybe it was because the team, apart from Eddy and me, was made up entirely of Italians. Bontempi and Leali were both from Brescia, the same region as Visentini, and they would have all trained together. Maybe, because of his win in the 1986 Giro, they believed that Visentini was going to win again and that everybody's life would be simple if I just accepted that. Maybe the Carrera bosses had spoken to them.

I do understand why Boifava supported Visentini in the Giro. He lived just 15 kilometres from Roberto in Brescia, a region where cycling is very popular. Boifava knew that if I won he would have to answer questions after returning to Brescia. He did not want conflict or argument and, for him, the straightforward solution was Visentini winning.

The first indications that the team was leaning towards Visentini came in their reactions to the first two time trials: the prologue and the downhill time trial on the Poggio. Visentini won the prologue and they were delighted. On the following day I was off four places ahead of Visentini on the Poggio time trial. All of the lads were watching back at the hotel, Patrick was with them in the room. When it was announced that I had recorded the fastest time they cheered. Then they waited for Visentini's time. When he failed to beat my time there was great disappointment in the room. Nobody was saying how great it was that I had won the time trial, they were all expressing their regrets that Roberto had not won. Patrick listened to this talk in disgust, then stood up and walked out.

Visentini wore the pink jersey after the prologue but lost it to Eric Breukink of Panasonic on the morning stage of the second day. Four days into the race Carrera won the team time trial to Camaiore Lido and I got the leader's jersey from Breukink. It was a well-controlled team performance; only one other team in the race (Del Tongo) managed to finish within a minute of our time. We had all remembered how Visentini had ruined our team time trial in the 1986 Giro by setting too fast a pace and because I was going well I decided to organize our effort this time. I told the other riders that if Visentini rode the way he had in 1986 they were to let him go. Just leave him ride off the front and not take his wheel. Any time I reckoned he was going too fast I screamed at him to cool down. When you are going well these are the things you can do.

Once I was in the *maglia rosa*, Visentini's attitude to me became clear and his ambition to win the race even clearer. He decided to follow me wherever I went, not letting me out of his sight. As long as he was close to me, he felt that he had his chief rival under control. There was no doubt in my mind that he saw me as his rival.

Later in the race Boifava asked why I did not complain about Visentini's tactics at the time. It was principally because it did not suit me to complain then. Visentini's presence at my back wheel was annoying but, when he was there, I at least knew where he was. There was nothing he could do unbeknown to me and as I too regarded him as my major rival I was glad to know where he was at all times. Of course his riding led to tension between us. On the day after the team time trial, the stage from Camaiore finished with a three-kilometre climb to Montalcino. Four riders attacked out of the leading group. Giupponi was one of the four. I let them go a bit and counterattacked and got across to them on my own. I looked under my arm and Visentini was towing the other riders from the original leading group up to us. When they rejoined us I turned to Visentini and asked what, in God's name, he thought he was doing. He said he had to chase because Giupponi was in the group. I reminded him that when I was also in the group there was no need for him to worry about Giupponi. But Giupponi was only the excuse. I knew he was riding against me.

Visentini's attitude was again clear on the first mountain stage of the race, the 134-kilometre sixth stage to Terminillo. It was a hard finish with a long climb to the summit of Terminillo and I attacked twice on the hill. A quarter of the way up I moved onto my big chain ring, a 51, and took off. The breakaway group which dominated that stage were four minutes up and not going to be caught. I attacked because I wanted to take time out of some of the leading contenders. In the regrouping which followed, Visentini, Millar, Lejarreta, Breukink, Giupponi and a number of others joined me. Argentin and Anderson were two of those left behind. It made sense for us to distance people like Argentin and Anderson and I asked Visentini to ride with me. He refused. Millar did ride with me and we took over three minutes out of Argentin. While he would not ride with me, Visentini covered every move I made and was on to me every time I got the tiniest gap. That evening I publicly criticized the way Visentini had ridden but the conflict between us was not yet out in the open. There was tension but the open hostility would not come until later. Visentini's refusal to help on the climb to Terminillo did upset me.

I suppose, looking back, it is easy to see that we were building up for a big confrontation. At the time, we sensed it as well. On that stage to Terminillo Eddy was in the break which was away all day and never caught. Because he was defending my pink jersey he sat on wheels in the break and was very fresh on the climb to the finish. At the very end the break was down to just Eddy and the Fagor rider Jean Claude Bagot. Eddy had a very good chance of winning the stage but, typical of Eddy, he did not care about that. He said to Bagot that he would not contest the finish if Bagot and the Fagor team agreed to help me later in the race. It was very good of Eddy because he could have won and he could not be honest and tell Boifava why he lost. Afterwards he simply told Boifava that he was on a bad day.

Later in the year I was talking to Boifava about 1988 and the possibility of my signing for Carrera again. Boifava complained about Eddy, that he had sold the Terminillo stage to Bagot and should not be taken on. I tried to explain that Eddy did not sell the race but had exchanged it for help from the Fagor team, saying that if the Fagors had not been around later in the race I probably would not have won. 'Davide,' I said, 'there were days when my own team was not so strong and I needed help from Fagor.' Biofava continued to protest, saying that Eddy should have consulted him before making any decisions. But Eddy could not do that because he was enlisting Fagor's help to help me in my battle against Visentini. In a situation where Visentini was away in a break and I was in the *peloton*, Eddy was going to call in his favour and get the Fagor team to chase down Visentini. The story helps to show how valuable Eddy was to me.

The first week of the Giro was hard because it appeared that everybody was trying to make things difficult for me. Because my form was sharp I was watching every move closely, trying to make sure that every break that included a rider of any consequence was covered. I was sometimes attempting to control everything on my own and I am sure that this angered some of the Italians. They retaliated by forcing me to work harder. An attack happened and I found myself boxed in. It took a little longer to counter the attack but that is what I did. Yet it is certain that I did far too much in the first week. In going after everything I was using up reserves that I was going to need later in the race and I am sure that my physical exhaustion at the end of the Giro had a lot to do with that first week. A part of the problem was that I considered there were many riders capable of winning: besides myself and Visentini, there were Argentin, Giupponi, Millar, Saronni, Breukink, Lejarreta and Van der Velde. It was a hard week and I did not help by riding so unintelligently.

It happened in this way: some guy who is not really a danger man but whom I consider to be a possible rival goes away in a break. His team mates have me boxed in and I have to push my way clear to get after him. I take some risks because it is on a descent and eventually I join up. At that point I decide that there is a chance to distance some other rivals who are back in the *peloton*. Instead of looking around and taking stock of the other riders in the break, I ride strongly at the front. Those behind are already engaged in a pursuit and we are caught.

I used up energy needlessly: if I had looked around and assessed the situation after joining up with the break, I would have realized that it was silly to ride. But this was the first time I wore the leader's jersey in one of the big tours and it was a very big test for me. It was a lesson and one which helped me to ride a much better tactical race in the Tour de France a month later.

I also found the pressure from television and newspapers far worse than anything I had previously experienced. Each day you had to do television and talk with the newspaper journalists. It was an hour and a half before you got to your hotel. In France it is difficult to cope with the demands but it is far more difficult in Italy. They talk to you anywhere, they come to your hotel at really inconvenient times and, basically, they do not give a damn. You go to do one television piece and end up having to do a separate piece for each station on the race. Italy has more sports papers than anywhere and they all want exclusive interviews. Of course if you tell one of them something that you have not told another, there is trouble. I am not complaining. It is part of the job but I found it particularly demanding in Italy.

Twelve days into the race, things began to go badly for me. Having defended the jersey for over a week and used up a fair amount of my strength, I was knocked back even further by the mass pile-up at the end of the tenth stage to Termoli. I could see the crash happening in front of me, bodies flying everywhere, and I had plenty of time to stop. But as I slowed, guys came crashing into me from behind and I ended up suffering some pretty bad bruises to my leg and backside. Ice packs were applied to the affected areas that night but I was still a bit stiff and sore the next day.

The stage to Osimo was not severe but it had a hard uphill finish and I was not feeling good. Visentini was dancing on the pedals and because of the way I felt, I asked him to take it easy. But on the first of the two cols he rode hard, increasing the speed as he got closer to the top. He attacked because he knew I was still sore from the previous day's crash. Once the sprint started for the mountain points, I was left behind and went across the summit about 200 yards behind the leaders. I got back on the descent.

At the finish we had to climb the second hill and it was steep for the final two kilometres. The last 500 metres of the climb were on cobbles, which made it even harder. Going around the corner before we got to the cobbles I slipped my chain; Visentini saw what happened and attacked. I went after him but the effort involved in pegging him back meant I was vulnerable when he attacked again. He finished about 50 metres ahead of me and reduced his deficit on me by seven seconds.

Journalists saw what Visentini did and asked me how I felt about the performance of my team mate. Because the important San Marino time trial was only two days away I did not want to make things worse than they already were and explained Visentini's attack on the grounds that it was his birthday (which it was) and that he simply wanted to win a stage on his birthday.

I was getting nervous about the time trial; I did not feel in good physical shape, my team mate was attacking because he knew I was feeling bad and, generally, the tension between us was at its highest point. Yet I do not accept that I disliked Visentini on a personal basis. That simply did not come into it. I only saw him as my *adversaire*, my biggest *adversaire*. The difference was that he happened to be in my team.

Many times over the last six months I have tried to figure out what went wrong for me in the San Marino time trial. At the time it was the most important time trial of my career, I liked the circuit, and the weather on the day was wet and windy, which should have suited me. I know I was not going particularly well: ten days in the pink jersey had taken quite a bit out of me and I was a bit sore from the Termoli crash. But, most of all, I believe that Visentini cracked me mentally. I am not sure that he deliberately set out to do this. But he did crack me.

On the morning of the time trial it was lashing rain. As is normal for me, I reconnoitred the complete circuit on the bike. Visentini intended doing the same and we went out to the start of the circuit together in the team car. Because it was raining we stopped under a bridge and changed into riding gear. He went to the end of the bridge, got off and just got back into the car. He followed in the car as I did the 46-kilometre course on the bike.

At the finish in San Marino I changed and got into the car. Visentini immediately began asking what gear I had used on the hill, how I had coped with the wind at such-and-such a point and what equipment I planned to use. I wanted to hit him. He was my chief rival in the time trial and the last person I wanted to have in the car. I was on edge and the circuit was going through my mind: what gears I would use, my choice of tyres, the wheels, the bike I would use. All these decisions had still to be made and Visentini was talking away nonstop. I could feel myself getting worked up. This went on all the way back to the hotel and when we got there it was time to sit down and have something to eat. I wanted to be alone but across the table Visentini kept asking the same questions. Because he was my team mate I could not say anything but inside I was burning up with anger. He was sneering and laughing, knowing that I was feeling the pressure of the pink jersey. He was relaxed, no nerves, and making jokes at me. It infuriated me.

Normally I depend greatly on nervous energy to drive me in the time trial but by the time I got to the start of this hugely important test, I had used up most of that energy. I never felt good, and struggled when riding into the wind. On the climb to the finish in San Marino I was using lower gears than was normal for me in a time trial and did not need anybody to tell me that I was losing the pink jersey. Even so, twelfth place was disappointing and that was made even worse by Visentini's very good performance. He won, beating me by two minutes and 47 seconds, and became the clear leader of the race.

I became more despondent when I saw the reactions of all the Carrera team, all except Eddy. It hurt me that there were some Carrera riders whom I had never seen as happy as they were that evening in San Marino. They were entitled to feel happy for Visentini, his perform-ance had been good and the team still had the pink jersey. But there was not a morsel of sympathy for me. I had owned the *maglia rosa* for ten days, lost it because of one very untypical time-trial performance, and nobody saw the slightest need to say, 'Hard luck, Steve.' They were otherwise occupied: Roberto this, Roberto that.

Maybe the result of the time trial was as much a relief to the Carrera riders as anything. To them, it was conclusive proof that Visentini was the strong man of the team. That meant that the issue of who was Carrera leader was decided. They believed Visentini would win and were looking forward to riding for him over the final nine days of the race. I could see they were making one obvious mistake: in assessing the merit of Visentini's time-trial performance they were using my time as the guide. But my performance was very bad. They talked of Roberto's time being *magnifique*. It was not. If judged against the times of the riders who finished second, third, fourth, fifth and sixth, Visentini's time was good, not *magnifique*. They reckoned he was invincible. I disagreed, but silently.

That night I lay in bed and all kinds of thoughts were going through my head. I was very down. The Giro was not in my grasp any more but, inside, I was not letting it go. Something reminded me that I owed Visentini nothing; something else said that I was too good to ride for this man. In all the races this year I had ridden well; as a professional I could not have performed better for Carrera. Now, because of one day, I was to lose the race I most wanted. I decided I was going to give myself a second chance. These were the thoughts which went through my mind. There are times when my thoughts can be egotistical. That night, I imagined, was one of those times and I was afraid to open up and reveal what I was thinking to Eddy, who lay in the bed alongside mine. Even though I was not letting go of the Giro I was still conscious that it was not proper for me to do anything directly wrong to a team mate.

But Eddy was thinking about the Giro as well. He began to say the things that I was thinking and that had the effect of multiplying my desire to do something. Eddy was very logical. He told me not to worry. He did not accept that Visentini's form was nearly as good as others were presuming. Throughout the year Visentini did nothing and the efforts he made in the time trial were sure to cost him. You needed a good foundation coming into a race like the Giro and Visentini did not have one. Eddy likened his situation to mine during the 1986 Tour de France: 'Remember, Stephen, you did the good time trial in Nantes and people thought you could win the Tour, but you didn't have any foundation and you suffered because of the efforts made in the time trial.' He said Visentini would suffer in the same way and if he did not it would prove that cycling was easy. We both knew cycling was not easy. It was time to have a look at the profiles of the stages over the following days.

On the very next day there was a completely flat stage to Lido di Jesolo which we dismissed. After that there was a medium-hard stage to Sappada; three mountains, not easy but not especially severe. Then there was the Marmolada stage; five big mountains to be climbed and easily the most difficult stage of the Giro. Eddy insisted that Visentini would expect an attack on that stage and would be prepared to go with everything. 'Stephen, you must try something when he's not expecting it and I think the Sappada stage would be the best. He isn't going to recover easily from the efforts in the time trial and it's better to try something as soon as possible.'

Regardless of whether I recovered from my bad performance in the time trial, I was going to attack on the stage between Lido di Jesolo and Sappada. The plan can be seen as a direct attack on Visentini but I know that at the time I did not see it as such. Rather it was an agreement between Eddy and me not to let go. An attack could have many results: it might lead to a stage victory with an insignificant time gain; it could enable me to take a significant amount of time on Visentini; it might force the other teams to chase me and so give Visentini an easy ride on what was a fairly difficult stage, or an attack could cost me everything . All I was taking was the opportunity. Too much had happened in the previous six months, even in the previous six years, for me to pass up the Giro d'Italia because of one bad day.

On the stage to Sappada I rode at the front of the bunch all the time, waiting for the right move and ready to go with it. It was a 224-kilometre stage, of which the first 100 were relatively flat. After that there were three climbs. On the first Bagot attacked and went clear. Further up Millar went and I went directly after him. He was making the descent fairly well but Visentini caught up with us and that was that. Ennio Salvador, an Italian who was 20 minutes down on general classification, attacked and even though he was not a man I would normally have chased, I was desperate at this point. I made an unbelievable descent, went downhill with the back wheel up in the air. I quickly caught Salvador and joined up with Bagot before the bottom of the descent. Occasionally I glanced backwards at the hairpins that had just been negotiated and I could see the confusion. Fellows were hanging out of trees, having overshot corners. Visentini missed one turn and was forced to take a short cut down one gravel bank to return to the road. They came down that descent in ones and twos and everybody was taking risks. It was very, very dangerous.

At the bottom Salvador, Bagot and I were together. I let them do the riding. Bagot did not object because he remembered the Terminillo stage and the agreement that had been reached with Eddy. But Bagot punctured soon afterwards and was swept up by the bunch. I was left alone with Salvador. We shared the riding. I did not consider it likely that we would stay away that long and was churning a nice sensible gear (53 x 16), trying to conserve my strength, pretty sure that I would need it for later in the day. I imagined that the Bianchi or Panasonic team was at that moment organizing the pursuit and I wanted to keep plenty in reserve for when we were caught. I was not going to wait for them but neither was I going to kill myself trying to stay clear of the entire pack. It was at that point Boifava pulled alongside in his car and began the conversations which led to enormous conflict and controversy.

'Hey, Stephen, what are you doing?' he asked.

'Just riding along,' I replied, 'waiting for the other teams to ride after me.'

'But Stephen, the other teams are not chasing you.'

'Well, then, that's their bad luck. If they're going to let me take 20 minutes they'll lose and Carrera will win.'

'But if you keep riding you will take 20 minutes and win the Giro.'

'That's what I want.'

'Why don't you just sit behind Salvador, let him do the riding and try to win the stage?'

'Salvador is going nowhere. He is creeping. Anyway, it's not the stage I want. It's the Giro.'

'Stephen, Visentini has the jersey. You cannot do this to Visentini.'

'Look, Visentini is behind. Somebody, the Bianchis, the Panasonics for Breukink, some team is sure to ride after me. Just wait a minute.'

'No, Stephen. The Carrera team is riding after you.'

'What?'

'The Carrera team is chasing you.'

'You go back and tell the boys that if they're going to ride behind me they had better be prepared to ride for a long time and that they should keep a little bit under the saddle because when they catch me, they're going to need it.'

Boifava slowed down, waiting for the pursuit to overtake him, and I carried on with Salvador. Finding out that Carrera was chasing was a shock and my reaction was to move from my sensible 53 x 16 gear into a 53 x 14. I was raging with anger. They were going to have to ride hard to catch up. The tension in the team had become open warfare.

I learned from Eddy afterwards the way things had happened behind. After I had made my escape on the descent there were bodies everywhere and it was only when riders got to the bottom of the descent that Visentini realized I was gone. He got Claudio Chiappucci to chase but they were not getting anywhere, and, as other Carrera riders joined up with the pursuit group, he tried to get more of them to the front. Leali disagreed with Visentini, saying that as I was up the road the team should not ride, but wait and see what developed. But Boifava came along and said they all should ride. For me that was the critical mistake. Both Breukink and Millar admitted afterwards that if Carrera had not chased, Panasonic would have done. The problem was that Carrera did not think, they simply presumed I was out to get Visentini.

So Carrera were told to ride by Boifava, who then drove up to me and ordered me to slow down. I refused and suddenly there was an open conflict between me and the rest of the team. They were riding their eyeballs out behind me and everyone in the bunch was laughing at them. And they could not catch me. That hurt their pride. By this point in the race Italian television was showing the race live and the *directeurs sportif* of other teams were being asked what they thought of this latest turn in the race. Most of them offered the view that I was the culprit and that if I were in their team, I would be sent home. Yet, I know that I was happy as I took on my own team. For me this was an exploit. Something big. I distinctly remember I was smiling on the road to Sappada. I could not feel any pain. I was so angry with everybody else and so happy with myself. Happy that I could do what I was doing.

There is one picture of that day which will remain in my mind. The sun was beating down, it was a glorious day and the heat seemed to rise from the road. My entire team were at the head of the *peloton*, chasing me. When I looked behind I could just about make them out, and I could see all the cars glistening behind the riders. There was a climb 20 or 30 kilometres further up the road and I knew that if I could stay in front until the climb I would get away again. They were chasing me, all of them except Eddy, but they were not catching me. That was a good feeling. They were going to talk about this day.

After Boifava failed to persuade me to slow down he went back and spoke with Patrick, thinking that I would listen to Patrick. So Patrick, who was in the second team car with the assistant *directeur sportif* Quintarelli, was sent up to talk to me. Like Eddy, Patrick is 100 per cent loyal to me and he was never going to ask me to do what I did not want to do myself. He told me Boifava asked him to ask me. I said I would not stop unless Carrera stopped chasing.

Patrick relayed my feelings to Boifava over the team's walkie-talkie. Boifava told Patrick he wanted to speak with me again and Patrick held the walkie-talkie out of the window of the car, close to my ear.

'Stephen, this is Boifava. You must stop.'

'Tell the team to stop and I'll stop. Not before.'

'I can't do that.'

'Well, then, I can't stop.'

'Stephen, if you don't stop I will come up personally with the car and push you off the road. This is not possible. Everyone is laughing.'

'It's not me they're laughing at but you. Tell the boys to stop riding, it's not right to ride after a team mate. I've been playing the role of joint leader in the Carrera team for the last two weeks and now when I have a chance to win you're telling me to stop. Tell the boys to stop and I'll stop.'

'No, no, Stephen. You stop or I will take drastic action.'

'You can do what you want.'

That ended our conversation. As he was still alongside I asked Patrick what he thought. He said it was for me to decide. He could not tell me what to do at such an important time. I agreed but still wanted his opinion. He looked at me with a bit of a smile: 'Steve, if you have balls, now is the time to show them.'

That was precisely what I wanted to hear. The *peloton*, led by the Carrera team, was not far behind. The roads were big, wide and open and I could see a long way back. I kept riding and riding, knowing that I was close to the climb. I had been out in front for 40 or 50 kilometres. On a false flat before the climb they were only 100 yards behind. I gave it everything, knowing it was double or nothing. Now the gap was down to 50 yards. I looked behind and I could see fellows dropping off the back. I kept going as hard as I could and suddenly Jean François Bernard counterattacked from the pursuing pack, Anderson just behind him. Still glancing behind I could see that the Carrera boys were dropping behind, paying for the efforts of their chase. Visentini was looking around for his team mates. I slipped down a gear and jumped in behind Bernard and Anderson. Staying on their wheel and glad of the shelter. We were on the hill and not going to be caught by any big group from behind.

On the climb Anderson, Bernard and I were joined by three Italian riders and farther on by a group of five which included Millar. At the top we were about a minute ahead of those chasing us. Visentini's problem was that he did not have a Carrera team any more and he sought help from other Italian teams. He approached Argentin's Gewiss-Bianchi team but was told to get lost. A couple of days earlier Visentini had been saying unpleasant things about Argentin to the Italian journalists. Attila agreed to ride with Visentini and with their assistance we were caught on the last hill. At least this meant that Eddy, who was in the group behind but not helping in the chase, was again alongside and offering encouragement. Without his presence on the critical part of that last climb to Sappada, I do not believe that I would have made it with the leaders.

That last climb to Sappada was unbelievably hard. On a false flat section the speed was so punishing that I just hung on to the back of the leading group. Eddy was with me, all the time talking to me. Visentini was in the same group now but a a bit farther back. Boifava came up to us and ordered Eddy to go back to Visentini.

'I can't,' Eddy said. 'Stephen is in a bad way too and he has asked me to stay with him.'

'Eddy,' replied Boifava, 'I'm telling you to go back to Visentini. If you don't, you're going home tonight.'

'I can't. Stephen is the one who looks after me. Visentini has never done a thing for me. Stephen has been out on his own all day and he needs help more than Roberto.'

On the way to my first stage victory in the Tour de France – the Aubisque, 1985

On the attack with Marc Madiot in the 1984 Milan–San Remo

The 1985 Tour de France: away in the Pyrenees with Delgado, Parra and LeMond

Riding hard in the '87 Giro to hold on to the pink jersey, with the crowd shouting for Visentini (just behind)

▲ Boifava tells me to slow down during the crucial Sappada stage of the Giro d'Italia. I was not interested in slowing down
◄ Winning the Giro and happy about it

I was in a dark tunnel during the 1986 Tour de France, injury saw to that

The crash which ruined a year. Riding the Paris-Six with Tony Doyle at the end of 1985, crashing and being helped away

I have always enjoyed time trialling and am fascinated by the choices of equipment in the races against the clock

The 1987 Tour de France – you hurt on the Ventoux. And (right) wearing the yellow jersey did not make the climb of Alpe d'Huez any easier

Delgado and Bernard raise my arms on the Champs Elysées, a very happy moment

Leading up St Patrick's Hill in the Nissan classic. Note the crowds!

Back in Dublin for the post-Tour celebration, Lydia and I enjoy ourselves

Eddy stayed with me. We knew there was a very steep bit coming up. Eddy talked about the great ride I had done and how everyone else in the race was so tired because they had been forced to ride so hard behind me. The steep section of the climb was still going to be hell for me. On that steep section I was like a yo-yo, Eddy would bring me up a bit, then have to ease as I recovered and we were just off the back of the lead group, hanging on for dear life. About 200 metres after the top Eddy blew. As he was going backwards he yelled at me, 'Stephen, you have got to get on to that group, this is the day that you win the Giro.'

There were five miles after the summit to the finish. It was a false descent. I was sitting on the point of the saddle, my knees up around my ears.

I chased desperately and eventually caught the group in front of me. I hung on and hung on until the finish line appeared. I did not have any idea what was happening to Visentini. Such was the pain I suffered all the way up that last climb and even after the summit to the finish that my thoughts were only for myself. I knew that I had not lost anything of significance to the other big contenders. At the start of the day I was second overall, two minutes 42 seconds behind Visentini. Everything hinged on whether he could finish within that time. I was so shattered I had no idea of precisely what was going on.

Three minutes passed, then four. No Visentini. It was clear that the *maglia rosa* was mine again. I was told to go to the podium. As I got to the podium Visentini came into view. Almost six minutes down. He looked towards the podium and saw me getting his jersey.

CHAPTER 15

The Aftermath

At the end of the Giro d'Italia Francesco Moser, who had not ridden, was asked to assess the seventieth Giro d'Italia. 'Roche has silenced everyone. He won in the mountains and won in the time trial, after having the leader's jersey for seventeen days out of twenty-two. No one can have any doubts as to who was the strongest man in the race.'

I was satisfied to have got the jersey back in Sappada but also a bit scared. There was certain to be trouble within the Carrera team. There was wrong on both sides: I should not have been riding against my team mates and they should not have been riding against me.

As soon as I finished in Sappada Patrick and Eddy both took me to one side and advised me not to say anything to the journalists. Franco Belleri, the Carrera team manager, warned me not to speak with the press or television; I was to take the pink jersey and head straight back to the hotel. Boifava asked me not to speak to the press. I could feel that everybody was talking about what happened, other *directeurs sportif* were giving their opinion, and it seemed to me that I would be sent home. Boifava was telling the journalists that 'Stephen should not have done this, should not have done that, and there will be very serious discussions when we go back to the hotel'. Journalists were trying to get to me but Eddy was pushing them away. He walked beside me like a bodyguard, making sure I was OK.

Back at the hotel I showered and Belleri came to my room. He said that what had happened had happened but I was not to speak with the press. To me this was unfair because I knew that Boifava and Belleri had both spoken to the journalists. I argued with Belleri, saying that if I refused to put my case to the journalists it would look as if I was accepting blame for what happened. That I had been the bad boy. After watching some television I went downstairs to eat and to meet my team mates again. At the bottom of the stairs about twenty journalists were waiting for me. Belleri saw me coming and shouted that I was not to talk to the journalists. I wanted to get my side of the story into the newspapers but I could not bring myself to speak with all the journalists so I selected two of them, to whom I would speak privately and they could tell their colleagues what I said. That was acceptable to them. Belleri again reminded me that I was forbidden to talk to the press. He caught me by the arm, trying to get me to come away from the journalists.

'Mr Belleri, my job is here. On this race. Your job is back in an office in Verona. You go back to your office.' He stood over me, fuming. I could see that he was really agitated but I just walked into the bar of the hotel with the two journalists.

After speaking with the two journalists I headed into the restaurant to eat. I did not know what reaction to expect from my team mates but suspected that it would not be pleasant. Bontempi, Casani, Ghirotto and Leali were the ones who reacted most strongly against me, telling me I should not have done what I did. Ghirotto, who used to be on my side, was the first to speak: 'Ah, Stephen, why did you do it?' The four of them cut me down, tried to make me feel like a child that had done something wrong. I could see they wanted to hit me. Now it all flashed before me again: how they had been delighted when Visentini won the prologue, disappointed when he lost the downhill time trial and again so happy when he won the San Marino time trial.

Later that evening there was a meeting of the Carrera team. I was not sure what was going to happen; originally there had been talk of all kinds of punishment. Sending me home, sending Patrick home, sending Eddy home; sending all three of us home. At the meeting it was decided that what had happened had happened and the only way to show that Carrera was strong and united was to defend the jersey, to ride together. To brush everything under the carpet.

I did not interpret this decision as Carrera supporting me. They were supporting the pink jersey and the publicity which goes to the team that owns the *maglia rosa*. Even as I rode past the finish line in Sappada I suspected that if I did not take the leader's jersey I would be sent home that evening. It could easily have been different. I took the jersey by just five seconds from the Swiss rider Toni Rominger. Doing what I did and taking the pink jersey was one thing, doing what I did and not taking it would have been another thing. It also helped me that Visentini finished so far down. He cracked totally on the final climb to Sappada and in losing almost six minutes to me, he was now out of contention. Carrera had only one chance of winning the Giro and that was me.

That evening the Carrera boss Tito Tacchella and his brother Imereo arrived on the Giro. They had come to see the next day's five-cols stage and to discuss with me the possibility of signing a new contract.

The next day's race to Canazei was the most difficult of the Giro and I was not looking forward to it. There were five big cols and the final one, the Marmolada, was particularly severe. Apart from Eddy, there was going to be no support for me from the Carrera team. Visentini was refusing to speak to me; every time we met he went red in the face and walked away from me. But the lack of team support did not worry me so much because on a big mountain stage, there should not be that many in the leading group. I was far more worried by my own physical condition. Even though I got the jersey back on the Sappada stage I was not riding that well – I survived on anger and the determination to hang on. What had been taken out of me before the San Marino time trial and led to that bad performance had not been replaced. I was still drained and lacking strength. And there was also the threat of the Italian crowds on the mountains. All the Italian newspapers reported how I attacked Visentini in the Sappada stage; one of them called me a 'traitor'. There was certain to be bad feeling towards me and I knew there might be trouble on the climbs.

Visentini complained about what I did on the Sappada stage and said what he was going to do on the Canazei stage. It was a really hard day, principally because I was not going well. But I was not going to give Visentini any leeway. He had said so many bad things about me and told so many about where precisely he would attack that if I had let him away, it would have been a victory for him. Each time he went, I went straight after him. There was a television camera overhead and it did not look very good as Visentini attacked and I chased. I was not helping myself with the Italian public. Some riders told me I was being foolish, I should have used somebody else, Munoz for example, to go after Visentini. Boifava came up and told me I was mad. If I wanted Visentini closed down immediately I should make sure that it was not Eddy or I who was seen to do the chasing. Maybe I was overreacting but the way I saw it Visentini had no right to attack me and I was not going to let him go anywhere.

I was also trying to bluff people, reacting quickly to Visentini and giving the impression that I was stronger than I was. The reality was that I was having a bad day. On one col I was riding at the back of the leading group and, as lads were dropping off the back, I was riding around them and staying with the front men. Once it split in the middle and with the crowds on the road I could not get around people quickly enough and was left with Eddy trying to close a gap to the leaders. That isolated us and gave people the chance to jump into the road and hinder our progress. They were punching and hitting and shouting as we went by. Towards the top of the col we were getting close to the lead group and, as we did, Visentini peeled off to one side and dropped to the back of the group in front of us. I was surprised because it appeared to me that he was actually waiting for us, at last prepared to give us a helping hand.

As we drew alongside him he veered to one side, forcing Eddy and me to slow down. An accident, I thought. Moments later, he did the same again. I barely got round him but Eddy had to put his hand out to stop himself falling. Visentini was trying to put us over the side of the mountain. I moved alongside him, placed my hand on his handlebars and asked what was wrong. He said it was the least he could do and the next time he would put his fist through Eddy's face. I told him to take it easy, that if either Eddy or I went down, he would be coming with us. That finished that.

After the stage, a journalist asked Eddy and me if it was true that Roberto had tried to put us on the ground. Not wanting to make things any worse I said no, Roberto just found it difficult to steer properly and the incident was not serious. Visentini was standing behind us and the journalist, who represented one of the TV stations, asked him whether my explanation was true. 'No, it's not,' he said. 'I tried to put them on the ground and the next time I'll use my fist instead.' That went out on television and Roberto was fined 3 million lire (£1500). At first he said he would not pay the fine. The authorities said if he did not pay, his licence would be withdrawn and he would be forced out of the race. Boifava said the team would not pay. Normally the money for fines comes out of the team kitty but I said not one penny of my share was to be used to pay the fine. Eventually Roberto paid up himself.

I will never forget the stage to Canazei, for as well as being over a very difficult route it was also the day when the Italian spectators gave me the most trouble. Because it was a Sunday the crowds on the mountains were enormous. They had seen and heard about what happened on the previous day's stage to Sappada but had only got the story from Visentini's point of view. The story I had given to the journalists in the hotel was too late for the next day's newspapers and only appeared in the Monday papers. They saw me as the bad guy.

Eddy and Robert Millar were protecting me on the climbs, riding at either side of me. Without the two lads that day, I do not believe that I would have got through the Giro. As Bob was a member of a rival team, Panasonic, I was particularly grateful to him for giving me a dig out that day. We have been close friends for a long time and I was very happy to have him close to me on that day. The behaviour of the people was bad. As well as the punching and pushing, they were spitting wine at me. There was also some kind of grain that they were spitting at me. At the finish I was really dirty from the stuff they had spat at me. At Canazei I spoke on Italian television, saying that I had not done anything wrong on the Sappada stage and that over a seven-year professional career I had always behaved in a proper way. My appeal to the Italian public did help because things were never as bad again as they were on the Canazei stage. They remained pretty bad all the same and as we were going into Brescia, Visentini's territory, things were not going to improve dramatically.

Brescia was full of Visentini supporters. They came to the hotel each evening with banners and I could not eat in the restaurant with the team because it was deemed unsafe for me. Visentini never tried to defuse the situation. When there were supporters around he would say, 'There is Roche, there.' Or 'There's the bastard, there.' Each day the newspapers were full of his side of the story. He had a way of giving his story in ten different versions. He had names for Patrick, Eddy and myself. I was Judas, Eddy was the Rebel and Patrick was Satan. Different newspapers also called us these names. I had never experienced anything like this in my life and it was getting me down. Eddy was on the other side, trying all the time to keep me up. I could see he was worried about me. Afraid that it would all become too much for me.

Boifava was suffering as well. He did not want confrontation. When he saw it coming he took Visentini's side. But that did not save him. He was nearly hanged. He was treated as a traitor, a man who had betrayed Visentini. He told me afterwards that his wife received threatening phone calls during the Giro. He was scared driving his car through the mountains, and always kept his windows up. People banged their fists on the front windscreen. Once a bike was torn off the roof by people who supported Visentini. They pulled at the bike, hoping to get him out of the car, but he kept driving, dragging the bike behind him. Later on, when clear of the crowds, he got out and refixed the bike to the roof. In the end he was almost putting bars on the windows of his car. He felt bad about this because he did not deserve it. He was on Visentini's side and was still being blamed for what happened to Visentini.

After the Canazei stage my form improved a little and I could feel myself coming out of the trough that I had been in over the San Marino, Sappada and Canazei days. Mentally I was taking a battering and my resistance was being reduced. Vincente Torriani, race director of the Giro, arranged police protection for me on the climbs and at the finishes. Three days from the end we arrived in Como and I was in a very bad way. Lydia joined the race in Como, having been made aware of how low I was feeling. Normally I do not like to see her on races as it is not possible for us to spend time together. But with three days of the Giro to go I needed to see her, and people like Eddy and Patrick would have detected this.

The Como finish was hard because there was a very tight four-kilometre circuit and ten complete laps to be ridden. On the circuit there were tens of thousands of people. Every so often on the circuit there was a group of people shouting, 'Roche, go home', 'Roche the bastard'. The initial group incited others to shout and as we did the laps the shouting increased. By the end it seemed that there was a group every 20 yards shouting these things at me.

Just before the final kilometre there was a crash and I narrowly avoided being brought down. I sprinted to get to the back of the group in front of me and went around the last few corners on the rim. Because of the crash and the hold-up, the police motorcycles could not get into the finish to protect me as they had been doing on other stages. I was edgy going over the line and was not helped by having to stop very suddenly immediately beyond the line. People were pulling me, some saying 'bravo', others shouting at me. Mostly obscenities. Fucker, cunt and that kind of stuff. And there was nobody to take me from my bike. I was shattered. People continued to push and punch me, and I could feel tears coming. I was painfully disappointed and tired by the reaction of the people. I turned around and Lydia was there but I did not want her to see me the way I was. She sees what I am doing from the outside and it looks glamorous. I did not want her to see me then because I was really bad, really down. It would have hurt her. Her coming was a surprise, I was glad to see her, needed to see her, but did not want her to see me as I was that evening.

That night I was calm. There were just two days left. A very hard mountain stage to Pila and the concluding time trial to St Vincent. Although I had defended the jersey for a week, Breukink was still just 33 seconds behind and the race was far from over. I could see that Eddy was worried about me. But Lydia's presence boosted my morale. As she had come I did not want to let her down. I slept well and tried to prepare myself mentally for the last two days. It was also good to see friends of ours from Paris, Bruno and Corinne, and my manager from Ireland, Frank Quinn. Bruno and Corinne came with a big banner. They had driven all the way from Paris in their Peugeot 104. Their coming cheered me and I did not want to let anyone down.

There were three climbs on the Pila stage and I struggled on the first. Eddy was sure I was gone. He tried to arrange help from this team, a combine with another, a deal with Lejarreta, a plea to Millar not to attack and, generally, he spoke with everyone. Some rider attacked and Eddy counterattacked, going alongside the attacker, moving a half wheel in front of him, trying to discourage. He would come back to me and ask how I was feeling. We had a code between us which meant that I would never say I felt bad. If I did feel bad I said I was *well* whereas I said I felt *great* when I was OK. In this way we were able to speak freely and Eddy always knew how I felt. On the final climb to Pila I began to feel genuinely strong and I noticed that Breukink and Giupponi were looking strained. Eddy was making a good tempo at the time.

I rode up to him and told him to 'take a rest'. After going past him I looked behind and there was a gap. I kept going. Millar and Lejarreta accelerated in pursuit and joined me. The rest of what had been a fairly big group were left behind. Millar and Lejarreta did a bit of riding on the flat parts of the mountain but I rode at the front most of the time and all through the final six kilometres. I totally surprised myself, keeping up a very good tempo and opening a big advantage on the group behind us. I could have won the stage in the end but, at the time, I did not believe I was going as well as I was and I did not have the confidence. There was no arrangement with Millar. Anybody who wishes can check back on the video of that stage and see that Millar was riding all out to remain on Lejarreta's wheel and Lejarreta was having to work hard to stick in behind me. With about 500 metres to go I realized that I could win the stage, that I was stronger than the other two, and I went to move onto my big chain ring. As I moved, Millar sprinted and suddenly there was only 200 metres to go and not enough time for me to get him back. But there was no disappointment for me in finishing second to Millar.

That attack on the climb to Pila strengthened my position. From being 33 seconds ahead of Breukink I went to leading Millar, who jumped above Breukink, by 1.27. This meant that I was very relaxed going into the final time trial. I am a better time-triallist than Bob and unless something very unusual happened, I was going to win the Giro. In the time trial I wanted to prove to the Italian public that I was a worthy winner of their race and I could do this by putting up a good performance. Getting time checks at all the different points on the route, I knew that I was on course to winning the stage and ended up 14 seconds faster than the second-placed Thurau. Millar was almost two minutes down but that did not worry him. He remained second overall and also claimed the mountains jersey.

Over the last four days of the race my team got fully behind me and rode better for me than they had ever done in my two years at Carrera. I think they were trying to show me that despite all the problems, they could still be professionals. I think they were also trying to encourage me to leave my share of the prize money in the kitty again. But that was the Italian way. I remember Chiappucci asking me for a pink jersey for his girlfriend a couple of days before the San Marino time trial. I gave it to him. When I was away on the stage to Sappada, he was the first guy to chase me. A couple of days later he wanted another jersey. This time for his girlfriend's mother. He did not even seem embarrassed asking for it.

Even the Italian public came round to the view that I had been a good winner of their race. The last two days showed that I was the best rider in the race. Visentini's crash on the stage to Pila did not affect anything. He was already beaten, and well beaten, before we got to Pila.

Despite the satisfaction of riding so well on the Pila stage and winning the time trial I had no wish to hang around Italy after the race ended. I did some interviews, television and press, and prepared for the homeward journey. Bruno and Corinne had been up all night and were very tired and I offered to drive their Peugeot back to Paris. We rolled down the back seat, they slept in the back, I drove and Lydia was in the passenger seat. Eddy drove my car, bringing Patrick and Frank Quinn. We left St Vincent at around 7.30, just three hours after I had completed the time trial. We arrived at our house in Sagy at 4.30 in the morning. Lydia's brother Thierry was waiting for us with some cake and champagne. That was our celebration of the Giro. We went to bed at 6.30 and at 9.30 Lydia and I went to the local shop to get some croissants for breakfast. After breakfast Eddy and I went out for a spin together. We rode for an hour and a half, having a really good talk on the way. We ate lunch together and then everyone went their separate ways.

That ended the Giro d'Italia 1987. Since then the race and the controversy have been discussed again and again. People ask how I would feel about going back to the Giro and taking on Visentini again. It is not a worry. My mind is clear. The 1987 Giro is over. I won it. Nobody can replay it. Visentini can never win it. Future Giros will be different. I know that if I am on form I have nothing to fear from Visentini. He is a good time-triallist, I am also good against the clock. I believe I am better than he tactically and can always beat him because of this. If he knows I am on form he will crack before the race ends. Mentally, I am stronger than he. Still, another race between us could be a good match. Whatever the road brings, it brings.

PART IV

The Head and the Legs

CHAPTER 16
Le Fidèle Equipier

At the end of the twenty-first stage of the 1987 Tour de France Eddy Schepers wheeled across the finish line at La Plagne in sixtieth place. It was one of those days when Eddy struggled and at the summit of La Plagne he was 26 minutes and 54 seconds behind the stage winner, Laurent Fignon. He climbed the last mountain in the company of Ruttimann and Bauer, did not push things because there was always the next day to consider. At the finish line nobody took much notice of Eddy and he wasted no time in finding his team's hotel. It had been a hard day: two big mountain passes followed by the long, severe climb to La Plagne. Eddy always said he cycled for the money and if he could find any other way to earn the same money, he would hang up his wheels. He thought of his life on the bike and muttered to himself. *Shit.*

Eddy was at one time considered a potential champion. As an amateur in Belgium he was regarded as an exceptionally good performer in stage races. He won the Tour de l'Avenir, a difficult stage race for aspiring champions. He is the only Belgian to have won that race. Eddy's graduation to the professional *peloton* was expected and a successful career was anticipated. But there is a great difference between professional and amateur racing and Eddy suffered in the transition. Soon, he realized that he was never going to be a great champion and he accepted that. For him it was simple: 'There are some riders who will win, and there are others who will not win. It is not difficult to see which is which.'

Cycling's hierarchical structure provides for the good rider who is not a winner. Eddy considered himself a good rider but not good enough to win. He decided to become a team rider. Not a rank-and-file *domestique* but a high-quality *equipier*. In 1978 he rode for Eddy Merckx's team C&A and got an insight into the kind of rider he wished to become. Merckx was then at the end of his illustrious career but Schepers could still see the greatness and knew that his destiny was to serve a leader like Merckx. When Merckx retired Eddy sought out a *patron*. He spent three years riding for the Daf team but there was no leader to whom he could dedicate himself.

Afterwards he drifted off to Italy, hoping that in a Saronni or a Moser he would find fulfilment. He rode for different teams but was never satisfied by the quality of the leaders: 'There are very few real leaders. They may think of themselves as leaders but through the eyes of their *equipiers* they are not leaders.' Towards the end of 1985 Schepers heard that his Italian team Carrera were signing Stephen Roche. He did not know Roche personally but he instinctively felt that he would be riding for this Irishman. Even before meeting Roche he resolved to ride for him.

1986 was the first year that Eddy Schepers put himself at Roche's service. It was not easy because an injured knee destroyed Roche's season. In the big tours he could not climb and was often 20 or 25 minutes behind the leaders. But Eddy saw something in this suffering star and he waited for Roche, paced him up the mountains, encouraged him in the hotel room and always treated him like a *patron*. Eddy never let Roche forget that his results in the past demonstrated that his problems in 1986 were explained totally by his injury. Once the injury went away, the real Roche returned. Once a champion, always a champion. Roche needed that kind of encouragement. Never before had any team mate taken such an interest in Roche and the interest came at a time when it was most useful.

At the end of 1986 Carrera analysed their team and concluded that Schepers was one rider they could do without. Roche was furious and pleaded on Schepers's behalf. The argument raged. Roche stood firm and Schepers was re-employed. Eddy expected that his leader would fight to keep him in the team because he knew he offered Roche a service which very few team leaders enjoy: 'Stephen knows there are few riders like me. Even the best team riders retain some slight personal ambition in the back of their heads. They think of getting away in a break which might lead to a stage victory or a good stage placing. Sometimes I think of that too but I know that my place is at Stephen's side. At all times.'

Early in 1987 Eddy discovered that his hunch about Roche was correct. He was a genuine leader. The moment of truth for Eddy came in the early season Paris–Nice race. Roche had lost the jersey on the stage to Mont Faron and was angry. The next morning he attacked in the first few kilometres, rode 100 kilometres on his own and when recaptured was strong enough to go with the counterattack. Eddy claimed he had not seen an exploit like that for ten years. Not since the time of Merckx.

Eddy and his leader went to the Tour of Italy knowing that they might have to beat their own team as well as everybody else if they were to win the race. Italy was Italy and Eddy understood how things worked there. When Eddy found himself in with a chance of winning the first mountain stage of the race at Terminillo, he thought not of himself but of his leader. His breakaway companion Bagot promised that his team, Fagor, would help Roche later in the race if Eddy allowed Bagot to win the stage. The deal was done. Roche was astonished by Eddy's devotion. He vowed that he would look after his lieutenant. If there was some appearance money at a race, Eddy got a share. If

Stephen was invited to ride a criterium he only accepted on condition that Eddy was also invited. Roche knew the value of his Sancho Panza.

It was in the moments of crisis in Italy that Eddy revealed his true worth. Nights when they lay in their bedroom and discussed strategy. Eddy understood Roche and helped his *patron* to do what both of them believed had to be done. It is unlikely that Roche would have had the audacity to attack on the stage to Sappada if it had not been for Eddy's prompting. On that stage Eddy experienced a personal crisis when the Carrera *directeur sportif*, Boifava, ordered him to abandon Roche and help the team's other leader, Visentini.

A difficult moment for Eddy because a refusal to obey might have led to a dismissal from the team that evening. Eddy did not want to disobey but neither did he want to leave Roche. He looked at Boifava, pleadingly. 'Davide, you can ask me to do anything else, but don't ask me to leave Stephen. That is something I cannot do.' Eddy stayed alongside Roche and helped him to win the Tour of Italy. When the hostility towards Roche reached its highest point in Italy, Eddy became as much a minder as a team mate. He put himself between Stephen and the punches, spits and insults. Eddy is not a big man but he was prepared to defend his leader against every kind of attack.

During the Tour de France Eddy found it impossible to be as helpful as he wished to be. Three and a half weeks of racing in Italy had left him tired and he was not as strong as he had been in the Giro. On the twenty-first stage of the Tour, Eddy experienced one of his worst days. As he cycled from the finish line to his hotel in the village of La Plagne Eddy was unaware of the drama which was enacted immediately before his arrival. He knew nothing of Roche's heroic comeback ride on La Plagne, how he ate into Delgado's one-minute advantage and finished just four seconds behind him. How he went so far beyond his limits to preserve the dream of winning the Tour.

Denis Roux could have told Eddy. He rode at Roche's side on the La Plagne climb and saw how deep his companion dug. When Roche accelerated for the line with about 400 metres left, Roux could not believe what was happening. Roche was shattered, wasted, and yet had the courage to go faster. The next morning Roux reminded Roche of what happened inside that last kilometre, in some way presuming that Roche would not have as vivid a memory. The photographers who waited at the finish line could have explained to Eddy how distressed his *patron* was. They wanted pictures but some of them were forced to switch roles as Roche reached out for support. His face was deathly pale and there was something chilling about an effort which left the cyclist unable to climb from his machine. Eventually they lifted Roche and eased the bike from under him.

The Tour's medical personnel lay him on the roadside and gave him oxygen. Dr Gerard Porte saw the life return to Roche's face and asked how he felt. Roche caught the doctor's eye and said he was OK, *mais pas de femme tout de suite*. At his side all through the crisis was Patrick Valcke, the man whose devotion to Roche matches that of Schepers. Patrick is an excellent mechanic and so much more. And Patrick, too, could have told Eddy about the ordeal at the finish of La Plagne. How worried everybody had been.

But by the time Eddy arrived at the finish the one-act drama was over, the various characters gone in their different directions. Nobody thought to wait around and tell Eddy the story. He checked the room list at the hotel and made his way to the room. Stephen was in the bath. Eddy asked how the day had gone. Stephen told him the full story of his pursuit of Delgado and of his collapse at the finish. Eddy felt ashamed: 'I saw myself as a small man. On the day when Stephen most needed me I was not with him. I promised him that whatever happened I would be alongside him on the following day's stage to Morzine. If he was prepared to go so far in search of victory, I knew that I must do the same.'

Eddy Schepers produced one of the best performances of his career on the twenty-second stage of the Tour de France. It was a severe mountain stage with five big mountains to pass. Schepers rode alongside his team leader all through the stage and helped him to make an important breakaway on the final descent to the finish in Morzine. A breakaway which turned the race Roche's way.

CHAPTER 17

Another Tour

On the continent of Europe it is said that 21 July 1969 was an important day in world history. For two reasons. A man called Neil Armstrong walked on the moon and a man called Eddy Merckx won his first Tour de France.

I have never regarded myself as being consciously ambitious. It is probably a fault. From my first year as a professional cyclist there were always people who believed that I would, one day, win the Tour de France. At no time in my career did I sit down and tell myself I would win the Tour de France. It was never an ambition. I might have said that I could win the Tour, I did have some talents and I was at my best in stage racing. But I did not earmark one race over another and nominate a select few that I had to win. That is not how I saw things.

I did want to improve my position as a professional cyclist. From season to season it was important that I improved and earned more money. In 1980 I had had to choose between staying on in France as a professional racer with Peugeot or returning to my job as a maintenance fitter at Premier Dairies in Dublin. I did my sums and calculated that I could earn at least as much on the bike as in the factory. And because I preferred the bike, I had not the slightest hesitation in deciding to stay in France. After that my aim was to do as well as possible.

I work at being a good and proper professional. During the months of December, January, February, March and April I train and race as conscientiously as I can and from there I will take what comes. If that means going away from home on 15 January and not getting home until 1 April, I will do it. What is important is that I get a good foundation for the season. Two and a half months away is a long time but I will accept the discipline. There are riders who cannot bear two and a half weeks away from their wives. If I can get a correct preparation, I make no other demands on myself. No telling myself that I must win this and this and this. For there are no small wins in professional cycling. Any victory is important. Sometimes the ones that people consider small are the hardest to win. In the big race the strong men watch each other very closely and the race is well controlled. In the smaller race, half the bunch are not interested but every member of the other half is desperate to win. Controlling a race with sixty riders striving to win is an impossibility. This can happen in the smaller races. You can see my ambition, or lack of it, in this way: I look upon my cycling career as a twelve- or thirteen-year segment of my life. During this period I must do as well as I can to make my life better. Doing well means earning money to provide for now and, hopefully, afterwards. There was never a fierce ambition to become a Giro champion or a Tour winner.

Because I do not set goals the way others do, the victories probably do not mean as much to me. Winning the Tour of Romandie for a record third time did not mean all that much. When at the beginning of the season in 1987 I won the Tour of Valencia it should have been a big occasion. It was my comeback victory, my first win for sixteen months. But I felt nothing. Winning the Tour of Valencia was not what I set out to do when I became a professional cyclist. But neither did I dedicate my career to the big tours. I am not sure what I really wanted from the sport. The negative side of how I feel is that when the victories have come, big or small, I have not been able to savour them as others can. For me a race like the Giro, the Tour or the World Championship is a battle like any other. You become absorbed in the attacking and counterattacking and you want to beat the other guys and you give it your best. After the Giro, Tour and Worlds they play the national anthem of the winning rider. It was only when everybody went quiet and the anthem played that it dawned on me that the Giro, Tour and Worlds were different. During the race itself, there are just another group of racers to beat, other mountains to climb and the same efforts to be made. The positive side to my attitude is that success does not in any way reduce my desire to be a better professional. Winning the Giro d'Italia was not an ambition of mine and when it happened there was no great feeling of fulfilment. I was satisfied to have survived in Italy, I knew the experience of winning would help me through my career, but I was also aware that directly after the Giro, there was another tour.

Another challenge. No more and no less important than the one that had just been overcome.

After the Giro I was on the rocks, physically and especially mentally. I needed to stay in France to sort out my contract for 1988. It looked as if I would be leaving Carrera and joining Fagor but nothing was definite and there was still a good bit of negotiating to be completed. But I also felt edgy and emotional. I could not talk to the journalists about the Giro without getting into a knot. I found that it upset me. They wanted to go back over the controversies; I wanted to change the subject. I had not the patience to argue. I was short-tempered. I had to do something. There was a reception for me in Dublin and I decided that I would spend some time in Ireland afterwards. Lydia was going to be there and it would give me a chance to relax again after the Giro.

In Dublin I worked on an old car, an MG, and that was perfect relaxation. Old cars are my favourite hobby and at a time when I needed to get away from the cycling world, the MG was important. Getting away from the cycling world did not mean abandoning the bike. I decided to ride the bike every day between the Giro and the Tour. Every morning in Ireland I did two or three hours, riding through the Wicklow mountains. That was really enjoyable for me because I grew up as a cyclist in those mountains and it was a good time to be going back to them. Besides, they are probably the best training roads anywhere. You can ride for hours and only come across a handful of cars.

A morning ride in the Wicklow mountains, a sleep in the afternoon, a few hours over the engine of the MG and I was on the road to recovery. In Ireland I slept as if I was dead, proving that Italy had taken a lot out of me. Journalists in Ireland were told that I was only spending two days there but I ended up spending eight days and was left alone. The crash I suffered in Italy had left me with a bruised back and it was causing some problems. Because of this I had to get back to France well before the Tour began and I returned to Paris on Monday 22 June, nine days before the Berlin prologue.

Back in France I saw my doctor and received treatment for my back. I went to him twice. It was important that every day between the Giro and the Tour helped me to recuperate. I needed to cycle each day but never for too long. Going into the Tour 100 per cent fit but mentally tired was what I most wanted to avoid and I was prepared to go into the Tour on 80 per cent physical sharpness as long as I was mentally fresh. If I was not mentally tuned into the idea of riding a good Tour de France, the race was certain to be a disaster.

I was apprehensive about my chances in the Tour. In Italy the weather had been greatly in my favour and that was an advantage I could not expect in the Tour. The Giro was hard and I did not know how much it had taken out of me. There were days in the Giro, around the time of the San Marino time trial and the Marmolada mountain stage, when I was going very badly. Days like those in the Tour de France and I was sure to be wiped out. I was also worried by the mountains of the Tour. Four times I had ridden the Tour; on three occasions the Pyrenees came before the Alps and each time I failed to survive the Pyrenees. Now the Pyrenees were again before the Alps and I was afraid that they would again kill my chances.

The Tour was a race without an outstanding favourite. Hinault's retirement and LeMond's injury meant that journalists were searching for a new favourite. My victory in the Giro gave them an excuse to pinpoint me and for the final week at home in Paris before the Tour began, I kept the phone off the hook. I wanted the quietest possible build-up and I did not want to be talking about myself as the Tour favourite. When asked by journalists immediately before the race I expressed what were genuinely felt doubts. I knew that I could win the Tour but I was not allowing myself to believe that I would. Tactically, I was going to have to be much cleverer than I was in Italy. My strength needed to be used far more sparingly than in Italy. The best Tour I could ride was one in which I did not get the yellow jersey until the Dijon time trial on the penultimate day.

Before the Tour it was generally believed that the Carrera team was one of the strongest, if not the strongest around. That was not a view I shared. The team does some things very well. It operates well in team time trials, it can organize a very effective pursuit in the final 40 kilometres of a stage, and there is no better team at pulling the *peloton* up to a breakaway group at the end of a race. But you cannot ride this kind of race in the Tour, it takes too much out of you. A team must be more intelligent in its use of resources, getting riders into breaks, ensuring that other teams do the chasing and never forgetting that the race lasts for three and a half weeks. But the average Italian team rider prefers to allow things to happen and puts everything into the organized pursuit at the end. Carrera could do this reasonably well in the Giro but it was not possible in a race as severe as the Tour. I tried to tell them that if they were prepared to get out of the saddle and go with the breaks, they would save themselves enormous work at the end of the stage. But they preferred it if they did not have to think about going with breaks. I remember riding at the front with my team mate Claudio Chiappucci, seeing that a break was about to go and shouting at Chiappucci to get after it. 'What?' he asked. By then, it was too late. It worried me that the Carrera team would ride the Tour as they rode other races and I knew that if they did they would be wiped out before the race got to the Pyrenees. Having no belief in my team meant that I went into the Tour believing the yellow jersey would be a burden on my back. I was going to have to be careful about when and where I undertook to carry this burden.

As I did not ride any races between the Giro and the Tour there was no way of knowing whether I had recovered from the physical and psychological demands of Italy. I was touched by the belief my friend Bruno showed in my ability to win both the Giro and the Tour before I turned a pedal in either race. Bruno had gone to San Remo on holiday to see the start of the Giro. Down in San Remo he passed me a piece of paper, saying, 'Steve, this is what you must do.' On that piece of paper he had drawn a map of Italy with Roche in pink and a map of France with Roche in yellow. He promised to return at the end of the Giro with a big banner showing both maps. Down in Italy at the end of the Giro, the Italians did not think too much of Bruno's banner and they exchanged the usual insults. The day before I left home to meet up with the team for the Tour, Bruno called round. He had the banner. 'Steve you have one half,' he said, 'you must get the other half.' His belief was blind but it helped.

So, too, did Eddy Schepers. He sat me down before the Tour began. He started by saying that I could win the Tour de France and listed the reasons why he believed in my chances. Eddy put things down on paper. What I did in the Giro: performances in the time trials, on the climbs. Proof that I could ride a very good Tour. When people who know you have such belief in you, it starts to mean something. There was hope.

CHAPTER 18
Calculations

The founder of the Tour de France was a journalist called Henri Desgrange. He wrote a book called *La tête et les jambes (The Head and the Legs)*. The book was published in 1894. Ninety-three years later Roche rode a Tour which would have earned the founder's eminent approval.

In some ways France was always going to be less difficult for me. Even though the French public wants a French winner they respect the effort of the other man. They look for the best man to win and will only say afterwards that it was a pity he was not French. They encourage anybody who makes the effort. Besides, I have always felt comfortable in France. I speak their language and get on very well with the people. French TV has been sympathetic to what I am attempting and I have enjoyed very good relations with French journalists. As soon as I left my home and arrived in West Berlin for the prologue I sensed that it was not going to be difficult in the way that the Giro had been. I was very relaxed, more relaxed than I imagined I could be. And I knew why. Whatever happened on the Tour, it was never going to be as bad as Italy. That feeling encouraged me, cheered my spirits. People asked whether I felt the pressure of being a Tour favourite. What pressure? After the Giro, nothing that could happen in France was going to upset me.

Prologues are interesting tests because they give you a feeling about your form. Before the six-kilometre prologue in West Berlin I wondered whether I would pay for the lack of racing in my immediate build-up. After all, I had not raced since the Giro ended and that was eighteen days out of competition. The prologue provided a very encouraging start as I finished third, seven seconds behind the specialist Nijdam, but faster than all the contenders for overall victory.

A day later there was the second test, the team time trial. Again I was very pleased with how I rode, being the strongest in the Carrera team, and we won the stage. The prologue had given me some confidence but I was still not prepared for how well I was going in the time trial. It really surprised me. Before it I was worried because guys like Bontempi are really strong in the team time trial and if you are not going well, you will suffer. But I was strong and tended to do 200-metre turns at the front whereas the other strong men were happy to do 100-metres. Maechler, Eddy and Bontempi were the other strong men in the team.

After the team test I was third overall, behind the raceleader Piasecki and Bontempi. For me that was too close to the jersey. I wanted to disappear from the race during the first week, returning to the front-line action on the tenth stage in the Futuroscope time trial. That was always destined to be the first major battleground in the race and I wanted to get there in the best possible condition.

I was encouraged not only by the prologue and team time-trial performances but also by a chance meeting with Jacques Anquetil in Berlin. We spoke about my victory in the Giro and how it would affect my performance in the Tour de France. Anquetil maintained that winning the Giro could be a very good thing for a rider setting out on the Tour de France. He recalled his own experiences of winning the Giro and reckoned that the rider has to go to his limits and beyond to win such a tour and then finds himself able to go even further in the Tour de France. Jacques told me that because I hurt myself in Italy I would be able to hurt myself even more in the Tour. Italy, he claimed, would have given me a foundation and I would be able to build on that.

All through the Tour I remembered what Jacques had said and found it to be true. When I was hurting in the mountains I convinced myself that I could suffer even more. Italy had given me that foundation. Four months after the Tour ended Jacques died. His passing was a source of great sadness. He was a very nice man.

If things began well for me in the Tour, they were not long changing. The early stages were marked by a fierce, humid heat and I was very uncomfortable. I have never liked racing when it is very hot and it was both hot and heavy in West Berlin and through the stages in West Germany and on into eastern France. If it was as hot in the mountains there was not the slightest chance that I would survive. My legs always felt tired and I was at my maximum to hold on. More than ever I became convinced that if I could get to Futuroscope without losing time to the big men in the race I would be doing extremely well. I thought if I could play my cards correctly and be tactically shrewd there was a chance that I would begin to feel better.

The third stage from Karlsruhe to Stuttgart was the hardest of all. A hilly route, intense heat and humidity, attacks all day, and when a breakaway group of over twenty went clear in the last 50 kilometres nobody wanted to chase. Mostly because nobody had the strength. Maechler was in the group and likely to win the yellow jersey for Carrera, so there was no reason why our team should pursue. However, the breakaway worked against my chances on two counts. It was not in my interests that Maechler should get the jersey, and Charly Mottet, a genuine contender for the Tour, was in the group and so granted a present of five minutes.

Maechler is an exemplary team rider and everybody in the Carrera set-up was very pleased that he became the new wearer of the *maillot jaune*. But I could see that the jersey would bring problems. Should we defend or not? Maechler was not a potential Tour winner and valuable strength could be lost in defending for a rider who could only have the jersey for a certain amount of time. My belief was that Maechler was deserving of team support because of all the service he had given to others over the previous two seasons. But I thought we should defend him intelligently. Try to keep him in the jersey but not by using tactics which meant Carrera controlling the race for every other team. If other teams believed that we were ready to ride after every break, they were going to exploit that situation to their own advantage. It was of little use to the team if everybody rode to the point of exhaustion defending Maechler and had nothing left for the remainder of the race.

But the defence of Maechler turned out to be an extension of the conflict which had taken place in the Giro. I tried to get the team to ride sensibly in defence of Maechler but found that I did not count. Everything was done according to what Boifava and Maechler said. At night Boifava would say that I was to make all the decisions on the road but when I did, they were ignored. On the sixth stage to Epinal they rode at the front for the final 80 kilometres. That is not the way I would have done things. You bluff a little, form alliances with other teams and do all you can to avoid putting eight of your team at the front and asking them to do it all. The result of that kind of manoeuvre is that you blow your own team apart. I knew from the efforts they were putting into defending Maechler that they were going to be of little assistance to me later in the race. At their best the Carrera riders find it difficult in the mountains and, after what they did for Maechler, they did not have a chance.

On one stage I recall Bontempi coming to me and asking what we should do: a break had gone clear and he wanted to know whether the team should chase. I thought we should sit and wait. He came back a few minutes later saying that the team had decided to ride. As the one making the decisions, I told him that the team was not to ride. But they just rode anyway. On the big stage to Sappada in the Giro d'Italia I had defied the lads. Now they had the opportunity to defy me and they availed themselves of it. Using a more intelligent approach and far less energy we could have kept Maechler in the jersey for the same length of time, but the Carrera riders would rather ride with their legs than their heads.

The problems on the road were not the only ones, because there was a flaming row between Boifava and me. A row which concluded with my threatening to leave the race and return to my *maison*.

It began on the morning of the sixth stage to Epinal, when Boifava ordered my mechanic, Patrick, out of his car, telling him that he would have to travel with the assistant *directeur sportif*, Sandro Quintarelli. But the roots of the problem concerned my team plans for 1988.

At the beginning of the Giro Boifava and I had spoken about 1988 and he wanted to keep me at Carrera. I outlined the conditions under which I would re-sign and Boifava agreed to speak with the Carrera bosses. On the night of the famous Sappada stage the Carrera people, Tacchella and Belleri, arrived, but the controversy of the day dominated everything that evening and nothing was decided about my contract. After Sappada I wondered whether it would be possible for the Roche–Carrera marriage to continue into 1988. Journalists asked me and my reply at the time was that 'one row between a husband and wife should not necessarily mean a divorce but if the husband comes home and finds his wife in bed with the next-door neighbour, he is going to think that things can never be the same again'. In a sense I did feel betrayed by Carrera. But I was still negotiating with them and, under different conditions, I believed it was possible for me to continue with them.

Between the Giro and the Tour, Boifava and I spoke on the phone and he said he would come to Berlin with an answer from the Carrera boss. He did not show in Berlin and only turned up five or six days after the Tour began.

While Carrera took their time to decide whether they could agree to my conditions, I was negotiating with Fagor. It is essential that a rider in my position does not get caught in a situation where he feels he has to sign for the team he is negotiating with because it is the only option open to him. In fact my talks with Fagor were pretty advanced and as Carrera refused to commit themselves, it looked almost certain that I would be going to Fagor. Under the deal we provisionally worked out with Fagor, Patrick was to become the *directeur sportif*. Consequently he was speaking to different riders during the Tour, sounding out the possibilities of certain people joining Fagor. As Maechler is such an honest and willing team rider, he was one that I wanted. Patrick spoke to him, saying that Fagor would be interested in talking to him about 1988 if Maechler had not already signed. Maechler had not signed. Nothing further happened until Boifava arrived on the Tour. Maechler, a very straight guy, went to Boifava and said he had to know what was happening in 1988 because Patrick had spoken to him about the possibility of joining Fagor. Boifava became extremely angry. He saw Patrick playing two roles: one as mechanic for Carrera and the other as *directeur sportif* for Fagor. And at a time when he was being paid solely by Carrera. So the next morning Patrick was told to take his tools out of Boifava's car and travel with Quintarelli.

That evening Boifava and Patrick spoke for hours. There was talk that Patrick was to be sent home. I decided to talk to Boifava. When I went to his room Quintarelli was already there. I asked what the story was. Boifava told me about Patrick speaking with Maechler and that Claudio Albasini, Zimmermann's *soigneur*, had overheard Patrick telling the Peugeot mechanic that he had already signed up Maechler. Boifava believed that Carrera was the laughing stock of the *peloton* as people heard that a Carrera mechanic was going around signing Carrera riders for another team. I told Boifava he was foolish to believe everything he heard from Albasini. They said that Patrick should not be even talking to Maechler about the following year. But Patrick had not approached Maechler with a huge amount of money and asked him to sign. He told Maechler to speak with Davide first and if, after that, he was still free they would talk about 1988. I tried to explain that if Patrick wanted to poach Maechler away from Carrera as they were suggesting, he would have mentioned money straightaway.

The argument went on and on and the further it went the more out of hand it became. Boifava told me it did not matter what I said because Patrick 'was being sent home anyway'. That was a shock to me and I replied that if Patrick was going home, then I was going home as well. A week of the Tour de France was not yet over and I was threatening to walk out. But, for me, it was not on to send Patrick home. He has been with me since 1981 at Peugeot and we have stayed together ever since. I know what he has done for me over the years and I could never allow him to be sent home from a Tour de France. Patrick never had much of a family life, he was left on his own when he was fifteen or sixteen, but he has been more devoted to me than any person I have ever worked with. If Patrick was being sent home, I was going as well. I meant it.

Over the years Patrick has always put me first. I remember being at the Nice–Alassio in 1982. Things were not going well for me and as we were driving away from the race an Italian policeman held us up. Words passed between the policeman and Patrick; the policeman was being very difficult and Patrick jumped out of the car and went for him. He ended up spending a few hours in an Italian jail and it was a real problem getting him out. We had to hand over a bit of money and Patrick was not allowed to return to Italy for two years. Patrick's anger with the policeman that evening stemmed from his disappointment that things were not going better for me.

On another occasion there was a row between myself and Bernard Thevenet. That was my first year at La Redoute. It was the 1984 Tour de l'Oise. I had been assured that a new bike which had been made for me in Italy would be ready for the Tour de l'Oise. When I got to the race, the bike was not ready. I told Thevenet that I was not riding. It was a Thursday evening. Patrick drove off to the factory which was supposed to have made up the bike. From the bare frame he built up an entire bike, returning to the race with it the next morning. He worked right through the night, not getting a minute's sleep. That was Patrick's style. I told Boifava that it simply was not on to send Patrick home.

Boifava accepted that Patrick need not be sent home but that he would be moved to the second team car, travelling with Quintarelli. Boifava could put Patrick in the second car but, in that case, the second car would be following me. My feelings were very clear: 'Davide, you can put Patrick where you like but he follows me. In the mountains, in the time trials. Whatever happens he follows me. If Patrick is not following me, I go home.'

Boifava asked me not to do this to him; he said that he loved me, that Quintarelli would back him up when he said I was the best and the most professional rider around. He was convinced that I was wrong: 'Stephen, you are letting certain things get out of perspective. You are letting things ruin your career. Patrick is a nice fellow but he should not be doing this job. He will never be a good *directeur sportif*. You are listening to too many people and being manipulated and I do not like seeing this happen to you.' But, faced by my threat, he backed off, muttering that 'things could not go on like this'. Shaking hands, we said good night.

Patrick travelled with Quintarelli and they were behind me all the time. Things had got completely out of control between Patrick and Boifava.

Even though Fagor were putting enormous pressure on me to sign I wanted to give Carrera the opportunity of re-signing me. They wanted me but they did not want me. At first they were desperate for me to re-sign. Boifava was offering Patrick his job, that of *directeur sportif*, if Patrick could persuade me to stay at Carrera. Boifava said he would move to the position of general manager. But the conditions I sought were not attractive to Carrera. I wanted certain non-Italian riders brought into the team. People like Millar and Sean Yates and a few French riders as well. Carrera wanted to keep the team predominantly Italian. One possible solution was that we create a French Carrera team with a French co-sponsor and an Italian Carrera with an Italian co-sponsor. Each team would have its own programme and for the big tours we would select a team from all the available riders. But they did not go for this. I believe that, ultimately, they saw Patrick and Eddy as their biggest problems. If they accepted Patrick and Eddy they were, in a sense, accepting all the bad things that had taken place. I think they saw it as a question of dignity. When the negotiations got to an important stage they spoke of having one mechanic too many. They wanted to drop Patrick. They also claimed that Eddy was getting too old, that he would not be able to climb the mountains any more. But Eddy was an exemplary professional and utterly loyal to me. In the end I think it came down to control of Stephen Roche. Without Patrick and Eddy around, they felt they could control me. I asked that they take on Millar but they argued against that, saying that Peter Post, *directeur sportif* at Panasonic, considered Millar a bad boy. That was nonsense and they knew it. They just did not want Stephen Roche with all his own people around him.

At the same time Carrera were saying that if Visentini did not shake himself up they were not taking him on in 1988. They gave him an ultimatum. At the end of it all I could not make out what the Italians had in their heads. They are a big team in a small region. They want to have a foreigner and they want the foreigner to win races but not all races, not the races in Italy. Those must be left to the Italians.

All this goes to prove that a rider does not go through the Tour de France thinking only of the next day's stage. There are always old contracts to be renewed and new ones to be drawn up. Everybody is on the Tour and it is an ideal place to get things sorted out for the following year.

The Carrera team continued to throw itself headlong into the defence of Maechler all the way to the first major test, the 87-kilometre time trial at Futuroscope. They succeeded in keeping Maechler in yellow but burned themselves out in the process. Maechler was also exhausted and that was a particular disappointment because he can ride the mountains reasonably well and, if he had been fresh, he could have been useful later in the race.

After the intense heat and humidity of the first few days, things got better. The weather became more bearable and the racing saner. From feeling that I would not survive a week, I grew more comfortable and was beginning to feel normal as the race got to Futuroscope. Still, there was no way I saw myself winning the Tour. That feeling changed after the time trial.

In previous Tours I failed to measure my effort properly in the long time trials. I started far too quickly and had nothing left for the last part. This happened even when I tried to ensure that my effort was more evenly distributed. As this time trial was especially long (the longest since the 1951 Tour), I had to be very careful. This time I was going to ride steadily all through and hopefully remain strong right to the very end.

In my own mind I set off at a very sensible pace but at all the time checks I was well ahead of the best time and coming towards the end I was beginning to lose some power. I could feel it on the hills, and in the final uphill ride to the finish, I was very tired. But my time was still the fastest of all. I won the stage by 42 seconds, my first victory in an individual time trial in the Tour.

For the first time in the race I thought that final victory was possible. Not only was the time trial proof that I was in good shape but it showed that others were not. Kelly, Fignon, Hampsten and Herrera all rode below their best form and lost out badly. Fignon finished four minutes 15 seconds down, Kelly five minutes 1 second, Hampsten six minutes 20 seconds and Herrera nine minutes 1 second. It was going to be very difficult for any one of them to win the Tour. Before the race began I had reckoned Kelly and Fignon to be two big rivals.

Because of the breakaway group getting five minutes on the pack in the third stage to Stuttgart, Mottet became the new leader of the race after Futuroscope and the next four places on classification were filled by riders who had been in the break to Stuttgart. I was sixth. Mottet was the only rider in front of me who had any chance of surviving the mountains and while he was now a big danger man it was good for me that he was in the yellow because his team, Système-U, would now have to control the race. Whatever else, I had to avoid taking the yellow jersey too soon because I was not going to have a team in the mountains. Eddy would be with me, beyond that I expected nothing.

The time-trial performance did not prove that I could pass through the Pyrenees without faltering. A year before I had ridden a good time trial in Nantes but lost over 50 minutes in the two Pyrenean stages. That time was lost because of my injured knee and the fact that my body never recovered from the efforts of the time trial. After Futuroscope there was a long stage to Chaumiel and, for me, an important day. I needed to find out what Futuroscope had taken out of me. Normally I do not recover that quickly from a time trial and when, on the road to Chaumiel, I felt as if I had not ridden a time trial the day before, my hopes of producing a really good Tour de France performance began to rise. There was no heaviness in my legs. It was confirmation of what Jacques Anquetil said in Berlin about the Giro giving the rider a foundation upon which he can build.

After Chaumiel we went to Bordeaux and that was the day Kelly crashed and had to abandon the race. It was a sad moment. Very sad for him because no rider likes to leave the Tour before it is completed and Kelly was leaving his Kas team without a leader. When I heard he had crashed I went back to try to cheer him up, not thinking that the crash would force him to pull out. I remember joking about the Tour being a three-week holiday; free hotels, good food, great scenery and a different town every night. Criquielion and Fignon both spoke with Kelly. The other Irish riders in the *peloton*, Paul Kimmage and Martin Earley, were back there as well. Three or four team mates of Kelly's were pushing him and we imagined that he would come round and be OK. Slowly it dawned on us that there was something seriously wrong with his shoulder and he would not be continuing. At moments like this you realize that professional cycling is not only about one dog eating another. We might have felt inclined to say that Kelly's departure meant one less rival but, deep down, we were sad. A rival he might be but a friend also and it was sad to see a friend having to leave the Tour.

Of all the mountain ranges that are traversed in European cycle races, the Pyrenees cause me most problems. The irregular gradients and the uneven surfaces make it difficult for me to maintain rhythm and that is the only way I can climb. Getting in and out of the saddle, as the pure climbers can, is not for me. On the morning of the first Pyrenean stage from Bayonne to Pau I was apprehensive. I was not sure I could survive, and survival was my only aim. I did not expect to gain on any of my big rivals and I knew that if I arrived into Pau with my Tour chances intact I was going to be satisfied.

The stage was good for me and not so good. I was not riding strongly and did not have any worries about maintaining my place in the front-line group, alongside people like Delgado, Millar, Hampsten, Fignon, Mottet and Lejarreta. But four riders, Breukink, Bernard, Herrera and Wilches, got clear and finished almost four minutes in front of our group. Of the four, Jean François Bernard was well up on general classification and it was a mistake to let him take such an advantage. Bernard attacked on the third climb, the Soudet, and I should have gone with him. He was dropped on the early part of the climb and I imagined that he would not get too far. Bernard did stop after about 100 yards and remained with that lead for some time but then he was gone. There were others in front of him, Herrera among them, but I reckoned that if he caught Herrera, the Colombian was not going to be much use to him on the flat.

In the back of my mind was the final climb of the day, the Col de Marie Blanque. A year before in the Tour I crossed the summit of Marie Blanque 21 minutes behind the leaders. I was not riding so well that I could be adventurous in the Pyrenees, and when Bernard went my natural response was to believe that he would come back or that, if he stayed clear, Système-U would organize a very good pursuit and his gains would be minimal. As things turned out, Bernard linked up with Herrera and they worked very well together, Herrera riding on the climbs and Bernard doing the work on the descents and on the flat. Eventually Système-U did get a pursuit organized and Fignon, especially, rode very strongly all the way to the finish in Pau. I believe that if Bernard had been seriously considered before the stage began, he would not have escaped as easily as he did. At the end of the stage Mottet still led the race but Bernard had jumped to second place, one minute 52 seconds behind and I was third at three minutes 23 seconds. Mottet, I felt, was going to lose some time on the big climbs and particularly at the summit finishes. Bernard was now a dark horse, and a dangerous one.

But the first day in the Pyrenees left me feeling reasonably happy. I rode up the Marie Blanque without any real difficulty and proved to myself that everything had changed since a year before. At the top of that climb I saw people like Millar and Hampsten getting the chop and that was a further boost to my confidence. I had worried about that first day in the Pyrenees since the Tour began, and getting through it was an achievement in itself. I rode sensibly throughout, not taking any risks and conserving my strength as much as possible.

The second day in the Pyrenees was even more difficult than the first with a summit finish at Luz Ardiden. The climb to Luz Ardiden is steep and irregular, the kind I most hate. Before reaching Luz Ardiden we crossed the Marie Blanque again and then the Aubisque. I climbed with Herrera, Delgado, Hampsten, Millar and Mottet. There were attacks all day, pursuits and periods when the group I was a part of refused to ride. At the summit of the Aubisque we were three minutes clear of Bernard and we should have distanced him; instead nobody wanted to ride and he got back on. Later in the Tour people would claim that Bernard was a little unlucky because he punctured and had mechanical trouble on the stage to Villard des Lens, but if he had been seen as a big contender on that second Pyrenean stage, he would never have rejoined us and would have lost far more than he did.

On the final climb to Luz Ardiden I found myself stretched to stay with Delgado, Herrera, Millar and Hampsten. Four kilometres from the top Herrera attacked and nobody even attempted to follow. The last two kilometres were desperately severe and I went beyond my limits to hang on. But it was another good day for me finishing with Delgado and Millar. I finished one minute 15 seconds up on Bernard, one minute 57 seconds up on Mottet and three minutes 26 seconds on Fignon. I stayed third overall but the time differences were now getting very fine: Mottet in yellow, Bernard at one minute 13 seconds and at one minute 26 seconds myself.

On Luz Ardiden Delgado got away but we caught him; he kept attacking, as did Hampsten. I tried to ride at my own pace, hanging in and hanging in. I was never able to go to the front (as I had been in the Giro) and set the tempo for everyone else. But the mountain stages in the Tour are more demanding than the mountain stages in the Giro and I was satisfied to be able to survive.

As the race moved on my objective became very clear. I wanted to preserve my chance of winning each day. To go as far as I could without losing it. Every time the crunch came I told myself that 'this could be the day the Tour is lost'. So I focused on the person who was getting away from me, or the group that was getting away, and I fought back. I was never riding to win the Tour. I was riding to protect my chance or riding to save myself from defeat.

Coming out of the Pyrenees, I was happy. My chance of winning was still alive and although I went dangerously over my limits at the end of the Luz Ardiden climb I looked forward to a couple of stages when I would be able to recuperate. The next day's stage to Blagnac should have been one of those stages but it wasn't.

Fifty kilometres from the finish in Blagnac a group of thirty, including Mottet, Fignon, Herrera, Delgado and Hampsten, got away. There was an all-out pursuit by Carrera, Panasonic and Toshiba to recapture them. Despite the fact that we rode very strongly all the way to Blagnac, the Fignon–Mottet group gained 67 seconds. It was a mistake to allow such a break to escape but I was fortunate that both Bernard and Millar missed it as well, for that meant Carrera were helped by Panasonic and Toshiba. I can still see the break happening. A torrential storm had just begun, there was a lot of crosswind and I was in the second echelon. There was no problem as the speed was not that high. Just in front of me Van der Poel pulled off to his left, then a Colombian and after him a Toshiba, and suddenly there was a gap between the first and second echelons. I presumed it would close but soon realized that the group in front were trying to ride away from us. I tried to get across myself but, in the conditions, that was not possible. I was relieved to find that both Bernard and Millar had missed the train as well.

I was disappointed to be outmanoeuvred by Fignon and Mottet. Both had lost time in the previous day's stage to Luz Ardiden and they used their heads to strike back at a moment when nobody expected.

But in the overall battle for the Tour the 67 seconds lost at Blagnac was not a worry, there were even advantages for me in the loss. Before the stage I was just one minute 26 seconds behind Mottet and that was dangerously close to the yellow jersey. Carrera was not in any state to defend the raceleader and it would have been a disaster for me to take the overall lead with eleven days of the Tour still remaining. Being a further 67 seconds behind Mottet put a little space between the yellow jersey and me and that was just fine. The key to my lack of concern was that I did not regard Mottet as a likely Tour winner. Each time there was an acceleration on the climbs, he was left behind and I did not see him getting through the Alps without losing time. As for my own team, they were realizing the fears I had felt when they were defending Maechler so vigorously. Eddy remained strong and was consistently helpful to me. After Eddy there was nobody. Bontempi either would not or could not ride after the big breakaway on the road to Blagnac. Maechler was shattered after his experience of defending yellow. Pederson, as is his way, spent most of his time at the back of the *peloton* and I rarely saw him. Perini and Ghirotto are strong team riders but when the going got tough in the Tour, they were not so courageous. Casani always seemed to have a fever or sore throat. Zimmermann just rode his own race.

The longer Mottet stayed in yellow, the better for me. With just two stages before the important Mont Ventoux time trial he was two minutes 33 seconds in front of me. I hoped he would hold the jersey to Ventoux and even beyond. That way Système-U would have to defend the jersey and that was what I needed. When you are there and another team is defending the jersey you can watch everything that is happening and you do not have to be too careful about who is going away. Every race has to have a pattern and the best pattern for me was one where I did not get the jersey until the Dijon time trial. At the end of the Blagnac stage I could look at the classification sheet, notice that day's 67-second loss and know that the loss actually helped my plans.

The next day's stage to Millau finished with a fairly steep seven-kilometre climb to the finish. I rode well but upset my calculations. I did not want to get time back on Mottet but was left with no choice. The climb to Millau was hard and the pace was up from the start. Mottet, Bernard, Delgado, Hampsten and Alcala were all riding at the front and I had to be there.

Halfway up the climb Hampsten attacked; Delgado counterattacked. They had a gap on Bernard, Alcala and me. Mottet was in trouble. I could not let Delgado away and accelerated to join him. Bernard followed me and he rode very aggressively in the final two kilometres, as if he wanted to show his anger at what had happened on the stage to Blagnac a day earlier. What Fignon and Mottet gained there, they were losing here, and while it was imperative for me to stay with Bernard and Delgado, it did not suit me to distance Mottet.

At the end of the stage I remained third overall but my deficit on Mottet was down to one minute 26 seconds again. Too close for comfort. There was now a good chance that I would take the yellow jersey on the Ventoux time trial, which came at the start of the final week. Taking the jersey at that point was not going to improve my chances of winning the Tour.

Before the Ventoux time trial there was a long, flat stage to Avignon and then the Tour's rest day. The stage to Avignon ended in a bunch sprint and I did everything I could to help Bontempi win. He had refused to ride with us after the break into Blagnac but on the following day to Millau he helped me, sheltering me from the wind at a time when Système-U were keeping the pace up. In the early part of the Avignon stage there were crosswinds and Bontempi brought me from the second echelon up to the front. I have always believed that if somebody does something good for you it does not matter what wrongs they have done in the past, your attitude should change towards him. So coming towards the end of the Avignon stage I asked Bontempi how he was feeling. 'OK,' he replied. From there I rode very hard at the front, keeping the pace so high through the last kilometre that nobody could attack. Bontempi got himself ready for the final sprint, so too did the Dutch sprinter Van Poppel. It was probably the best sprint of the race. Bontempi and Van Poppel were side by side for the final 150 metres. Van Poppel made it by a fraction. My work for Bontempi did not get him the stage win but it was a good try. The Avignon finish was a nice little distraction from the bigger issues that lay in the immediate future.

Our rest day was spent in the Novotel at Avignon. It would not have mattered where we stayed because the only thing on anybody's mind was the Ventoux time trial and the final week of the Tour. I was not sure how things were going to go in the Alps. All I knew for sure was that after two and a half weeks my chances of winning the Tour were still alive. From the beginning I had calculated on the basis of preserving my chance. So far, I had succeeded.

CHAPTER 19
To Hell and Back

'Roche arrived at the finish line in La Plagne and collapsed, suffering from a total lack of oxygen. He was given oxygen for what seemed a long time. It was a day when he showed he had the heart and character of a true champion: one who succeeds in going beyond himself and so reaches the zenith of sporting performance.'
Jacques Goddet, Tour de France director for fifty years

Sunday afternoon at the summit of Mont Ventoux, the eighteenth stage of the 1987 Tour de France, had just ended. There was a week of the race remaining. A difficult week: four days through the Alps, a time trial and two flat stages. Nobody had the right to say that the Tour was over, but everybody thought it. Jean François Bernard won the mountain time trial to the summit of the Ventoux and left us feeling that maybe he had taken a winning lead. In the eyes of many, he was the natural successor to Bernard Hinault, and his victory on Mont Ventoux reminded people of the *blaireau* at his best. Bernard was now two minutes 34 seconds ahead of me as the time trial had taken us both over Charly Mottet, who finished almost four minutes behind. But it was no compensation to me to be second overall. Suddenly all my calculations did not count for much. Bernard was a dangerous rival and his advantage was a major worry.

It was not that I had calculated badly or failed to perform on the Ventoux, it was more that Bernard was far better than anyone expected. I thought he would win on the Ventoux but never imagined that he would destroy everybody else. I was satisfied with my own performance. Fifth in a mountain time trial on the Tour is about what I expect. Losing 40 seconds to Herrera and 28 to Delgado did not disappoint me. And I knew that the Ventoux ride had not left me as exhausted as other time trials. I still had something left and was not simply going to disappear during the final week. But I was disappointed that I failed to get my bike equipment right for the Ventoux time trial. The equipment I use in a time trial is very important and for the Ventoux I got it all wrong. It is I who decide precisely what equipment to use in the time trials but I could not make up my mind what to do for the Ventoux.

The particular difficulty in deciding for the Ventoux was that the first 18 kilometres were flat and then there were 18 kilometres of climbing. I was worried about the Ventoux and wanted to get things right. I rode the flat part of the course during the rest day and made my choice of gears and bike after that. I did not know that Bernard was using two bikes. If I had it would not have made any difference because I did not believe it would be an advantage. It was only when I was riding the time trial that I realized how valuable it could have been. For the flat part of the course I selected 13, 15 and 17 sprockets but, because there was a slight headwind, I needed a 16. I felt I was pushing too much when I used the 15 and was pedalling too much when I tried the 17. If I pushed I lost the strength that I was going to need on the climb; if I pedalled I lost time. For the first part of the Ventoux I needed a 20 and 21 and as I had those there were no problems. Towards the top I needed an 18, did not have it and ended up using a 17 but was not really able to turn it.

What I should have done was to change bikes as Bernard did. Use a low-profile bike with a disc wheel and a 13–20 block. Change then to an ordinary bike for the Ventoux and every gear that I might have wanted for the climb. During the Tour, the Ventoux time trial was a worry to me because I knew that if I blew up towards the end, as I sometimes do in time trials, I stood to lose many minutes and my chance of winning the race. As a result I did not think enough about material and it was only as I rode the time trial that I realized the mistake I was making. At the end of the test I knew I was going to have a bloody hard job to get Bernard out of the yellow jersey. It was not impossible. He was not Hinault. During the two stages in the Pyrenees I noticed that he was not good on the early cols but grew stronger as the stage progressed. He was always strong on the final climb. Everything depended on whether others would ride if Bernard was in trouble on the first climb of any Alpine stage. I was also aware that if he managed to stay in yellow for a couple of days his confidence would grow and he would be even more difficult to dislodge. Knowing

Bernard well, it was clear that he had taken an enormous amount out of himself on the Ventoux and the time trial must have hurt him. He was going to be most vulnerable in the days immediately after Ventoux.

If you looked at the Tour route you would have studied the four days in the Alps and decided that the first Alpine stage to Villard des Lans was not severe enough to change things. You might also have thought that after the Ventoux time trial, the top riders would want a fairly easy day. Most people were thinking that way and so I became convinced that I had to see things differently. Bernard had to be attacked when he least expected it. It was like the Giro all over again, trying to plan an attack on a day when it would not be anticipated. Before the Tour began I reckoned that the Alpe d'Huez, La Plagne and Morzine stages were going to be critical, but the events of the race forced a new assessment. The Villard des Lans stage was going to be decisive. Bernard could not be permitted one easy day in yellow. That was sure.

There was also the probability that the Système-U team were planning something. They could not have been happy with the way things went on the Ventoux, for Mottet was the big loser. And as the up-and-coming rider in a rival French team, Bernard was their number-one rival. Better for them if anybody other than Jean François Bernard won the Tour. The thing about Système-U is that they had the talent to do something about the situation.

The stage began in the town of Valréas and from early morning I felt that plans were drawn up to attack Bernard. I was not the only clever one in the *peloton*; others were certain to have reached the same conclusion as I. I had to be ready to react when others put their plans into action. Eddy studied the route for the day and warned me to be well placed at the feeding station which came directly after the first climb and directly before the second. I spoke with the RMO rider Bernard Vallet who is from the region, and he told me that the feeding station at Léoncel was going to be very dangerous. After that feeding station, there were a series of climbs all the way to the finish. From my knowledge of the route, my suspicions about how others were thinking and knowing what Bernard did the day before, I was sure that the Valréas to Villard des Lans stage was destined to be interesting.

My attention was focused most sharply on Fignon and Mottet. Fignon and his *directeur sportif*, Guimard, are calculators and they were certain to see the opportunity for an attack at Léoncel. As we set out that morning I happened to be speaking with Paul Kimmage, another Irish rider in the *peloton*, and I told him to be well positioned at Léoncel because something was going to happen.

Different riders attacked in the early part of the stage and I was surprised that Bernard allowed so many of his team mates to go with the breaks that were escaping. I knew that was a mistake. He was going to need all his team mates near him before the stage was over and it did not make sense to allow some of the best ones to disappear with the breaks. Eventually eighteen riders got clear, but they were mostly riders well down on classification and nobody was too worried. Eddy was in the group but I was not sure whether it was a good idea. I always like to have Eddy alongside me. But as things began to happen in the early part of that stage Eddy went to the back of the *peloton* to get a few Carrera riders to the front so that if a break went away we would be represented. Eddy could not get any of them to the front and when the break went, he decided to go with it himself. As things worked out, it was ideal for me to have him in the break but it was not planned.

The pace was very fast during the first two hours, which were flat. On the first col, the Tourniol, I tried a couple of small attacks but Bernard countered quickly. Near the top he punctured but I did not realize that at the time. After the descent we came to the feeding station and, sure enough, I noticed the Système-U riders Gayant, Mottet and Fignon moving to positions at the front. It was Gayant who attacked and he really went. I went with him, so too did Mottet, Fignon, Delgado, and a few others. Herrera and Alcala got on soon afterwards. We knew that Bernard was chasing in a group not far behind us and the tempo was severe. We soon caught the break that had escaped earlier in the day, and that meant that I had Eddy with me. He was fresh and ready to ride at the front.

Eddy was a great help. He rode as if the finish was around the next turn. He pulled the group in the valleys, on the hills, on the descents. It did not bother him that there were certain riders not doing a thing, just sitting at the back. Our lead over the Bernard group was between a minute and a minute and a half for a long time and the pressure at the front was constant. As well as Eddy, the Système-U riders were very strong and they played a big part in distancing Bernard.

The finish for Eddy is when his legs can take him no further and that happened as we began the climb of the last hill, the Châlimont. He pulled alongside and whispered that he was gone and I was to be careful. I made the tempo on the Châlimont but not all out. Delgado was in the group, which was now down to about six or seven, and as he had not done a tap of work it was certain that he would attack. I wanted to be ready for that and so I was not prepared to show my full hand as I climbed the Châlimont. Mottet and Herrera came past me, wanting a faster tempo, and I told myself to hang back. If they wanted to make it faster that was fine by me but I was waiting for Delgado to attack and any energy I had was being saved for that.

Halfway up the Châlimont Delgado attacked, going about 20 yards clear. I countered immediately, knowing that if Delgado got a gap he would be very hard to bring back. Even though I was all out to get to him and was suffering as I rode with him, I bluffed by riding just half a bike length behind him, at his shoulder. If I was in behind him he might have attacked again to get away from me and I did not want that. He rode at the front to the top of the Châlimont but I rode on the descent and the flat sections before the finish. Over the final two kilometres he began to hedge as he thought about the stage finish. As I was going to take the yellow jersey I did not mind allowing him to have the stage victory. He sprinted early and I let him go, not having much left anyway.

We then had to wait to see how much time we had taken on Bernard. Four minutes and 15 seconds after we crossed the line Bernard made it. He had suffered badly on the Châlimont and lost much of the time on the climb. For the first time in my career I was going to wear the yellow jersey in the Tour de France, but I had mixed emotions that evening in Villard des Lans.

It is an honour to wear the *maillot jaune* of the Tour de France and I was pleased to have it. There was also satisfaction that the plan to get rid of Bernard worked. Afterwards there was talk about his puncture and that he was unlucky. But I think it is foolish to come out of a Tour de France complaining about the ifs and buts of the race. Each rider has his own collection and he considers himself the most unlucky rider in the race. At the time of the attack at Léoncel Bernard was back in the *peloton*, and it must also be said that the Système-U team had decided their attack long before Bernard suffered his puncture.

But even with the yellow jersey in Villard des Lans I was very apprehensive. My team was not going to be of much assistance to me. I was also concerned about the following day's stage to Alpe d'Huez. Of all the climbs in the Alps, Alpe d'Huez is the one I fear the most. As I stretched the jersey over my shoulders my thoughts were already on the 13-kilometre finish to Alpe d'Huez a day later. I knew there was a very good chance that the jersey would be my property for only one day. What has always worked against me on the Alpe d'Huez is the severity of the early slopes. There is no way you can maintain a rhythm on those slopes, instead you are changing gear, getting out of the saddle, sitting down. All the different motions. For a pure climber these things come naturally and such gradients provide an opportunity to distance rivals. For somebody like me who is not a natural climber, those early slopes are a nightmare. Try to go with the best guys and you may blow up farther on in the climb. But if you let them go, you will never see them again. In all the times I had climbed Alpe d'Huez in the past, I never climbed in the front group. There were always some guys who had ridden away from me. OK, I had the yellow jersey in Villard des Lans, but for me it was time to go back to the drawing board. I had to see whether I could lose at Alpe d'Huez and still win the Tour. It was time to calculate again.

Looking at the classification table it was clear that I still had three rivals; Mottet, Delgado and Bernard. Mottet was in second place, just 41 seconds behind, but I worried least about him. Although he was backed by the strongest team in the race he was not climbing well enough to get through the Alps. His form was good, he rode well on the flat and could make a good tempo on the climbs, but when there was an acceleration, Charly was generally distanced. Delgado was third, one minute 19 seconds down and a very big danger. He was on form and one of the best climbers in the race. Far better than I on the steep slopes. During the early part of the race he was rarely seen near the front of the *peloton* and I knew that he was in very good condition. I worried about Delgado. Bernard was one minute 39 seconds behind me but still close enough to be a danger. I did not know what Bernard was capable of in the Alps. His failure at Villard des Lans might have stemmed from the puncture or it may have been that he was not on a good day after his time-trial effort on the Ventoux. I worried about him less than about Delgado but he was a contender.

I knew that I was not likely to climb Alpe d'Huez with Delgado and calculated how much I could lose to him and still retain my chance of winning the Tour. Always, my aim was to preserve my chance of winning. I had one minute 19 seconds to play with. Even more, because the Dijon time trial on the penultimate day would give me the chance to take time back on Delgado. It was not a long time trial, just

38 kilometres, but long enough for me to get 30 seconds back. Knowing Alpe d'Huez I felt that if I was within 20 seconds of the yellow jersey at the end of the stage, I would be satisfied. The prospect of losing the yellow jersey did not worry me in the slightest – the only *maillot jaune* that mattered was the one presented on the Champs Elysées. Working it out I estimated that I could finish between one minute 30 and one minute 50 seconds down on Delgado and keep alive my hopes of winning the Tour. More than anything I wanted to remain calm on Alpe d'Huez when Delgado attacked. I had some time in hand and I wanted to use it.

The nineteenth stage of the Tour de France from Villard des Lans to Alpe d'Huez was every bit as hard as I imagined it would be. Although there were almost 190 kilometres to be covered before we arrived at the foot of Alpe d'Huez, Delgado, Bernard and Mottet were content to allow things to be decided on the Alpe. Not that the race was easy before Alpe d'Huez. We climbed the Col du Coq and the Côte de Laffrey rapidly but I was fairly comfortable on both. But Delgado was also going very well and it was sure that he would make a big bid for the jersey on Alpe d'Huez.

Eddy was with me until the start of the final climb but he could not survive the first accelerations on Alpe d'Huez. I was in a group with Herrera, Delgado, Bernard, Mottet, Hampsten, Lejarreta and Loro. Herrera flew away from us on the first slopes. Delgado counter-attacked and my immediate reaction was to go with Delgado. He stayed a certain distance in front of me for a long time. I would look at his jersey and tell myself that he was not getting that far ahead of me but there was a long, long way to the top. Then Delgado appeared to find new strength and attacked again. This time more fiercely than before. I did not attempt to follow. I was going to have to ride to the summit at my own pace and hope that he did not get too far in front.

At the time you are convinced that you can do nothing. When Delgado accelerated I did not have it in me to stay with him. But I knew that I had some time to play with and that I could let him go, cut my losses and save my chance of winning the Tour. I am sure that if somebody had held a gun to my head on Alpe d'Huez and told me to stay with Delgado on those early kilometres of the climb, I could have done. But at what price? Going all out I could have stayed with Delgado and because I was with him, he might not have ridden so hard. My presence might have discouraged him. On the other hand he might have kept up the pace and because of the efforts I made in staying with him, I might have blown up and lost four or five minutes in the final seven or eight kilometres. That was the risk I was not prepared to take. Having calculated all through it did not make sense to start gambling foolishly in the final five days of the race. Delgado went away to do his ride on the mountain and I settled down to do mine.

Hampsten was with me for a time and he rode at the front. That was a help. Lejarreta, too, rode with me and that took me another bit of the way. Eventually I was with Loro and Bernard. The Italian Luciano Loro was a rider in the Del Tongo team. Because Del Tongo are an Italian team like Carrera we had an arrangement with them that they would help us on the flat parts of the stage to Alpe d'Huez, but there was no agreement whereby they would help on the climbs. But Loro did not need any encouragement from me. He wanted to ride in front of Bernard and me. As we were not going that well, that was fine. His pace was right for us.

People claimed afterwards that I must have had an alliance with Loro but they were wrong. There are riders like him who like to show how strong they can be. He was on a good day on the Alpe, there were television cameras in front of him and he enjoyed every moment of it. The next morning he was telling the journalists that it was a dream for him to be riding alongside people like Bernard and me. He said that he saw himself as more than an ordinary *domestique* and that he could sometimes climb the big mountains in the company of the best.

With the help of Loro, I made it to the summit of Alpe d'Huez in fifteenth place, one minute 44 seconds behind the seventh-placed Delgado. Riders who had escaped in early breakaways took the first four places. Delgado was the new leader of the race but only by 25 seconds. My disappointment at losing the jersey was slight. I knew that I could recapture the 25 seconds; he knew that he would have to increase his lead on me if he was to be sure of winning the Tour. I would have preferred not to lose the jersey but the fact of losing did not discourage me. Delgado would have to bear the responsibility of the jersey and that would make his life more difficult.

In other ways the Alpe d'Huez stage was good for my chances. Mottet finished over a minute behind and in my eyes was now not a contender. Bernard was dropped from our group on the first slopes of Alpe d'Huez but came back to us and was strong over the final kilometres of the climb. But he did not make any worthwhile inroads on the one minute 39 seconds of advantage I held over him. More than ever it looked as if Delgado was my principal *adversaire*. I had not enjoyed a good day on Alpe d'Huez but the Tour was not lost. My overall aim was to keep myself in contention for as long as possible and now, with just five days remaining, I was still there.

With Alpe d'Huez out of the way, I was happy. No mountain in the race would cause me as much difficulty as it and even though the next day's stage also finished at the summit of a mountain, La Plagne, I was not too worried. La Plagne was hard but nothing like Alpe d'Huez and I felt I could handle it. Eddy and I spoke about how I should ride the La Plagne stage and we agreed that the best thing would be to ride with Delgado all through the stage and to attack one kilometre from the summit finish.

Things worked out differently. It was a hard day from the start. A few guys attacked on the Galibier and as that came early in the stage it was clear that many riders were going to be in trouble getting inside the time limit for the day. The Colombians were riding like crazy men on the Galibier and I told Herrera that he had better tell his cowboys to ride sensibly or they would find themselves in some ditch. Lots of the non-climbers in the race were desperately tired and it needed only one fierce day in the mountains to eliminate twenty of them. But the Colombians are not easy to deal with. Herrera does his own thing and I reckon that the other really strong Colombian, Parra, has adapted far better to the European way of doing things. On the descent of the Galibier I got together with Mottet and Bernard and we rode as hard as we could to get rid of a few of the Colombians.

After descending from the Galibier we climbed the Telegraphe and then continued on down the long descent into the valley leading us to the Col de Madeleine. In the valley a few riders well down on classification attacked. There were the French riders Sanders and Bernaudeau, the Spaniards Fuerte and Munoz, the Dutch rider Theunisse and the Colombian Parra. I saw the chance to join this break and went for it. Bernard reacted a fraction too late and when he counterattacked to join us the gap was too great. He rode on his own between us and the Delgado group for about 10 kilometres, never more than 300 yards behind. Afterwards people said I made a mistake in not slowing and allowing Bernard to join us, maintaining that he would have given the breakaway group some added power. I saw it differently. To me, he was a big rival. He could have joined us, ridden with us to the final climb and then accelerated clear. I was not going to help him to do that.

Our lead grew to one minute 40 seconds by the time we reached the Madeleine, but I knew that I had to be careful. If I went all out on the Madeleine to stay clear of the pursuing group I risked losing everything. When I attacked from the original group I went away from Delgado, Mottet and Herrera, but they had been rejoined by Fignon and his presence was sure to strengthen the pursuit. With all those guys chasing me I had to keep something up my sleeve, because it was likely that they would catch me. I rode up the Madeleine at a good tempo but the group behind still pulled back a minute. That was evidence that they were going to recapture us and I tried to preserve my strength as much as I could. They eventually caught us at a feed station about 40 kilometres from the finish.

Everybody criticized me for what they saw as a foolish attempt at a breakaway. Maybe it was but I do not look back on it as such. For me it was another exploit. Earlier in the season I had pulled off exploits in the St Tropez stage of Paris–Nice and the Sappada stage of the Giro d'Italia. Those performances helped my confidence greatly and I wanted to try another.

I was now feeling the other side of the exploit: the disappointment when it does not come off. I was out in front and knew that I was going to be caught. I felt like a fool, knowing that I was going to be vulnerable to a Delgado attack on the climb to La Plagne. They were going to say I was an idiot but, in the back of my mind, there was the thought that if my breakaway had come off, the very people who criticized would have been the ones to say, 'This man does it like Merckx.' They would have said how brave I was to attack from so far out, how I had regained the race lead with such panache. They would have made me out to be God Almighty. Because my attack did not work, I was a fool. The tactics were deemed stupid. But that is the way things go.

When Delgado attacked on the early slopes of La Plagne there was nothing I could do. His acceleration was violent and I knew that my only hope was to let him go and hope that I could cut my losses. If I went with him, I was sure to blow up and lose the Tour. For the first time in the race I was staring defeat in the face. I told myself to stay cool, not to panic. My only chance was to ride as strongly as possible, but at my own rhythm, until five kilometres to the top, and after that I could give it everything. I could go all out for five kilometres and not fall apart. On the previous day Delgado suffered in the last five kilometres to the summit of Alpe d'Huez, and I hoped that he would again be weak on the last section of La Plagne. I rode up La Plagne with the French rider Denis Roux and Loro, who was again going well. I was getting time checks on Delgado, some of them official, some unofficial. He was at least one minute up on me, probably a bit more.

I kept telling myself to be patient, not to make my all-out effort too soon. Five kilometres before the finish sign I increased my tempo, hoping to take back some time on Delgado. I kept going as fast as I could. For the final 400 metres I went to the absolute limits, putting my chain onto the big ring and surging for the line. I could see a car in front of me but I was sure Delgado was in front of the car. At the line I was shattered. I stretched out for somebody to take my hand but there was nobody there. Because of the crowd I had to stop pedalling a few yards after the line and that meant I went from the all-out effort of the final 400 metres straight into a huge group of photographers and journalists. There was no air. I felt awful. I wondered where Patrick was and then I heard his voice telling me to try to get off the bike. As soon as I did I fell. There was no power in my legs. Nothing. Patrick got me to lie down on the road. I was conscious but powerless. He told me that my legs were crossed and that I should straighten them out, if not I would be trampled on. I understood what he asked me to do but when I tried to move my legs nothing happened. A minute or two later the Tour doctor was over me with a mask in his hand. I was vaguely aware that he must be giving me oxygen. After a few minutes I began to feel better and was well enough to be able to say that there was no need for them to take me to hospital. I wanted to get back to my hotel and rest for the following day's stage to Morzine.

The big thing for me was that I saved the Tour. My fight back on La Plagne cut Delgado's lead down to four seconds on the line. His 25 seconds' advantage over me in the race jumped to 29 but he knew and I knew there was still everything to ride for.

That night the race *commissaire* penalized me 10 seconds for taking food from the team car. I was furious because it is seldom that a rider is penalized so severely for such an offence. Delgado's lead was up to 39 seconds and things were very much in the balance. There was no way I could be sure of taking 39 seconds out of him in the time trial and even if I could there was still the chance that one puncture in the time trial could cost me the Tour. I appealed against the 10 seconds' penalty and even spoke to the race director, Jacques Goddet. He expressed sympathy but appeals do not work in the Tour de France.

My collapse after finishing on La Plagne worried me because of the psychological boost it would give Delgado. He had seen me lying on the road, receiving oxygen, and he was going to believe that I was weak and ready to surrender. That would help him. It would encourage him to attack on the stage to Morzine, which included five big passes. Against that, I felt I was OK.

Back at the hotel I took a bath and tried to relax. I went down the stairs of the hotel as a test for my legs and was surprised at how lively they were. As far as I could see I was fully recovered from the La Plagne experience. In one way I would have been happy to get through the Morzine without losing to Delgado but I also believed that it would not be enough to stay with him. His 39 seconds' advantage had to be reduced. Before the Tour began I had looked to the Morzine stage as the one that would decide the winner of the race. So much that I had not expected had taken place and yet Morzine was still to play a big part.

I bluffed as well as I could on the early climbs, trying to convince Delgado that I was fully recovered from the previous day. Again he was happy to leave everything until the final climb, the Joux Plane, which came just before the descent into Morzine. Eddy was having an exceptionally good day and he stayed alongside all through the stage. He was super on the Joux Plane, making a strong tempo which suited me and eliminated many. Towards the top of the Joux Plane there were only Eddy, Delgado, Bernard, Lejarreta, Parra and I. I felt good and reckoned that I was at least as strong as Delgado, if not stronger. I tried to get away before the summit and moved about 20 yards in front of the other four. Eddy worried that Lejarreta would pace Delgado up to me and that Delgado would counterattack. So Eddy sprinted to join me. Lejarreta did lead Delgado and Bernard up but, with Eddy alongside me, there was no fear of a successful counterattack. I resigned myself to riding over the summit with the others and attacking on the descent. If things worked for me, I could use Eddy to get away from Delgado on the descent into Morzine. No matter what else, that 39 seconds' deficit on Delgado had to be reduced.

At the start of the descent Bernard led from Eddy, Delgado and me. I wanted to attack from fourth position, getting Eddy to take my wheel as I flashed past, knowing that Eddy would let my wheel go on a sharp corner and that Delgado would then have a real problem closing the gap. But Delgado saw what I was trying and pushed Eddy to one side as he came after me. He moved quickly enough, but I still got a gap.

Once I had the gap I tried not to take any risks on the corners, feeling that I could stay clear of Delgado on the descent. My lead was never more than seven or eight seconds on the descent but it was enough. The final five kilometres of flat road to the finish turned out to be a pursuit between Delgado and me. That suited me and my eight seconds' advantage jumped to 18 by the time we reached the finish.

Delgado's overall lead in the race was down to 21 seconds and I was happy. On all known form I stood a very good chance of taking more than 21 seconds back in the Dijon time trial. Even more importantly, the breakaway on the descent to Morzine was a major psychological blow for Delgado. In interviews he was conceding that 21 seconds would not be enough. While I was now getting very close to Tour victory I continued to play things cautiously, saying that my chance of winning the race remained alive and that I was pleased about that.

The stage to Morzine concluded what had been five very hard days of climbing. We were now out of the Alps and heading for Paris. After Morzine there was a flat stage from Saint Julien-en-Genevois to Dijon. It changed nothing. Everything was down to the Dijon time trial. I wanted to get my build-up right for the time trial. Over the years I have learned that it is crucial to get your mind into the correct state before a time trial. In 1983 there was a Tour de France time trial in Dijon, close to the end of the race. Before the test I met Lydia's grandmother, who is from that city. We spoke for a while. I met somebody else I knew and spent another few minutes talking. I ended up losing the stage by a fairly small margin to Fignon. Afterwards I met Raymond Poulidor, Anquetil's great rival in the sixties. Poulidor told me that I lost the time trial before the start. How? I asked. He explained that as I was chatting away with different people before the start I could not have been properly tuned in mentally. He was right. My mind was not concentrated on the job that I had to do.

Four years later Poulidor's advice helped me to get my preparation right for Dijon. I decided that I would not see anybody, I was not talking to anybody, and on the morning of the test I ate in my room. My night's sleep was sound and undisturbed and I never felt too nervous. Eddy was wonderful, acting as a bodyguard, refusing to let anybody near me and ensuring that every wish of mine was seen to. In the cubicle before setting out on the time trial there was a song going

The hectic moments before the start of a Tour de France stage. On this particular morning, I am wearing the yellow jersey and trying to look relaxed

One of my main rivals for the 1987 Tour – Pedro Delgado

On the slopes of La Plagne, the 21st stage of the Tour, I took myself to the limit

The 1987 Tour is over and I am happy to speak with all of the journalists

Back in Ireland with Sean at the end of the 1987 season. The photo tells its own story

One of the great honours of my career: the only sportsperson to become a freeman of Dublin. From left, Lydia, Frank Feely (Dublin City Manager), and Lord Mayor Carmencita Hedermann

Friends and family turned up for the ceremony. From left, my granddad Ned, my parents and Lydia's parents

Winning the Tour is a wonderful feeling

through my mind. This often happens before or during a time trial and I find that it helps. I never think of the dangers or the risks and never consider that I might not be able to perform. I knew that I could take the required time out of Delgado but I also felt that I had to be on a bloody good day to do it. With the yellow jersey on his back he could be inspired. The Tour was not yet won.

In a time trial I try to calculate where I can gain time on my rival and I knew in the Dijon test that my race ended at the top of the climb, a little after halfway. If I had not taken the time out of Delgado by that point there was no way I was going to be able to do it in the second part of the course. The 22 kilometres before the summit of the hill was my kind of territory, up and down, and I had to make it count. Afterwards there was a descent and flat roads and I was not going to gain much. I had different people posted at different points to give me time checks and so I was constantly aware of how well or badly I was doing.

At the foot of the hill I was one minute 14 seconds up on Delgado and knew then that barring accidents I was going to take the yellow jersey. It was wet and the roads were slippery and I rode with great care over the final 16 kilometres of the course. I was prepared to lose some of my advantage but I was not prepared to take any risks on dangerous corners. Delgado did cut my advantage down to sixty-one seconds but that was not important. The yellow jersey was mine by 40 seconds. The time trial had run true to form.

Lydia was at the finish with our two children, Nicolas and Christelle. My mother and sister Carol were also there. There were lots of Irish people around and it was a very happy occasion. There was just one day left in the Tour, the final leg to the Champs Elysées, and normally nothing changed on the last day. But I pinched myself and said that the race was not yet over. There was the final stage to Paris and who knew what would happen? It was most unlikely that anything would happen but after calculating so well for the previous three and a half weeks, I was not going to start taking things for granted on the final day.

The Champs Elysées stage was uneventful. Bontempi and Eddy stayed very close to me all the way and I enjoyed a fairly comfortable ride into the centre of Paris. There were people on the roadsides whom I recognized and I was able to wave to them. After the finish line it was pretty hectic, going through all the interviews and ceremonies. I find it hard to feel the elation that others feel at such moments. In my mind it was another race and the satisfaction was that I survived it better than anybody else. Of course, when the Irish national anthem was played I experienced very strong emotions. Everything quiet, tears coming to my eyes and the realization that the Tour de France was *the* race.

PART V
A World Apart

CHAPTER 20

The Class of '87

On Wednesday 26 August 1987, four Irishmen collected in Dublin. They had come from Belgium, France, Spain and Italy. Expatriates, if you like. Their coming together was for the purpose of forming a team. A team which would represent Ireland at the World Professional Cycling Road Race championship twelve days further on . Normally they rode for their commercial team sponsors but on one day each year they rode for their country. For at the World Championship road race they were permitted to wear the green of their country and they enjoyed that. It might be wrong to say they were in Dublin solely for the business of forming a team, because they were also present to ride a city-centre race in Ireland's capital city, and other such races in Wexford and Cork. As they were professionals and had contracts for the races in Ireland, they were being paid to appear.

The four members of Ireland's professional cycling class were Sean Kelly, Stephen Roche, Martin Earley and Paul Kimmage. Kelly had been officially ranked number one for the last four years in cycling. Roche was number two in the rankings but, as winner of the Giro d'Italia and the Tour de France, the outstanding cyclist of 1987. Earley and Kimmage were two respected team riders. Their value on the cycling exchange would have been reflected in the fees they earned for riding that Wednesday evening in Dublin. Kelly and Roche might have made £2000 each; Earley and Kimmage would have settled for £200 each. Money, of course, is what makes the wheels go round, but these four Irishmen were conscious of the other reason for their Dublin rendezvous. They needed to get into the mood for the World Championship road race at Villach in Austria, and for giving Irishmen a feeling of Irishness, Dublin was a pretty good starting point. Kelly and Roche had not seen much of each other in 1987 and needed to get together before riding in Austria. They also felt it was a good idea having Earley and Kimmage around. They could be useful at the World Championships and the five days spent in Ireland would help to stimulate that team feeling.

The time spent in Ireland was central to what was to happen in Austria. Through the years in the *peloton* Kelly and Roche enjoyed each other's company. Each admired what the other tried to achieve. Ireland was the common bond and they liked people to see them as 'the two lads'. Most of all they never wanted people to be able to say that 'the two lads do not get on'. In this they broke with cycling tradition. A tradition which ordained that two cyclists from the same country and of the same era disliked each other. Bartali and Coppi in Italy in the forties; in France Anquetil and Poulidor in the sixties, Moser and Saronni in the seventies, Hinault and Fignon in the eighties.

At different moments in their careers Kelly and Roche leaned on each other's shoulders. Roche helped Kelly to win his first classic. That was the Tour of Lombardy, Italy, 1983. Kelly offered the wisdom of his experiences when Roche was thrown back against the ropes. Neither ever sought to score points over the other. Ireland is small and they saw no virtue in being Ireland's best. Sights were higher. Friendship genuine. Coming together for a week in Ireland before the World Championship would be a laugh and interesting preparation for the world road race.

Roche did not seriously entertain the notion of winning the World Championship. He had no right to. Since winning the Tour de France his life had swirled around on a planet far above cloud nine. Adulation, such as he had never known, descended. He was besieged. Once he was out training and on returning found that a man had called while he was away and left an enormous crab. Roche did not have a notion who left the shellfish but appreciated the generosity. Some called to pay homage, others to let their young son behold the champion, and others were content to write. Hundreds of letters, all congratulatory. It turned Roche's head, momentarily. He was tired anyway. Training was hard and the circuit for the World Championship race was not severe enough to give Roche a chance. As a professional and an Irishman he had a responsibility. Kelly.

Roche decided that he could ride a useful race in Austria by doing what he could for his friend. The circuit suited Kelly. He sprinted well and the world road-race circuit was made for those with rapid finishes. Kelly had prepared assiduously for the race and was certain to be in excellent condition. His season had been a misery. Denied victory in the prestigious Tour of Spain because a cyst on his groin could not wait to be removed. Forced out of the Tour de France because of a crash. All Kelly could hope for was the world title. Roche understood and said he would help, if he could.

Although the city-centre races in Ireland were nothing more than one-hour circus shows, Kelly and Roche decided to milk them for all they could get. They started by playing little games with their rivals. They roped in Earley and Kimmage, formed a team and raced against the pack. The pack was comprised mostly of British-based professionals. Given that the Dublin city-centre race was his first in Ireland since winning the tours of Italy and France, it was expected that Roche would be encouraged to win by all his rivals. Cycling, particularly when professionals compete, acknowledges a sense of decorum and only a fool would wish Roche to be vanquished at the Dublin circus.

Roche did win but some of his rivals acted out the serf's role with unusual vigour. They may not have been acting at all. By the time the second city-centre race started the following evening in Wexford, the rival factions were lined up in opposing trenches. Kelly and Roche summoned Earley and Kimmage to a team meeting. Strategy was agreed and a match was put to the fuse of defiance. Their rivals numbered about forty but the four comforted themselves that quality could count for more than quantity. All they had to do was take Kelly to the finish and let him sprint.

In Wexford they did just that. Kelly flew at the end and won easily. Given the odds, the exploit pleased them enormously. After the race they went to a reception. Local dignitaries welcomed the legends to town. Kelly nominated Kimmage to reply on behalf of the gang of four.

When the reception ended all four felt like doing something. A quiet pub where they could sit and maybe sip a beer. Life in the *peloton* was hard, it was seldom they got home and even more seldom they were asked to ride just a one-hour race each day. And they had beaten the English in Wexford. There was something to celebrate. So, a quiet pub. But, for Kelly and Roche, there is no such thing as a quiet pub in Ireland. Everywhere recognition was instant. Cutting their losses they returned to White's Hotel, where they were staying, and went to their rooms. There they ordered tea, biscuits, and fresh fruit salads (without cream of course). They sat in the corridors and talked and laughed. And decided how they would beat the English in Cork. Kelly and Roche might have been imprisoned by their own stardom in Wexford but they were not complaining.

What had been nervous tension in Wexford became bare-knuckled fighting in Cork. The English wanted one prize to take away but the natives wanted all three. Earley and Kimmage rode very strongly, Roche showed that Tour de France winners are versatile athletes, and Kelly, dogged Kelly, won the sprint again. As Roche opened the way and ushered a flying Kelly through, he moved to one side. Behind him a battalion of fiery Englishmen banged on the door, wanting to follow Kelly. Roche pretended not to hear and left less room than was necessary. One of the English, Walsham, persisted in banging and his bike touched Roche's.

That was all it needed. Eleven riders, including Roche and Walsham, tumbled from their machines. Keith Lambert broke a collar bone but the surprise was that only one suffered serious injury. In Roche's mind Walsham was being silly. Could he not see that there simply was not enough room? Walsham, angered, accused Roche of deliberately causing him to crash. Englishman and Irishman arguing, as their ancestors have for centuries.

Walsham and others threatened violence as Roche lay on the road. Spectators threatened violence on the English. Roche tried to stem the tide of aggression but chose a curious method: 'After all, lads, the score is now Ireland 3 England 0 and the game is over.'

And the game was over. The next morning Kelly, Roche and Kimmage (Earley had returned to Dublin the previous night) headed for Cork airport. It was 6.30 in the morning and their flight left Cork at 7.15. There was barely time to intercept a man going about his business of delivering the local newspaper, the *Cork Examiner*. They wanted to see what the *Examiner* said about the race.

Sometimes it is useful to be a star. The man plucked a newspaper from his bundle and presented it to his heroes. On the front page they found what they were looking for. Kelly's quote. *The* quote. 'After giving me a great lead out, Stephen was obviously not too sure that I was going to win for he felt he had to wipe out everybody else.' Boy, did they laugh at that on the way to the airport.

In the aisle of the airplane Roche met Walsham and asked how he was feeling. He wanted to forgive and forget. Walsham spurned the peace offer and the bickering began again. Kelly joined in, explaining that the English professional should consider growing up. For an instant, Kelly and Roche could have been brothers. All their previous exploits merged for one glorious second and they stood utterly together.

The four Irishmen met again in Austria. Kelly, Roche and Earley cycled up from Italy after riding a race there. Kimmage arrived by car from his home near Grenoble. Kelly and Roche began working on the two younger ones. Quiet, subtle stuff, making sure that the two lads understood the importance of the World Championship. Convincing them they had a part to play. Earley and Kimmage were listening and willing to do as much as they could. For them winning was not a possibility but they could help one of their team mates to victory. They were pleased, even proud, to get the chance to help. Never did Kelly or Roche treat them as anything other than equal team mates. All the time Earley and Kimmage felt it was going to be Kelly's World Championship. Something about his mood. His deadly seriousness, the appetite for training and the obvious hunger for victory. When training with Roche they were overwhelmed by his natural class but presumed that Stephen's condition was not good enough for an attack on the world title. They were also conscious of the unsuitability of the circuit for Roche. And, logically, riders without a sprint generally do not win one-day races.

Two days before the race an Italian journalist turned up at the Adolf Piber Hotel in Villach to interview Roche. During the course of their conversation Roche spoke about his relationship with Kelly and said he would willingly ride for his compatriot in the World Championship. The journalist noted the comments with scepticism. Roche noted the scepticism and reminded his interviewer that he and Kelly shared rooms. Two great stars in one room! This was beyond the Italian imagination and Roche had to produce the hotel room list to prove the sharing arrangement was as he said.

As the rain lashed in Villach on the morning of the race there was despondency all around. The Italians did not like the rain, neither did the French. Cycling was hard enough without the miserable feeling of wetness. Earley wears glasses, even when he races. You need not ask how he feels about rain. Kimmage hates rain for his own reasons. His legs react against it. What baffled Earley and Kimmage that morning in Villach was the good humour of Kelly and Roche. The two big contenders sat across from them in the makeshift pits, the rain making a loud noise on the roof, and laughed and joked their way through it. By the time the starter called the riders to the line, Kelly and Roche were ridiculously cheerful. 'It was not that they liked the rain,' said Kimmage, 'nobody likes rain. But they knew that moaning about it would not make it go away. They are professionals in every way, even down to not complaining when there is no point in complaining.'

Through the first ten of the twenty-three laps Kelly rode in the front fifteen or twenty of the 179-rider *peloton*. But that is Kelly's way. Rain means slippery roads and crashes. Position yourself in the front line and there is less chance of somebody else's crash bringing you down. Roche saw less need to be so protective of his chances and moved along in the middle of the pack. He felt stiff and lifeless. Earley was comfortable but Kimmage found those early laps trying. At one point Roche drifted back towards Kimmage and offered encouragement: 'Come on, Paul, keep going. You have to finish this race. I'm going to try to finish.' If Roche is prepared to try to finish, thought Kimmage, then the least I can do is try.

In their own ways, Roche and Kelly both rode exceptionally well. Roche's performance benefited from the total lack of expectation. He was present to assist Kelly and knew that he was equipped to offer quality service to his friend. Roche was also encouraged by Kelly's strength on the day. Every time he looked at Kelly he saw a man who was riding like a winner.

With a little over four laps to go, the race for the rainbow jersey began in earnest. At that point Moreno Argentin from Italy, the unusually hot favourite, attacked. With him went Holland's Teun Van Vliet, Spain's Juan Fernandez and Belgium's Jan Nevers. To many, it looked like the winning break. The Italian, Dutch and Spanish teams were happy to let it go, Belgium were undecided, and of the teams which were counted as serious twelve-rider teams, only the French wanted this breakaway quartet recaptured.

Laurent Fignon and Charly Mottet led the pursuit for France. But after cutting the deficit from 50 down to 25 seconds they could give no more. The effort of the chase cost both dearly and they abandoned soon afterwards. Argentin and his three companions rode onwards, leaving the French trailing in their wake.

Roche read the warning signs and pushed up the pace. Gone was the lifelessness which so worried him in the early part of the race; he was now riding extremely well and felt in control. On the second of the two climbs on the circuit he accelerated and sustained the effort for about two kilometres. The 25 seconds' advantage of the leaders dwindled to 10 seconds. Suddenly the escapers were catchable and the door was open for Kelly again.

As Roche eased to take a breath, Earley streamed past him. Ireland's little team was working far more effectively than anybody had anticipated. The race commentator at Villach could hardly believe what was happening and announced that Ireland was conducting the pursuit in a voice that carried as much incredulity as admiration. By the time Earley concluded his surge at the front, the four breakaways were within touching distance. Earley spent the last morsels of his strength in the effort to recapture and he abandoned almost immediately. His contribution more than satisfied his team mates.

With Argentin safely in the clutches of the *peloton*, eyes focused on Kelly. Other riders noted how tirelessly Roche protected Kelly's chances and concluded that Kelly had to be the big favourite for the rainbow jersey. In most situations it is enough to take Kelly to the finish and allow him to contest the sprint. Few can beat him when the final all-out surge takes place at the end of a seven-hour race. But Roche, so sure of his powers, sought to do more for Kelly.

Through the last lap but one he did a head count of his fellow riders and decided there were far too many and, more importantly, there were some in the company who might actually outsprint Kelly. Roche worried about Vander-aerden and Bontempi, two of the most rapid finishers in the pack. The seventy-two riders who formed the lead group had been on the road for six and a half hours when the bell sounded for the final lap. Roche moved closer to the front, Kelly moved in his slipstream. The time to eliminate rivals had come. On the long climb which presented itself soon after the start/finish line, Roche moved to the right-hand side of the road and upped the pace. Kelly dug deep just to follow. In an instant the tightly grouped pack splintered into a series of small, uneven groups. Roche's acceleration looked smooth, almost effortless, but the faces of the others gave the lie to that. They were hurting.

Only eleven of the seventy-one could follow Roche's pace. At the top of the climb the twelve breakaways were 15 seconds clear of the rest and the advantage increased through the final 10 kilometres to the finish. Kelly's reputation as a sprinter prompted a series of counterattacks from the leading group. Golz, Van Vliet, Sorensen, Bauer, Rooks and Winterberg all attacked at different moments. Roche chased one down, Kelly another and then Roche another. And when Van Vliet attacked again with a little over two kilometres to go it was Roche and Golz who pursued. Sorensen and Winterberg tagged along. After that there was hesitation. A gap dividing the five from the remainder appeared. Those in the rear group waited for Kelly to lead them back to the front. Argentin, in particular, expected Kelly to shift himself.

In one of those bizarre twists that was inconceivable moments before, Kelly found himself playing for Roche: 'If I made the effort to close the gap and Argentin beat me in the sprint, which was a possibility, then the race would have been a disaster. Stephen was my team mate. I told the others I was not chasing. It was up to them.' Argentin, Fernandez and Bauer could not believe that Kelly was prepared to forfeit his chance. They were sure he was bluffing and waited for him to move. Argentin taunted Kelly: 'Well, it's your gold medal going down the drain.' Kelly sat still, expecting that the others would accelerate and join the Roche quintet which was less than 200 metres ahead. He waited. They waited. Roche, constantly looking behind, grew anxious.

To him, it appeared that a day's work was being wasted. He was one of five in the breakaway group and with his sprint that meant fourth or fifth. If only Kelly were alongside. With about 500 metres to go Roche glanced back for the last time and knew there was no comeback for his friend. Roche understood that he had to try something.

There was maybe 450 metres to go when Roche made his surge for glory. He was fourth in the line of five, behind Sorensen, Van Vliet and Golz. Only Winterberg saw Roche lift himself out of the saddle and accelerate. Winterberg tried to follow but did not have the strength.

As Roche sprinted through a narrow passageway between the line of three riders and the barrier on the left side of the road, Van Vliet turned to see if Golz was reacting. Golz wondered if Van Vliet was going to chase. It only took that second's hesitation. Roche had flown. Out of the saddle, turning a big gear, moving smoothly clear. Towards the very end, as the little incline to the finish line grew steeper, he had to fight with his big gear, grinding out the last thirty or forty pedal strokes. Behind Argentin, Kelly and their companions joined up with the four left behind by Roche, and Argentin sprinted magnificently for second place. Fernandez claimed third, Golz fourth and Kelly fifth.

Kelly's heart was not in the sprint. Early in the finishing straight he saw that Roche was clear, knew that the gold medal was safe and the rest did not matter. As Roche crossed the line he shot his two hands upwards. At the same time Kelly's two hands went upwards and for a few precious seconds the four green arms remained raised. After the line they embraced. Tears fell from Roche's eyes.

Forty seconds later the main bunch crossed the finish line. In the middle of that pack Paul Kimmage pedalled home in forty-fourth place. A very satisfying performance for Kimmage, but he was despondent. Through the last kilometre he tried to make out the race commentator's description of the finish. Kimmage was sure he heard the commentator say that Steven Rooks had won. Rooks, an accomplished Dutch rider, was a member of the Kelly–Roche breakaway group. Kimmage had expected to hear Kelly's name and was astonished to hear that Rooks had beaten him. Seconds after crossing the line he saw some smiling Irish eyes and was bewildered. What had happened?

Kimmage's joy matched Kelly's. Earley was equally moved. They would have said before the race that it mattered not a whit whether it was Roche or Kelly that won, and their reactions confirmed that their togetherness was genuine.

That night all four Irish riders celebrated at the Adolf Piber Hotel. It was the kind of cycling celebration that you expect: all talk and no action but wonderful all the same. Roche recounted the story of the race as a Boy Scout might recall his first camping trip. Kelly spoke about Roche. Of the class. What a year! Kelly then pleaded on his friend's behalf: 'Nobody should ever expect Stephen to repeat what he has done this year.'

But the talk continually returned to Roche and his class. To ride a World Championship for your team mate, to do all the work which goes with that kind of task and still win. That left us all a little baffled. There were about thirty Irish supporters in the hotel that evening. People who had begged and borrowed to be present, hoping that an Irishman might do something. Kelly, Roche, Earley and Kimmage dedicated their evening's celebration to their supporters. Not in any ostentatious way but simply by moving from one huddle to another, making sure they got around to everybody. Thanks for winning. Thanks for coming. We watched them mingle and admired.

Roche, Kelly, Earley and Kimmage. Roche and Kelly. Roche. The class of '87.

CHAPTER 21
Digging a Grave

On the morning after Stephen Roche won the Tour de France the *Irish Times* editorial said of the achievement: 'More dramatically, certainly more colourfully, than all the Ministers travelling in and out over the years for EEC conferences, more than all the MEPs attending at Strasbourg and Luxembourg, Stephen Roche this weekend brought Ireland to the centre of European attention and awareness.'

Living abroad, I can't tell what impact professional cycling is making on the people back home. I get indications from the Irish journalists who come to the Tour de France and from Irish people that I meet in France. It was clear that the country was taking more of an interest in the Tour in 1987 than ever before and when I heard that the Taoiseach Charlie Haughey was going to be at the Champs Elysées finish, I felt it was an honour for the sport of cycling and for the Tour de France. Yet when it was proposed that I return to Dublin the day after the Tour ended for a public parade and reception I was nervous. I wondered how many people in Ireland had seen the Tour, worried about how many would turn out for a reception and thought to myself what a let-down it would be if I arrived home to find the streets of Dublin empty. I knew that Barry McGuigan had received a great reception in Dublin after winning his world boxing title but McGuigan was a world champion. The Tour de France did not make me a world champion. And what did the Tour mean to Irish people? I imagined I was going to look stupid, parading through Dublin and people wondering what was happening.

The reception turned out to be an extraordinary experience for me. Ask me now what was the most memorable moment of 1987. Beating the Italians in the Giro? Winning the Tour de France? The World Championship? The great memory is of the Dublin reception. I cannot explain it and I cannot forget it. There is no word that describes what it meant to me.

Arriving at Dublin airport I was amazed to see so many people present and I reckoned that everyone who cared had come there. After a reception at the airport we headed into the centre of Dublin and I was totally taken aback by the numbers of people. Various estimates were put on the crowd, 250,000 being quoted in many reports. To me it appeared that the entire population of the city had turned out. I have a video of the parade on the double-decker bus through Dublin. I felt shy at first, being the centre of such attention. But soon I began to enjoy it. I am, and always have been, like an orchestra: I play better when the hall is full. What really surprised me was the number of people who stopped their cars and got out to cheer. People who were in a hurry but suddenly found the time to greet a cyclist. I found it very touching. They valued what I had achieved. I wondered how they would have felt if I had lost, and tried not to think about that. It was far better to enjoy the moment. There was a thrill in knowing that my victory could bring so much happiness. I was glad that I had not let all these people down.

That day in Dublin I smiled for twelve hours and there was not a single second when I had to force myself. It all came naturally. I could live for a long time and never be able to describe how I felt when I saw all the people in Dublin. But the reception could not last for ever and I was contracted to ride a criterium in Holland on the following day. Many bike racers make a significant part of their money in the criteriums and it is important that the very top riders make the criteriums because without them, there will be no public. There were times when I needed the criteriums more than I do now and in those days I was very glad of the money. Now I feel an obligation to support the criteriums, knowing they are so important for many pros. The criteriums, for example, give me a chance to repay Eddy for the work he did in the Giro and the Tour. Organizers permit the big name riders to nominate some of their team for certain criteriums and I would not accept a contract unless Eddy was also offered one.

On the day after the Dublin reception I rode in Stiphout, near Eindhoven in Holland. A day later there was another Dutch criterium, this time in Caam. On my way to that race I passed an overturned BMW which was the same colour as Eddy's. When I arrived at the start of the race I heard that it was his. Eddy had crashed on his way to the race and was taken to hospital. I rang the hospital and spoke to him. He told me that he and his wife and daughter were very fortunate not to have received serious injuries. It was a reminder to me that even after the Tour de France life goes on.

I might have wanted to take things easily in Caam that evening but I did not have a choice. Because I raced with the yellow jersey of the Tour de France on my back, people expected things. Every time I hit the front, the reaction of the crowd was unbelievable. They were standing on their heads to get a view. With the Carrera jersey I could have slipped around quietly at the back and nobody would have noticed. But as Tour winner I had to perform before the race, during the race and after the race. It was exciting but I was killing myself and I knew it.

Between the Giro and the Tour, I had ridden fifty days of the hardest stage racing in cycling. Those tours had come after a very demanding three months of competition. I was very, very tired and sensed that I was digging a grave for myself. The day after Caam I rode a criterium in Belgium which was over a circuit that included the Mur de Grammont. I crashed on the Grammont and felt very sore. That crash struck me as the clearest message from my body telling me to stop. I was doing too much. After the crash I cancelled all my criterium commitments, pulled out of the Tour of Britain and forced myself to rest. I needed to decide what I wanted from the rest of the season.

I wanted to ride the World Championship. That was certain. Everybody informed me that the circuit for the race was totally unsuited to my kind of rider. It was supposed to be flat and easy enough to give the sprinters a winning chance. But I wanted to be there in any case. I felt I could be of some help to Sean Kelly and there was no way I could or would pass up the chance of helping him in the World Championship. If the two of us were going well it was possible that one of us could win and, because of the circuit, he was by far the more likely contender.

After the fall on the Mur de Grammont I was badly bruised and decided on a few days' rest. I was desperately tired. I went with Lydia and the kids to the holiday home on the Ile d'Oleron but took my bike with me. The weather was very hot and I went for a few long spins, each time returning to the house in a bad way. But those spins got me back into some kind of condition and I knew I should be going back to Paris where the weather would be cooler and better for training. So I left Lydia, Nicolas and Christelle and headed back to Paris. It was now mid-August and there were three weeks to the World Championship road race. I found it difficult in Paris. Although I wanted to ride the World Championship I did not believe that there was any chance of winning and although I was happy to go there and help Sean, I was not too enthusiastic about the prospect.

In Paris I found it difficult to get into a training routine. Out on the bike I wanted to return after an hour and a half and generally did. For me it is always a problem to maintain a strict and disciplined approach when I am not racing. The problem is overcome by going for long training spins and organizing my day around that training ride. But because of all the exertions in the Giro and Tour I could not bring myself to train for more than an hour and a half at a time. This meant there were spare hours during the day and less tiredness at the end of the day. I ended up eating slightly more than I should and going to bed an hour later than would normally be the case. As there was still a constant stream of callers to the house, people coming to say congratulations on the Tour and journalists coming for interviews, I had no difficulties filling each day but I knew I was not doing anything for my chances of winning the World Championship. But then that prospect was far from my mind. Since the Tour ended the tiredness had caught up with me.

It annoyed me that at such a time in the season I was letting things slip. The only way out for me was to start racing again and exactly two weeks before the World Championship I went to Italy for a small race. I did not leave Paris until the Saturday night before the race, taking a 9 p.m. flight to Milan. By the time I got my bike through customs, something that always adds an hour to the travelling time, it was close to midnight, and it was near 2 a.m. when I arrived at the hotel where the Carrera team stayed. I was up the next morning at six, eating breakfast. My preparation for the race over the previous week had been slight and on the night before the race I had just four hours' sleep. It was not the ideal situation but it was important that I got back racing. As it turned out, the race did not go too badly. I rode well for much of the way, trying to keep things together for Bontempi, and I got tired only towards the final 20 kilometres. But it seemed to me that I was a long way from a cyclist who was ready to challenge seriously for a world title. I did not finish that race in Italy. That was unusual for me and proof that things had gone backwards in the four weeks since the Tour had finished.

Maybe what I was feeling in those weeks after the Tour was the natural response to the efforts made in winning. There was the tiredness and also the desire to sit back and take things easily. After all, I had won the two most important tours in the world and there appeared to be no chance that I could win the World Championship. I know that the thought of my winning all three – Giro, Tour and World Championship – did not enter my mind until the feat was achieved. I am sure that if I had raced all the criteriums and the Tour of Britain in the month of August I would never have been able to do anything in Austria. As it was, only by thinking of the race for the rainbow jersey as an opportunity to help Kelly could I look positively towards Austria. And that was the way I saw it.

CHAPTER 22
Finding the Rainbow

Paul Kimmage rode on the Irish team at the World Championships in Villach, Austria. 'About halfway through the race I saw Stephen slowing down to have a pee. As he peed from his bike I went over to give him a push, to ensure that he would not lose too much ground. But he asked me not to touch him as the organizers of the Worlds are really sticky about riders getting a push, regardless of the reason. Anyway, then he said, "OK Paul, let's go up this hill fast and get ourselves to the front." We both attacked the climb at the same time. I gave it everything. I looked up and, unbelievably, he was at least twenty places in front of me. He was moving so gracefully, like a bird, floating past people – or perhaps more a gliding process. I could not have been more impressed. There is nobody in the *peloton* who can ride like that. Absolutely nobody.'

Even though I went to the World Championship expecting nothing, I now believe that my performance in Villach was the best single-day effort of my career. I don't think I have ever ridden better in my life. And I am sure that the victory proves the truth in my belief about motivation. After winning the Giro and the Tour I did not feel motivated to win the world title. But I have never been what people would regard as a highly motivated rider. They look at Phil Anderson on the bike, always stretched to one side or another but never actually sitting on it. So everybody says that Phil is a horse of a man, that he really hurts himself to win. That he is *really* motivated. They see me, looking so relaxed and cool. Even when I am dead, I look as if I am riding steady, the movement and the flow are still there. 'How can Roche win?' they ask. 'The chap never hurts himself.' Journalists have told me after races that I gave up without a fight. In reality I was on my knees. They believed I was a fighter when I needed oxygen at La Plagne but it took that to convince them.

I did not go into the Tour de France feeling that this was the race of my career, or feeling more motivated or less motivated than I had been in the Tour of Italy. As I've said, I have never been able to divide up races like that, putting some on a much higher plane than others. For me there is no such thing as a small victory. That has been a fundamental belief of mine and one that I have always kept in mind. I do not target some races and try to generate a special motivation for them. That has not been my way. My motivation, if it can be called that, is to do my job well. I am competitive and I have always been conscious of the fact that I do not like to lose. It was not that I especially wanted to win but that I did not want to lose. If you can understand the difference!

Rather than working on my motivation I just try to get my preparation right beforehand and then do the correct things in the race. I genuinely believe that motivation does not come into it. Before the World Championship I wanted to get into the kind of shape that would allow me to ride well, to be of assistance to Kelly or more simply to be able to finish the race. That race in Italy got me back to competition and from there I went to Ireland where I was contracted to ride three criteriums: one in Dublin, the second in Wexford and the final one in Cork. It was going to be my first race in Dublin since winning the Tour and the Giro and I was looking forward to it. The three criteriums meant five days in Ireland and it was sure to be helpful in terms of the build-up to the Worlds. Racing the criteriums would help to bring back the sharpness that had been lost since the Tour ended. They lasted just one hour but were very fast and provided high-quality speed training. In between the races there would be long training spins which were necessary before a World Championship.

The time in Ireland worked out better than anybody could have expected. The fact that Sean Kelly, Martin Earley, Paul Kimmage and I were all home for the criteriums gave us a chance to be together before going off to the World Championship. We only get one chance in the year to ride together and we wanted to make the best of it. The lads all thought that whatever happened I should win in my home town. Normally I would not fret too much about criteriums. Even in Ireland. The races themselves carry no importance and are only a means of showing the riders to the public. And criterium racing does not suit me very well as the finishes are, more often than not, contested by the sprinters. Yet, on this occasion in Dublin, it was slightly different. I was the returning hero and the huge crowd had turned up to see me win if possible. I was going to try as hard as I could. It was an opportunity for me to say thank you to the people of Dublin.

But there was no certainty I could win. Being a Tour de France winner does not make you a champion in one-hour criteriums. There were over forty British professionals in Dublin for the race and they are more accustomed to city-centre criteriums than I. We expected that many of the British teams would combine and try to carve up the race for themselves. In the circumstances there was a danger that the four of us could get into a big battle with the British professionals over a race that had no significance. We did not want that to happen. We wanted to put on a good show for the public but far more important than that was the build-up to the World Championship road race.

There was a meeting of the riders before the Dublin race. Sean proposed that, as I had just won the Tour de France and this was my first race back in my own home town since the Tour, an agreement should be reached whereby I would win. In a similar situation on the continent, there would not have been any need to ask. Everyone would have understood that the guy back in his home town after winning the Tour would simply *have* to win. His fellow professionals would want it as much as the public. It is a kind of admission that the criteriums are more spectacles than madly competitive races. That is the way we understand them and I am sure that is the way the public sees them as well.

But the British professionals knocked down Sean's proposal straight-away. Sean argued that if it were not for me the Dublin criterium probably would not have been staged in the first place. But the British pros dug in, saying that they regarded the criterium as important and were not agreeing to anything. Allan Peiper, the Australian who rides for the Panasonic team on the continent, said it was crazy for anyone to argue against the Tour de France champion winning a small criterium in his home town. Peiper told the British pros that he did not mind saying they were a pain in the arse and he was sick and tired of their mentality. Sean spoke again and the arguments went on. Paul Sherwen, an English pro who spent his career riding on the continent, spoke totally in favour of my winning in Dublin. The issue became money. The English pros would have to be compensated financially if I was to be allowed to win. Paul Kimmage became disgusted with the attitude of the British professionals and walked out of the meeting. I met him afterwards and he said it sickened him to hear riders who had not the right to lick my cycling shoes trying to lay down the law.

At the end of the meeting there was no firm agreement but a presumption that we would have to pay them something for the privilege of their allowing me to win. Something around £1000 to be divided between them. During the race I did not have the impression that the British riders were allowing me to win. I rode very strongly and worked right through until getting away from Joey McLoughlin and Bob Downs late in the race to win. I had been away in other breaks during the race and was exhausted at the end of the hour. But, at least, I had won and the Dublin public could not have been more pleased. My victory added to the spectacle. The crowd did not see any great importance in the win, and I certainly did not attach any importance to it – a good occasion had been made better by the fact that I won.

Afterwards the English professionals said they had let me win. It did not appear that way to me. I had ridden my eyeballs out. They presumed that we Irish would not seriously contest the following evening's criterium in Wexford. But there was no mention of their giving us anything in return. They met among themselves to decide how best to divide up the race. We were not invited.

As part of our preparation for the World Championship we rode a part of the way from Dublin to Wexford. We knew that the English were planning without us and decided that if they did not come to us and reach an agreement, we would go our own way. The least the English pros should have done was to come to us and say that because we were allowing them to win in Wexford, this cancelled out what they did in Dublin and neither party would have to pay any money to the other. Our feeling was that if they were not prepared to do this then to hell with them. But we were kept totally out of things as the English guys made their plans about which of them should win. As we saw it, the race was *open*. Sean, Martin, Paul and I discussed what our tactics should be during the race and we decided that the best thing for us was to stay near the front at all times and to take things from there. In the back of our minds was the fact that if we could keep Sean in contention his sprint would give him a chance of victory in the finish.

Wexford went well. We were able to keep things together and going into the final few laps I saw that if I could give Sean a lead out, he would be hard to beat. Throughout the final lap Sean was on my wheel and just before the last corner he came past me. I accelerated as he

overtook me, moving as if I intended to take his wheel. In doing so I cut
the English sprinter Malcolm Elliott tight on the corner. I felt that
what I was doing was dangerous and I quickly moved to the other side
of the road. But as Elliott tried to figure out what I was doing, he was
forced to brake slightly and Kelly was gone.

After that there was war. The English guys were furious. We were
painted as the Irish mafia ripping off the poor English pros. They
claimed that it had been agreed that one of their riders would win in
Wexford. They said they had let me win in Dublin. We did not accept
that there had been any agreement for Wexford, since they had not
discussed the race with us beforehand. Neither did we accept that they
let me win in Dublin. The arguments ended with a threat from them
that we 'would see in Cork'.

Paul and Martin were a little worried. They had never been involved
in this type of situation before and did not know what to expect. We
told them to ride at the front as much as they could and there would be
no problems. We needed Paul and Martin to ride well. I reckoned that
I could again give Sean a winning lead out for the sprint but not if I had
to ride at the front all through the race. We all sat down together and
decided what had to be done. Martin was particularly worried because
he had never previously finished the Cork criterium. It was always too
fast for him. Things were dirty from the start, mostly because of the
tactics used by the English riders. The important ones were riding
together. With their vastly superior numbers they should have been
well able to beat us but I had the impression that even though they
worked together they did not have a definite idea of which one of them
should win. Some of the big ones were watching out for themselves.
With us, it did not matter in the slightest who won but Sean's sprinting
ability meant that he was our best chance. It always helps to have a
plan and our idea was to take Sean to the finish and leave the rest to his
sprint.

It was a very good race with attack after attack but the circuit was
too short for anyone to get clear. Martin and Paul rode really well,
staying at the front for long periods and reducing the pressure on Sean
and me. As the finish loomed, I could sense the atmosphere becoming
tense and the tactics dirtier.

I was away with three or four laps to go and after being recaptured I
slipped back into the middle of the *peloton* to take a breather. As I
made my way back to the front there were many English riders who
tried to block me. I had to fight to get back to the front but I was more

determined than ever to give Sean a good lead out. If they were being dirty about it, the least we could do was give it everything. I suppose it also meant that our tactics at the finish were going to make things as difficult as possible for them. Normally, when I lead out somebody I ride very straight and that makes it easy for rivals to come past me and challenge the rider I have worked for. Not everybody rides the same way. If you watch Sean in a sprint you will see that he switches this way and that, making it very hard for anybody to go around him. His little changes of direction discourage people from trying. Before the Cork criterium we decided that in order to surprise the English sprinters Sean should go a little early.

On that last lap I gave a few switches, just to make others think a bit. Sean knew what was happening and was not in the least bothered. Before the last corner Sean reached out with his hand and hit me on the hip, letting me know that he was coming through. He came around me but I did not alter my line. I came out of the corner on his wheel and when the English guys realized what was happening they tried to come around me. There was not much room and I was not going to facilitate the pursuit of Kelly by moving out of the way. One of the English sprinters, Mark Walsham, was a little too hasty in his efforts to get past me and he ran into me from behind, pulling the bike from under himself. He fell, I fell and lots of those coming behind us fell. Walsham claimed I switched him but that was not the case. There was no need for me to switch anybody. The bird had already flown. He hit into me once and then pulled his bars too sharply and got in under me. I hurt myself badly, particularly my knee. There were many bruises and I felt very sore.

The English pros said that I deliberately caused the crash to help Kelly win. That was the most silly argument of all. I am a professional. I have a wife and two children and I don't go around causing 30-mile-per-hour crashes. Anyway there were only ten days to the World Championship and nobody wants to be involved in a crash at such a time.

Sean's victory pleased us greatly. We had set out with a very definite aim in mind and we had achieved it. There was the extra satisfaction that one gets from being involved in a united team effort. And the four of us were united. We went to the World Championship road race committed to each other.

After the three races in Ireland I went to Italy and rode another three races in four days. I could feel that I was coming round but this always happens when you get into the routine of the profession. A massage each evening, carefully selected food and an early bed. The Italian races brought me nearer to top condition and I was beginning to look forward to the World Championship. Not that I was thinking of winning myself but at least there was the likelihood that I would be of real assistance to Sean. We rode the final preparatory race in Italy and cycled from there to Villach in Austria. A number of Sean's team mates were with us; Acacio da Silva, Stefan Joho, Alfred Achermann, Tomas Wegmüller and Steve Hodge. Wegmüller is called Merckx by the lads because of his odd notions. He would tell you of some extraordinary exploit of Merckx's during his career and that he was going to do the same thing. Wegmüller is a strong boy, really strong, but no Merckx. Still, in his own mind he was going to be world champion. He had no doubts.

For me Villach was a little like Goodwood in 1982 when I went to the World Championship with the purpose of helping Sean. Not every circuit suits me; most circuits suit him. It could be said that I went to Villach lacking personal ambition and that would be true. I began to revise my opinion slightly when we first went round the circuit on the Thursday, four days before the race. All of the talk of it being a flat circuit and one which suited the sprinters was off the mark. It was a circuit for strong men, essentially for people like Sean and Argentin, but I knew that I would go OK on such a circuit. On the following day we trained over the circuit and I could not believe how well I felt. I had suddenly clicked back into top form and told Sean how well my legs felt. They were really good. We spoke about our gears. Sean said he was putting on a 13 straight through to 19 block. I decided to go for a 13 up to 18 but would use a 20 instead of the 19. I thought the hill was quite hard and, particularly in the early part of the race, I wanted to act on my belief in pedalling and use the 20 whenever possible. In this way I would preserve my strength.

We took things easily on Saturday, the day before the race, and we looked forward to the big test. We were ready to do our best. As well as Sean, Martin, Paul and myself there was a fifth member of the Ireland team, Alan McCormack. An old comrade from my amateur career. Alan now rides as a professional on the US circuit and although he was a part of the team he did not stay at our hotel and never really got into the spirit of our team atmosphere.

At important moments in 1987 I was helped by the weather. It might have been much warmer during the mountain stages of the two major tours, Italy and France, and it is certain that if it had been I would have found the going more severe. I do not like to race when the temperatures are really high and many of the problems that I have suffered on past Tours de France have happened at times when the days were really hot. It was never likely that the temperatures would be very high in Villach but there was the chance that the day would be warm and over the seven hours of the day that would take its toll. But, true to the way things went for me in 1987, rain lashed down on the morning of the race. It was miserable. But, at least, it was miserable for everyone. I have always been able to ride well in the rain. It is not that I like rain, it is simply that I don't mind it while others positively hate it. Neither Sean nor I was too disappointed to find that the rain fell in buckets as the World Championship road race went on its way. Before the start I regarded Argentin as the most likely winner. He was the defending champion, he had prepared specifically for this race, he was in super form and he had the backing of the strong Italian team.

To me it seemed that our best chance of doing something lay in Sean. If things were kept together and Kelly could arrive at the finish with a winning chance, he would go very close. We could see from the ten days we had spent together in the build-up that Kelly was very determined to ride well and that he was in good shape. The circuit at Villach was just 12 kilometres long, which was a bit shorter than the circuit one normally finds at a World Championship. The shortness of the circuit meant that there were twenty-three laps and the race was going to take almost seven hours. Because of the rain and slippery roads Sean wanted to ride near the front during the early laps and, in this way, to give himself the best chance of staying out of trouble. I might have done the same but I did not feel strong during the first ten laps. My legs were heavy and stiff and I wondered if I was going to be able to finish. The thought of actually winning the race did not enter into it. Even though I was not feeling good I survived the first half of the race easily because the World Championship builds up very gradually into a hard race. At first it is steady as everybody tries to find their legs, and because there is such a long way to go nobody wants to be too adventurous during the first part of the race. There were a few unimportant little breaks but nothing to worry anybody.

After a while the rain eased off and as the race went through the first twelve laps and past halfway, I began to feel stronger. I positioned myself nearer the front and I began to take a closer interest in what was happening. I could see that Sean was going well. Martin was going OK and, after suffering a little in the early part of the race, Paul was also going nicely. Our little team was surviving exceptionally well. Because the circuit was not severe the elimination process was happening at a much slower rate than at previous World Championships I have ridden. As far as I could see, most teams were still very strong.

With about six laps to go I could feel the pace increasing and riders thinking that the time for decisions had come. Our plan was that Sean and I would ride fairly close to each other and if there was any big attack from the front we would both react in the same way. When Argentin attacked with three others five laps from the finish we all knew that it was a dangerous move. Teun Van Vliet was one of his breakaway companions and Van Vliet was very strong. Their presence in the breakaway meant that their teams, Italy and Holland, would not chase and that created problems. It was a crisis but I knew there was no sense in taking up the pursuit immediately. There were other teams which had nine or ten riders capable of chasing, we were just four riders and we would burn ourselves out if we spent too long in pursuit of the breakaway group. We had to gamble that others would chase Argentin.

Fignon and Mottet of the French team did and I was happy to let them do the riding. They reduced the deficit but destroyed themselves in the process. By the time they had finished riding at the front they had nothing more to give to the race. After they stopped chasing I looked around and could not see anybody ready to pick up the chase. I knew the time had come for me to play my cards for Sean. I rode at the front on one of the hills and kept the pace up very high and further narrowed the gap on the leaders. Then Martin rode at the front, giving it everything and helping to ensure that the breakaways were finally recaptured. Once they were caught, others counterattacked and the last three laps of the race were a continuous series of attacks and counterattacks. I felt really strong and was enjoying the challenge of trying to control things for Sean. We both felt good about the way Martin and Paul had ridden for us: both of them had given it everything and performed as well as anybody could have expected. Nobody could have asked for more.

On the penultimate lap I knew there was plenty in my legs and I tried to make sure that it was used in the best possible way. Sean was still in the lead group and so there was everything to ride for. But there were far too many good sprinters in that lead group and Sean was not likely to beat all of those guys if it came to a mass sprint. Bontempi was still in contention, Vanderaerden was there also and they were both, possibly, faster than Kelly. We had to reduce the lead group before the finish. Sean knew it. I knew it.

After hearing the bell for the final lap we accelerated as gaps appeared at the front of the seventy-plus lead group. On the long hill at the start of the lap I went as hard as I could go. Sean was on my wheel. I wanted to put the other sprinters under pressure but I could not believe it when I looked behind at the top of the hill and saw that there were only ten or eleven guys still with me. I did push the speed up but I had no idea that it was fast enough to get rid of about sixty riders. Getting the field of potential winners down to twelve suited Sean and me well.

Looking around we knew that Argentin was the only member of our twelve-rider group who was capable of outsprinting Kelly at the finish. The others did not like the idea of sprinting against Kelly, and the attacks started coming from every direction. I covered most of them and the ones that I did not go with were covered by Sean. After each attack there was a general regrouping of the twelve and everything pointed to a sprint finish. That suited us as I was present to give Sean a lead out and he was still going well.

With about three kilometres to go there was an attack from the Dane Sorensen, countered by Van Vliet, Golz, Winterberg and me. Once Sorensen realized that he was not going anywhere he slowed; we all slowed and waited for the others, who were just behind us, to come up. I looked behind and could see that they were stalling. I became anxious. I wondered what was happening. How could Kelly lose contact at this late stage? What I did not know was that Kelly and Argentin were having their own private battle of nerves, Kelly refusing to lead the pursuit of a breakaway group that included his team mate, Argentin refusing to lead Kelly because he feared Kelly would then beat him in the sprint. As they deliberated I was faced with a problem. As a sprinter I do not compare with Golz or Van Vliet and I knew that if I was in a sprint with these four riders for the rainbow jersey I was likely to get fourth or fifth with only an outside possibility of a bronze.

I looked back again and again to see if Kelly and his group were going to rejoin us. I was not too pleased, feeling that Kelly had landed me in a mess. After the year that I had enjoyed, a bronze medal at the World Championship was not worth aiming for and it was obvious to me that I had to attack. With about 500 metres left I took one last look behind and decided that Kelly's group was not coming back in time and so I prepared for the attack. The remarkable thing was that there was still something in my legs and when I went I tried to use every available ounce of energy. I was turning a big gear when I attacked and just kept turning it. After about 300 metres I glanced under my arm and got the most beautiful surprise of my life. The others were well behind me and I was going to be world champion. I kept turning my big gear but close to the line the incline got a little more severe and I struggled through the last 50 metres. But, by then, it did not matter. I was not going to be overtaken.

At the finish it was chaos. Because the victory was so unexpected I was overcome with joy. Sean, who finished fifth, was the first to congratulate me. I could see that he was genuinely delighted for me and that added to my victory. Martin and Paul were soon congratulating me too and there was a marvellous night ahead of us. Our celebration took place at the team hotel and was very enjoyable. Many of those Irish people who have supported us over the years at the World Championship were present and it was good to be able to share the night with them. Everybody was talking about the fact that I had achieved the great Giro, Tour, World Championship treble, and reminded me that Merckx was the only man in cycling history to win all three in one season. I was now alongside Merckx in this regard. It was going to take a long time for all this to sink in.

Maybe the achievement will never sink in. For me the great source of satisfaction was that on the day I rode so well. After the season that I had ridden I should have been exhausted by the time the Villach race came around. I had imagined that I would be unable to produce my best, that the accumulation of all the efforts made throughout the season would have left me shattered. But things turned out quite differently on the day. Now, months after the Villach race, I look back on it as the best one-day performance of my career.

CHAPTER 23

The Life and the Lads

'Stephen's greatest quality and greatest fault is his generosity. Some people will try to take advantage of him. For me he is a great friend. I hope that when we both finish cycling, our friendship will carry on. During your life you will not meet any more than about ten friends like him.'

Sean Kelly

Life on the bike has been good to me. I have worked hard for the things that have come my way but it has been a good life. I am conscious of the fact that I am a professional and that I signed for Peugeot in 1981 because I could earn more money racing in the *peloton* than working in a factory back in Ireland. It is important to earn as much as you can during the good years but the rider must not be governed totally by the financial side of things. At certain moments during my career it was clear to me that I needed a break from racing and even if this meant giving up ten or twelve criteriums (£15,000) or a contract to ride a stage race, I had no hesitation in taking the rest. In the overall sense I have done well financially. But then if the guy who wins the Giro, Tour and World Championship does not do well, something is very wrong. Before 1987 I had not earned nearly as much from the sport as most people imagined. When, at the end of 1986, I was told that my knee was so bad I would have to give up cycling, I reckoned on starting immediately in another job. I was not going to be able to afford to hang around.

As a first-year professional with Peugeot I earned £500 a month and had to pay the usual contributions and tax out of that. My justification at the time was that it was as much as I would have earned working in the factory and I enjoyed the life on the bike more. After winning

Paris—Nice Peugeot gave me an increase of £200 per month and the use of a Peugeot car. All first-time contracts are for two years and at the end of my first season there was little I could do. Peugeot had me for two years and the salary was fixed. Although they were not obliged to, they increased my salary to £900 per month during my second season. At the end of my second season Peugeot pointed to my lack of results and said I could not ask for an increase. They offered to keep me on the same salary for another season and if I did not like that, I could go elsewhere. I felt I had not achieved enough with them to go to another team and, anyway, I was happy where I was.

Eventually they gave me about £1200 per month during my third season. For the next Bernard Hinault it was not very much. My third year was reasonably successful and at the end of it Peugeot were offering £2000 per month to keep me for a fourth year. I knew I was worth more than that and the protracted contractual wrangle which subsequently took place all came down to money. During those early seasons I was spoken of as a future champion but I was not being paid as one. I lived out of a suitcase so that I did not have to get a place of my own in Paris. I stayed on the road as much as possible so that when I returned to Paris I could stay with Lydia's parents, but I did not want to abuse their hospitality. As a result I spent most of my time racing and at training camps. It was cheaper. When we got married in 1982 all my money went on the wedding and we did not have the money to go too far away on the honeymoon. We drove to Lourdes, spent a few days there and drove back. Well, it was going to be Brittas Bay in County Wicklow or Lourdes, and Brittas Bay in October did not seem like a good honeymoon idea.

At the end of 1983, my third season in the *peloton*, I signed for La Redoute and my salary went up. My contract with La Redoute was for two years and it enabled me to get my house started. Over the two years with La Redoute I put everything I had into the house, believing that it was as good an investment as any. After La Redoute I signed a two-year contract for Carrera and because my second year with La Redoute had been so good, I got a good contract with Carrera. I was fortunate that I came into the sport at a time when the big sponsorships were happening. In Hinault's time, 1978 to 1982, he was getting good money but he was the only one getting it. Nowadays there are a number of fellows making good money; myself, Kelly, LeMond, Argentin, Delgado, Fignon, Bernard and a few others. But it is still only a handful. It helps that we all have a fair idea of what the other fellow is getting and that means we know what to look for. Sean has been very helpful to me in this respect because he was earning the big money before me and when I started doing well he knew what I should be getting. It is also helpful that the new generation of rider does not *have* to ride at any price. He can pick and choose and ensure that organizers of races treat him better than was the case in the past.

I think I have enjoyed good relations with the sponsors who put money into cycling. I have found that they are always very good on the first day or at the time when they want you. After that they are always nice and good and it is never their fault that things go wrong. The big boss will continue to smile and stay out of the way. It is not he who creates the difficulties but the general manager or the *directeur commercial*. I am still on good terms with all of the sponsors who have employed me, even the big bosses at Peugeot.

Sometimes sponsors can be naive. At the end of 1987 La Redoute wanted me to go to their factory and sign autographs for their employees. There were 7000 employees and it was going to be a big deal. The big boss at La Redoute thought that since we had got on so well in 1984 and 1985 it would be nice for me to go back to the factory after all my success in 1987. Through the general manager of the Fagor team, Philippe Crepel, I informed La Redoute that I was not prepared to meet their employees for nothing. They nearly went through the roof, asking if it was because Stephen Roche had won all the big races that he thought he could do this to La Redoute. They said I was a friend of the boss and yet I wanted money to come to his factory. But to me it was straightforward. If La Redoute wanted to use me to keep their employees happy they would have to pay for it.

I would like to think that I get on well with most of my fellow riders. The people I get on especially well with are Kelly, Millar, Yates, Peiper, Kimmage and Earley – our own lads. Continental pros have a different mentality from us. Maybe it is because we went over there on our own and had to dig in to get somewhere. We appreciate the value of friendship. The continental guys do not have the same needs and, from our point of view, you cannot fully trust them. But, I suppose, the mistrust is mutual. Within our group people are always loyal to each other. Over the years I have learned that with Kelly, Millar, Yates and Peiper, their word is their word. You never, ever, doubt that. It makes a difference. Twice during 1987 I was let down by the Norwegian Dag Otto Lauritzen. Once in a race: the Grand Prix de

Frankfurt when he agreed to combine with me against a Dutch group. Yet he continued to ride against me. Then at the end of the year I tried to get Lauritzen to join the Fagor team but he did what I had asked him not to do: he used our offer as a bargaining tool with his own team, 7-Eleven. That kind of thing is not on.

Kelly is a special friend. Before I turned professional I admired what he had achieved and then when I got to know him as a person I found that he was dead straight and good fun. We have had some great times together. In my early years as a pro I wanted to ride in the same team as Sean, at least for a couple of seasons. But as I progressed and he maintained his position as one of the very best professionals it became clear that we were never going to be able to ride in the same team. We became too big to fit into the same team. But we have always tried not to damage each other's chances when we have ridden against one another. I think we were fortunate that neither of us was ever jealous of what the other one did. And we never counted the things we did for each other. When people compare what I have won to what Kelly has won my reaction is to ask them not to compare but to combine. Instead of asking what each has won, it is better to put our victories together and say, 'Here are two Irishmen who between them have won almost every race in world cycling.'

As well as trying to help each other in races whenever we can, Sean and I use the knowledge we have acquired to help each other. When I am renegotiating my contract I will speak with Sean. He made mistakes during the early part of his career and knows the pitfalls. But I am learning as well and Sean will speak with me before he signs his contract. I tell him what I am getting and what I think he should be getting and he does the same thing for me. From the start Sean and I were able to talk, we were able to discuss things and that is the key to our relationship. Sure we can be rivals on the road and there are times when we are all out to beat each other, but it is still on the condition that neither of us will damage the other guy's chance. If I cannot win a race, I would rather Sean wins than Laurent Fignon or Jean François Bernard. He feels the same way.

Robert Millar and I always got on well. Or at least we have got on well since our days at Peugeot in 1981, 1982, and 1983. I remember how Millar rode in the 1983 Tour of Romandie and how much admiration I felt for him. He and Pascal Simon were Peugeot's two leaders for the race. Bob got the jersey and I rode for him. But in defending his jersey I went away with Veldscholten and ended up taking the leader's jersey. Bob was disappointed but that did not affect his attitude to me. He immediately took up the role of team rider and defended my lead without question or complaint. That was Bob.

Even when Bob and I ended up on different teams we invariably combined and helped each other. It worked on the basis of not harming the other's chances. When he shouted I was always there and the other way around. We have total trust in each other and it also gives you the confidence of knowing that you are not on your own. My first good performance in the mountains of the Tour de France happened on the Morzine stage of the 1983 Tour when I rode side by side with Bob from beginning to end. I think we finished sixth and seventh after I had suffered all kinds of mechanical problems in the early part of the stage. Bob and I have gone to the Alps together to train and I think I have learned a bit about climbing from him. The importance of just sitting back and pedalling, I learned that from Bob. His friendship was never more important than it was during the 1987 Giro. On the day to the finish at Canazei, over the five big cols, I was in danger of being assaulted by the Italian spectators. Eddy rode at one side of me, Bob rode at the other. I can never forget that. No matter which team I joined in 1988 I wanted Bob to be with me and that is what happened.

I would also class Sean Yates as a good friend. He has plenty of ability but maybe not that much ambition. His chief concern is not to have to return to England to race. You could give Sean a handful of five pound notes, even a barrow full, but it would not make the slightest difference to him. All he wants to do is race but it must be continental racing. He is very sincere, one of the gentlest people I have ever met, and childlike. As a professional racer, I have always believed that Sean needs a cause. He has a good body, a lot of power, but he needs somebody to ride for, some big leader whom he would respect. He has not been prominent in recent seasons simply because he has not had this kind of leader. But he can do it. This is why I am happy to be joining up with Sean again. I remember what he was like at Peugeot and if he was not already at Fagor I would have worked to bring him into the team.

I would have liked to take on Allan Peiper as well because he fits in very well with our English-speaking group. But Peiper has made a very good career for himself with Panasonic and he likes the Flemish/Dutch system. I like him a lot and it would have been good to have him in the team but you cannot have everything.

Phil Anderson and Greg LeMond have never been a part of the informal group of English speakers. I get on OK with Phil but I would never want to race in the same team as he. Phil wants things for himself and sometimes this makes him selfish. He lived for a good few years in France and he learned very little French. Then he lived for a number of years in Belgium and he cannot speak a word of Flemish. Everything is Australian or American and Europe is a third choice. Phil spends a lot of time trying to put you down. He used to live in Saint Niklaas in Belgium. He claimed it was paradise. He told Peiper that he should live there. So Peiper got an apartment in Saint Niklaas. A month later Phil moved to Courtrai, telling Peiper that Saint Niklaas was shit. But that is Phil. A good guy, maybe, but you have to know him.

I never had that much to do with Greg LeMond. My impression is of a rider who will leave the sport as soon as he has made his money. He will want to get out when he is thirty whereas most guys would be happy to go to thirty-five if they were still riding well. Both Greg and Phil reckon that another English speaker should never ride behind them, but they think it is OK if they do it themselves. Greg will ride after me more quickly than he will ride after most other fellows. But Phil and Greg can be funny to watch. You see them in the bunch, never far away from each other. If one of them goes with an attack the other will counter immediately. These are the guys who say that the English speakers should not be working against each other. If Sean goes away in a break you can be sure that I will wait for somebody else to make the first effort to bring him back. Same for Millar. I believe that Kelly, Millar, myself, Yates, Earley and Kimmage are all for one, one for all. Greg and Phil tend to be one for one and one for one.

But that is the way in the bunch, there will be some you like more than others. I have met so many people, made many good friends through cycling. And while it is a very hard and sometimes very cruel profession, my love for the bike remains as strong now as it was in the days when I first discovered it. I am convinced that long after I have stopped riding as a professional I will be riding my bicycle. I never want to abandon my bike. I see my grandfather, now in his seventies and riding around everywhere. To me that is beautiful. And the bike must always remain a part of my life.

Freewheeling Champ

The exploits of Stephen Roche during the year 1987 touched a great number of people. In his own country he won a special place. Dublin, his home town, bestowed its highest honour when it made him a Freeman of the City. The first sportsperson to receive the award. Everywhere, people warmed to Roche's performances and were cheered by his success. Davoren Hanna was moved by the exploits of his fellow Dubliner. Now 13 years of age, Davoren has cerebral palsy. He cannot speak, sit up, walk or control most of the muscles of his body. It is hard for him to breathe and swallow. He can only write when sitting on someone's knee, usually his mother's. Thus positioned he shifts his weight through his pelvis and uses his legs to indicate to his helper the letter which he wishes to use. It is a cycling movement and Davoren found it easy to relate his struggle to that of his sporting hero. Like Stephen Roche, there were times when Davoren was down. Like Stephen Roche, he fought and triumphed. Davoren has won a number of major literary awards and has been described as a poet 'of maturity, control and brilliance, with a Celtic gift of imagery'.

Davoren called his poem 'Freewheeling Champ':

> I listened to the roar
> of victory in my ears,
> Inch by painful inch
> I rode with him –
> plummeting downhill,
> swerving, gliding,
> rising with his wry
> Dublin humour
> rolling in my spokes.
> Satin ribbon roads
> slipped under my wheels,
> but undaunted came I
> to vanquish all doubt
> riding in triumph
> onto the Champs Elysées.

Principal Performances

AMATEUR

1979 – Winner of Rás Tailteann

1980 – Winner of Paris–Roubaix classic, winner of Paris–Reims classic

PROFESSIONAL

1981 – Winner of Tour of Corsica, Paris–Nice, Tour of the Indre and Loire, Etoile des Espoirs; second in Grand Prix des Nations

1982 – Second in Amstel Gold classic; third in Four Days of Dunkirk and Baracchi Trophy

1983 – Winner of Tour of Romandie, Grand Prix of Wallonia, Paris–Bourges, Etoile des Espoirs; third in World Championship road race; fifth in Grand Prix des Nations; thirteenth in Tour de France

1984 – Winner of Nice–Alassio, Tour of Romandie, Subida-Arate; second in Paris–Nice; third in Criterium International, Grand Prix des Nations; twenty-fifth in Tour de France

1985 – Winner of Criterium International, Tour of the Midi Pyrenees; second in Paris–Nice; third in Tour de France; seventh in World Championship road race

1986 – Forty-eighth in Tour de France

1987 – Winner of Tour of Valencia, Tour of Romandie, Tour of Italy, Tour de France, World Championship road race; second in Criterium International, Liège–Bastogne–Liège; fourth in Paris–Nice, Flèche Wallone classic

Index